Best Summer Weekends Cookbook

BEST SUMMER WEEKENDS
Cookbook

Jane Rodmell

National Library of Canada Cataloguing in Publication Data

Rodmell, Jane, 1938 -
Best summer weekends cookbook / by Jane Rodmell.

Includes index.

ISBN 0-9696922-4-2

1. Cookery. 2. Summer. I. Title.

TX829.R618 2004   641.5'64   C2003-907238-X

Published by
Cottage Life Books
54 St. Patrick St.
Toronto, Ontario, Canada
M5T 1V1
www.cottagelife.com

Trade distribution by
Firefly Books Ltd.
66 Leek Crescent
Richmond Hill, Ontario
L4B 1H1

Printed in Singapore

Publisher Cataloging-in-Publication Data (U.S.)

Rodmell, Jane, 1938 -
    Best summer weekends cookbook / Jane Rodmell. –1st ed.

[352] p. : ill., col. photos. ;   cm.

Includes index.

Summary: Cookbook with 300 easy to prepare recipes for summer weekend cooking.

ISBN 0-9696922-4-2

1. Cookery. I. Title.

641.5/64 22   TX829.R63 2004

Published in the United States by
Cottage Life Books
Box 1338
Ellicott Station
Buffalo, N.Y., U.S.A. 14205
www.cottagelife.com

Trade distribution by
Firefly Books (U.S.)
Box 1338
Ellicott Station
Buffalo, N.Y., U.S.A. 14205

For Michael, Alex, Katie & Rebecca – the cottage kids

Photography (including cover) by
Robert Wigington

Food styling by Ruth Gangbar and Jill Snider

Propping by Maggi Jones and Sue Florian

Illustrations by Heather Holbrook

Edited by Ann Vanderhoof

Design by Steve Manley

Colour by Colour Technologies

Additional photography by:
Laura Arsiè: p. 304
Kevin Hewitt: pp. 49, 261, 269, 318
Suzanne McCormick: pp. 75, 113, 121, 143, 187, 220,
257, 265, 315
Ken Rodmell: author photo, back cover
Olga Tracey: p. 272.

Additional food styling by:
Claire Stancer, Debbi Charendoff Moses,
Jennifer Danter, and Sue Henderson

All recipes by Jane Rodmell, except as noted below:
Monda Rosenberg: Citrus-Glazed Salmon, p. 92
Keely Schierl: Bus-Stop Chicken, p. 114
Jill Snider: Ultimate Bran Muffin, p. 262; Mix-in-the-
Pan Cake, p. 276; Chocolate Banana Cake, p. 277; Easy
Apple Cake, p. 284; Chocolate Toffee Crunch, p. 286;
Lemon Squares, p. 288; Caramel Almond Squares,
p. 291; Espresso Ice Cream Loaf, p. 308; Chocolate
Nests & Crunchy Peanut Butter Shells, p. 309;
Chocolate Chip Crisps, p. 332; Raisin Soda Bread,
p. 333; Chewy Butterscotch Bars, p. 334; Quick Tricks,
pp. 280, 286, 308, 309.

The following recipes (or variations) were winners in
Cottage Life magazine's annual recipe contest:

Barbecued Marinated Brie, p. 34: Tina Roberts
Barbecued Pork Tenderloin, p. 76: Gaylen Racine
Caramelized Peaches, p. 310: Nancy Weese
Cedar-Smoked Salmon & Trout, p. 98: Gaylen Racine
Chilled Cantaloupe Soup, p. 225: Susan Steinberg
Cottage Canoes, p. 43: Fran Stephen
Double-Chocolate Peanut Bars, p. 289: Karen Dolan
Double-Crust Mixed-Fruit Pie, 324: Moira Elsley
Green Beans & Feta, p. 155: Nancy Weese
Grilled Pound Cake, p. 282: Nancy Weese
Lazy-Day Sticky Buns, p. 267: Lydia McClure
Muskoka Blueberry Pie, p. 323: Ross Burwell
Napa Cabbage Salad, p. 150: Judy Anderson
Overnight French Toast, p. 254: Danielle Stewart
Raspberry-Spinach Salad, 138: Peter O'Hare
Stuffed Tortilla Wedges, p. 38: Nancy Weese
Tabbouleh with a Twist, p. 147: Laura Robinson
Very, Very Green Salad, p. 158: Karen Dolan

Front cover photo: Garlicky Shrimp Kebabs, p. 90

Introduction

Great summer weekends invariably include great food. There is a problem, however: All things considered, I would rather spend my weekend lazing on the deck with a good book than wrestling with grocery carts at the store, or dicing for hours in the kitchen. The cook wants to relax, too!

This cookbook is designed to help you easily create uncomplicated, wonderful-tasting food for your summer weekends. It combines updated versions of favourite recipes from my previous two books, *Cottage Life's Summer Weekend Cookbook* and *More Summer Weekends*, with many new recipes and tips, to give you a whole summer's worth of ideas and inspiration for entertaining relatives and friends, and feeding the family, too. The focus is on relaxed, simple cooking using fresh, seasonal ingredients. Many of the dishes can be made partly or entirely ahead – the tips with the recipes tell you how – so that last-minute fuss is kept to a minimum.

The recipes are also meant to be flexible: They include ideas for variations and substitutions for those times you don't have a particular ingredient on hand. And you'll find suggestions of what I like to serve with various dishes, making it easy for you to put together a whole meal.

Since many of the recipes were first developed for my column in *Cottage Life* magazine – and cottages aren't always equipped with all the conveniences of home – they don't rely on a lot of fancy kitchen equipment. Although a food processor or blender often makes life easier (especially when cooking for large groups), I still rely on my good chopping knife and trusty pestle and mortar. Because cooking outdoors is an essential part of summer, a good number of recipes use the grill. Not only does barbecuing help keep things

Jane Rodmell's "Cottage Cook" column appears regularly in *Cottage Life* magazine. For subscription information, contact: *Cottage Life*, 54 St. Patrick St., Toronto, Ontario, Canada M5T 1V1; tel.: 416-599-2000 or 877-874-LAKE; fax: 416-599-0800; www.cottagelife.com

cool inside, but the barbecue also becomes a focal point for social activity. Friends gather round to review the day's events, plan what they're going to do tomorrow – and give advice to the cook, of course.

The recipes in this collection rely on a core group of basic ingredients (see "Stocking the Cupboard," which begins on the next page), supplemented by seasonal vegetables and fruits, meat, and fish. While Mediterranean and south-of-the-border flavours remain among my favourites, more and more often the food my family and I like to eat includes spices and flavourings from other cuisines, particularly Thai, other Asian, and north African. But the recipes remain simple, and I provide options in case an out-of-the-ordinary ingredient isn't available in your supermarket.

Lastly, though the recipes are mostly based on healthy, fresh food, there are some that are definitely special-occasion dishes. For sure, Caramel Pecan Sticky Buns and Chocolate Raspberry Terrine are not on the spa food list, but it is the weekend after all, and no one needs to eat a *big* piece.

The preparation and enjoyment of good food is best shared with good friends – likewise, the creation of a cookbook. My sincere thanks to Ann Vanderhoof and Steve Manley, a talented editorial/design team beyond compare; to photographer Bob Wigington and food stylist Ruth Gangbar, who always make food look irresistible; to Heather Holbrook, for her lively illustrations; to Penny Caldwell, Al Zikovitz, Wendela Roberts, and all the creative folk at *Cottage Life* magazine, who provide consistent support and encouragement; to the magazine's enthusiastic recipe-contest contributors; to Sari Bercovitch, for making the all-important index work; and to my inspiring and much-appreciated cooking companions. Among them are chef Julie St. Jean, who shares the passion for fabulous food and the pursuit of ultimate flavour and who spent hours in the kitchen testing many of the recipes in this book; master baker Jill Snider; David Moore, skilled artisan bread-baker; Sue Bowman; David Cousins; Mario Totaro; and the many talented chefs and bakers at All the Best.

I hope your summer weekends are long and lovely, and filled with good friends and good food. Enjoy the book.

—*Jane Rodmell*

TABLE OF CONTENTS

At the start of each section, you'll find a complete list of the recipes included in that section.

Stocking the Cupboard

After years of leaving the city on weekends with a hastily gathered collection of odd cans and packages, I have developed a few strategies that make it possible to enjoy good food on summer weekends with a minimum of anxiety and effort. The trick is in stocking the kitchen cupboards. With some basics in place, it's easier to whip up delicious spur-of-the-moment meals, cope with last-minute guests, and still have time to enjoy the day outdoors. Here are some of the ingredients that are useful to have on hand for preparing the recipes in this book:

Herbs and spices

Fresh: basil, coriander (also known as cilantro), and flat-leaf parsley (also known as Italian parsley); occasionally called for: chives, dill, mint, oregano, rosemary, tarragon, and thyme.

Dried: bay leaves, basil, black peppercorns, cayenne, cinnamon (ground and sticks), cumin (seeds and ground), curry powder, oregano, paprika, hot red pepper flakes, rosemary, salt (see Tips, at left), and thyme; occasionally called for: allspice, cloves, coriander seed (ground), ginger, nutmeg, mixed peppercorns (black, white, green, and pink), poppy seeds, saffron, sesame seeds, and turmeric.

Many kitchen cupboards – especially those at seasonal places – contain jars of dried herbs and spices that have been around for years, if not generations. This summer, throw out the old and get new; you'll be surprised at the difference in taste. Buy them in small quantities that you'll use up this year, and store them in airtight containers in a cool, dark place. For better flavour,

buy your herbs in leaf form rather than ground, then crumble as you add them to a dish. Better still, plant a few favourite herbs in pots, so they're on hand fresh when you need them. Fresh herbs *really* make a difference in taste.

Canned and jarred foods

Every family has its favourites, but I find it particularly helpful to have the following cans and jars in the cupboard:

At the top of my list is canned seafood – crab, tuna, salmon, clams, smoked oysters, and shrimp. They can be used to make a spread or hors d'oeuvres for cocktail hour, turn a salad into a main dish, or provide the basis of a quick pasta sauce. I usually keep a can of anchovies in the fridge, too.

Canned beans are also extremely handy – they can be added to salads and main dishes, or turned into a tasty dip. Stock a variety: red and white kidney beans, pinto beans, chickpeas, black beans, black-eyed peas, and lentils. Rinse canned beans thoroughly before using to remove the preserving liquid. Organic Eden-brand beans are excellent for flavour and retaining their shape.

Tomatoes in various forms are useful pantry staples for the recipes in this book: canned plum tomatoes, tomato paste either in a can or in a handy tube, and cans or jars of good-quality regular and chunky tomato sauce. I also make sure my shelves are stocked with marinated and plain artichoke hearts, pimentos, capers, and olives. Canned, pitted black olives can't compare in taste or texture with the intensely flavoured olives sold in bulk in some delis, supermarkets, and specialty stores, and sometimes also available in jars: fruity black kalamatas, sharp cracked green olives, wrinkled sun-dried ones from Morocco, small ripe ones from Italy, ones with herbs or hot red pepper flakes. Good olives make a lively snack, add flavour to salads and main dishes, and can be turned into tapenade, a tasty spread.

Peanut butter (chunky and smooth) is essential not just for sandwiches and cookies, but also for Thai-inspired sauces. Tahini – a paste made from sesame seeds – is used in some Mediterranean sauces, dips, and spreads. Look for it in bulk-food stores (near the peanut butter), as well as in jars.

TIPS:

• A couple of well-chosen jars in the cupboard can serve as the basis for instant emergency hors d'oeuvres. Excellent homemade-style antipastos and spicy salsas are available ready-prepared. So too is tapenade (black olive paste) and roasted eggplant caviar (also known as "poor man's caviar"). All you have to do is find the crackers and open the jar when guests arrive unexpectedly.

• While unopened cans and jars will keep quite well in the pantry, many items – even so-called "shelf-stable" foods like flour, nuts, and dry cereals – will deteriorate over time. To maximize shelf life (and to keep out pests), transfer boxed and bagged foods to clean, dry glass or plastic containers with well-fitting lids, label them, and store them in a cool, dry cupboard. And don't go overboard: Buy in quantities and sizes you will use within a month or two.

• Heavy-duty zipper-style plastic bags in several sizes are extremely handy. Marinate meats and vegetables in them; the bags take up less room than bowls or other containers in a crowded fridge. They're great for storing salads, too.

TIPS:

• Check the preparation instructions on the packages of couscous you buy. They may differ slightly, depending on the way the couscous was processed.

• As a general rule 1 medium lemon produces about 6–8 tbsp (90–120 ml) of juice; 1 lime, 4–6 tbsp (60–90 ml). To get the most juice, squeeze the fruit when it is at room temperature.

• Parmesan cheese will stay fresher if you buy it in a chunk and grate it as necessary. Buy the real stuff – Parmigiano Reggiano – and taste the difference. It has a rich nutty flavour the others don't approach. Serve it sprinkled on soup, grated over pasta, slivered on a salad or antipasto platter, or just to nibble as a special snack.

• Some of the recipes in this book call for "deli-style cream cheese." This refers to the type sold in bulk and scooped into plastic containers. Not only does it taste better than the packaged kind sold in blocks, but it also spreads and blends more easily.

• If you have a summer place, at the beginning of the season compile a list of the essentials in your cupboards and make photocopies of it. Use a copy to check supplies every week or so, then take it with you to the store. It's much easier (and more reliable) than trying to remember what you're out of after you're back in the city.

Condiments and other staples

Although you can use a good red or white wine vinegar for all the recipes in this book, give yourself some variety by adding a few others to your shelf: balsamic vinegar, sherry vinegar, cider vinegar, and sweet mild rice vinegar. Supplement a basic vegetable oil with a mild, fruity extra-virgin olive oil. A more robust extra-virgin olive oil and a flavoured olive oil (such as garlic oil) are also handy.

Sun-dried tomatoes and dried mushrooms (such as porcinis, portobellos, and shiitakes) keep almost forever on the shelf and add intense flavour to sauces and stews. Yes, they're expensive – but a few go a long way. Look for them in the produce section of the supermarket; they're usually sold in small plastic or Cellophane packages. Soak them in water for about 30 minutes to soften before using.

A good Dijon mustard (Maille or Grey Poupon) and a box of Keen's powdered mustard – plus your family's favourites for burgers and hot dogs – should serve nicely. Other staples to have on hand include: mayonnaise, horseradish, Worcestershire sauce, and honey. Homemade-style preserves and real maple syrup are breakfast essentials. Ready-made chicken, beef, and vegetable stocks are a time-saving alternative to homemade stock. Search out good-quality, low-salt options in cans, Tetra Paks, and cubes.

Grains, legumes, and pasta

Good-quality dried pasta, made from durum wheat, has excellent flavour and texture, and blends with sauces much better than most commercially made "fresh" pasta. Dried pasta keeps well and is available in so many different forms that the meal possibilities are endless. In addition to spaghetti and fettuccine, I like to have penne or fusilli, orzo (a rice-shaped pasta), and egg noodles on hand. Grains such as bulgur, couscous, and wheat berries are great for making salads and side dishes. They also provide a choice of texture and flavour for creating healthy meals for the vegetarians of the group, as does a selection of rices – basmati, jasmine, arborio, long-grain brown rice, and wild rice – and dried lentils and dried beans (instead of, or in addition to, the canned varieties).

For the baking cupboard

Even if you're not much of a baker, it's well worth having a few baking supplies: all-purpose flour, instant yeast, baking powder, baking soda, old-fashioned and quick-cook oats, cornmeal, cornstarch, skim-milk powder, white and brown sugar, icing sugar, cocoa, and vanilla. Graham crackers or crumbs are handy, too, for a quick crust.

Don't forget chocolate – unsweetened, semi-sweet, milk chocolate, and white chocolate – in squares, chunks, and/or chips. For the ultimate indulgence, use the finest quality imported chocolate; my favourite is Callebaut. A supply of nuts is also essential, to add crunch to salads as well as for baking: pecans, walnuts, peanuts, hazelnuts, pine nuts, and sliced or slivered almonds. Raisins, apricots, and dates are the old standbys, but you can now buy other dried fruit – cranberries, cherries, and blueberries – in packages in the supermarket or in bulk-food stores. They last almost forever and can be used to add intense fruit flavour to cookies, cakes, and salads. Unsweetened coconut and crystallized ginger (if you like it) are good additions to the cupboard, too, and instant espresso powder can be used to add a real shot of coffee flavour (to ice cream, say, and dessert sauces) and to intensify the taste of chocolate.

After all, it's nice to know that if it rains all day, *someone* can whip up a batch of cookies or squares. Also, you never know when you'll be confronted with a birthday and need to come up with a cake. (Make sure you tuck away a package of birthday candles!)

Asian ingredients

This book includes some recipes with Asian flavours – Thai, Indonesian, Malaysian, and Indian. Having a few basic staples on hand will make preparing them easy. Most of the following are now readily available in the oriental/Asian section of large supermarkets, and all have a very long shelf or refrigerator life: soy sauce, rice vinegar (it may be shelved with other types of vinegar), pure sesame oil (used for flavouring, not frying), fish sauce (see Tips, facing page), hoisin sauce, dried rice-paper wrappers (great for making various seafood and vegetable rolls), rice stick noodles or vermicelli, soba

TIPS:

• Baking powder, baking soda, and yeast lose their leavening power over time, so replace them every year. Do the following test to see if your baking powder still has its oomph: Put ½ tsp (2 ml) into a small quantity of warm water; if it's still good, it will fizz and bubble. To test baking soda, combine a small amount with an equal quantity of vinegar. If it doesn't bubble vigorously, it's time to get a new box.

• Buttermilk powder – available in bulk-food stores – is a handy staple. If a recipe calls for 1 cup (250 ml) buttermilk, put ¼ cup (60 ml) of the powder in a 1 cup (250 ml) measure, fill with cold water, and mix well. If you are baking or making pancakes, add the powder to the dry ingredients and the water to the liquid ones. (Buttermilk powder meant specifically for baking is sold in cans in some U.S. supermarkets; follow the directions on the can.)

• Toasting nuts helps bring out their flavour: Put them in a shallow baking pan in a 375°F (190°C) oven for 3–6 minutes, stirring often, so they become evenly and lightly browned.

• A 4-oz (114-g) tin of Thai curry paste will likely be enough to make 2–3 dishes serving 6 people each. Use what you require, then wrap the remaining curry paste in foil packages of about 1 tbsp (15 ml) apiece and store in the freezer; they will keep for 2 months.

• Fish sauce, an essential element in Thai and Vietnamese cooking, is a light-gold liquid condiment produced by layering fresh anchovies or squid with salt in wooden barrels and allowing them to ferment. I like to use the light-coloured brands imported from Thailand or Vietnam. A bottle, once opened, lasts indefinitely in the cupboard. There is no substitute for fish sauce, but you can just leave it out of most recipes or add a dash of light soy sauce instead.

• A small can of chipotle peppers in adobo sauce goes a long way. (They're devilishly hot.) To store the unused portion of a can, purée with a couple of tablespoons of vegetable oil. Spoon into an ice-cube tray and freeze, then pop the cubes into a freezer bag, ready to use.

noodles, and canned coconut milk. (It may be shelved with the other canned milks.) Canned baby corn and water chestnuts add instant oriental crunch to salads and stir-fries. Some Asian recipes call for red chili paste or sauce – sambal oelek is a readily available option – but you can substitute hot red pepper flakes (or leave out the heat, if it's not to your family's taste).

Ready-prepared Thai and Indian spice pastes – sold in jars, cans, and envelopes – are a great shortcut for making curries as well as marinating food for the grill. Let the ingredient list on the jar be your guide: good-quality pastes include few additives and lots of authentic herbs and spices.

South-of-the-border flavours

This book also includes some recipes whose origins are south of the border. Although they may call for chile peppers in some form, none of them is fiery hot. If you follow the quantities given, you'll end up with a modest degree of heat. Adjust the recipe to your own taste by increasing or decreasing the amount of "hot" ingredients called for.

Here are some south-of-the-border basics to have on hand: a bottle of hot sauce (Tabasco is probably the best known, but there are now countless brands on the market, with varying degrees of heat), hot red pepper flakes, a good quality chili powder, and chipotle peppers in adobo sauce. Chipotles are smoked jalapeño peppers that add heat and a lovely smoky flavour. Although they are sold dried, they are easier to find in cans, packed in adobo sauce, a rich, thick tomato sauce. (Look on the Mexican food shelf of the supermarket, or in a store specializing in Latin American foods.) You can chop or purée them and add to a variety of tomato-based stews and sauces, egg dishes, or marinades.

With these items in the cupboard, and garlic, onions, ginger root, lemons, and limes on hand, you have the basics in place for most of the recipes in this book. Just add the meat, fish, seasonal produce, cheese, and dairy items for your selected menu, and you're ready for the weekend. And don't forget the bread and milk!

Get the heat out of the kitchen

Cooking outdoors is an essential part of summer, and a good number of the recipes in this book use the barbecue or provide an option for barbecue cooking. For the true grillmeister, barbecuing is an art form; for the more casual practitioner, here are some refresher tips:

• Remove food from the refrigerator a half-hour before grilling, so it will cook more quickly and evenly.

• When cooking marinated meats, pat them dry before putting them on the grill. This will help them brown.

• Always preheat the barbecue. Brush the grill rack vigorously to make sure it is clean, and oil lightly just before putting on the food.

• Place an oven thermometer inside your barbecue if it doesn't have an accurate one on the lid. Have an instant-read thermometer, too – it's the best way to tell when a large cut of meat is done the way you like it.

• Get yourself a good pair of stainless-steel hinged tongs (available in restaurant-supply stores). A vegetable grilling basket is also a handy barbecue accessory, as you can use it for grilling all sorts of small delicate food (including mussels, clams, and small fish).

• If you baste with the marinade in which raw meat, chicken, or fish has been sitting, make sure the meat continues to cook on the grill for at least a few minutes after basting. Don't serve the marinade as a sauce, or glaze the meat with it after cooking, unless you first bring it to a boil and simmer it for 5–10 minutes.

• For smoke flavour, soak chips of hardwood such as hickory, mesquite, apple, or cherry in water for an hour before using. Or use branches of aromatic herbs such as thyme, rosemary, or sage. Drain and place directly on the coals of a charcoal fire. Some gas grills have a special spot for wood chips; otherwise, place the wood in a shallow metal container (such as an aluminum pie plate) with holes punched in it and put the container on the rocks over the flame.

TIPS:

• Use bamboo skewers to grill strips or cubes of meat, fish, and veggies – short ones for appetizer-size snacks, longer ones (10"/25 cm) for dinner. Soak them in cold water for about an hour beforehand so they don't burn. Metal skewers work well for potatoes because they transfer heat effectively and speed up the cooking.

• If you include vegetables with meat or fish on the same skewer, choose varieties that require the same degree of heat and the same cooking time. It's often easier if you grill them separately. Cook vegetables on skewers first and set them to the side of the grill, then quickly grill the meat or fish, which is best enjoyed piping hot straight from the fire.

• For a special presentation, skewer meat on trimmings from grapevines or the woody twigs of fresh herbs such as rosemary or sage. They provide aromatic smoke and look attractive. Soak the vines or twigs in water for an hour and pierce the pieces of meat with a wooden or metal skewer before threading them on. You can use the same technique with slender stalks of lemon grass for Asian-flavoured chicken skewers.

Barbecuing with indirect heat

Indirect heat is great for barbecuing larger cuts of meat or bone-in chicken. With this method, the meat is cooked without a direct flame under it, so your dinner doesn't turn out charred on the outside and raw inside.

With a gas barbecue, place a foil drip pan on the rocks over one burner. Preheat the barbecue to high with all burners on and the lid closed. When the barbecue is preheated, turn off the burner under the drip pan, put the meat on the grill above the pan (and the unlit burner), and close the lid. The heat from the lit burner(s) then circulates throughout the barbecue, cooking the meat. (The technique may vary slightly with some makes of barbecue, so check the manufacturer's instructions.)

With a covered charcoal grill, place a foil pan in the bottom and bank the hot coals on either side of it. Put the meat on the rack over the pan, and set the cover in place. Add more fuel to each side every hour or so of cooking time. Preferably, preheat these coals in a small Hibachi or metal chimney so they are ready when needed and the heat remains constant.

I. APPETIZERS, STARTERS, & SUNDOWN SNACKS

Classic Summer Cocktails

There's nothing wrong with that old standby, the gin and tonic, but here are some other ideas for refreshing drinks that are guaranteed to enliven your summer gathering. Each recipe makes one drink, but can be multiplied to serve a group (or for individual indulgence).

Mojito

6–8	fresh mint leaves	
1½ oz	white rum	45 ml
1 tsp	sugar	5 ml
	juice of 1 lime	
	soda water	

Watermelon Daiquiri

¾ cup	watermelon, *seeded*	175 ml
1½ oz	white rum	45 ml
1 tsp	sugar	5 ml
	juice of 1 lime	

Gin Fizz

	juice of ½ lemon	
1½ oz	gin	45 ml
1 tsp	sugar	5 ml
	soda water	

QUICK TRICK:
Berry Bubbly: Splash a bit of Berry Syrup (p. 305) or cassis or framboise liqueur into a glass of sparkling white wine or champagne. Garnish with fresh berries.

Mojito

Said to have been one of Ernest Hemingway's favourites: In a tall glass, crush the mint. Top with lots of ice, then add rum, sugar, and lime juice. Top with soda water and stir well. Garnish with a sprig of mint and a slice of lime.

Watermelon Daiquiri

A twist on the old classic: Chill glass in freezer. In a blender, purée watermelon, rum, sugar, lime, and 6–8 ice cubes. Strain into chilled glass over fresh ice. Garnish with a wedge of watermelon.

Gin Fizz

Gin is the traditional spirit in this drink, but you can also make Vodka Fizzes and Rum Fizzes. Vigorous shaking is the secret to the fizz: Whirl lemon juice, gin, sugar, and 6–8 ice cubes in a blender, or shake vigorously for several minutes. Strain into a tall glass over fresh ice, and immediately top with soda water. Garnish with a lemon wedge.

Mai Tai

	juice of 2 limes	
1½ oz	dark rum	45 ml
½ oz	orange liqueur	15 ml
2 dashes	grenadine *(approx.)*	

Berry Margarita

1	lime	
	salt *and/or* sugar	
1 oz	gold tequila	30 ml
½ oz	orange liqueur	15 ml
2 oz	Berry Syrup *(p. 305)*	60 ml

Bloody Caesar

1	lime	
	celery salt	
	hot sauce	
	Worcestershire sauce	
1½ oz	vodka	45 ml
	Clamato juice	
	salt and pepper	

Ginger Beer with a Kick

	juice of ½ lime	
1½ oz	rum *or* vodka	45 ml
	ginger beer *or* ginger ale	

Mai Tai

Makes you feel like you're in the tropics: Combine all ingredients in a blender or shaker with 6–8 ice cubes. Blend or shake well, then strain into a glass over fresh ice. Garnish with a maraschino cherry and a lime wedge – and a paper parasol, if you really want to get into the spirit.

Berry Margarita

A north-of-the-border version of the traditional margarita: Chill glass in freezer. Rub rim of frosted glass with a cut lime, then dip in a saucer of salt, sugar, or a combination. Combine remaining ingredients and pour into glass over crushed ice. Or whirl in a blender with 6–8 ice cubes until smooth and frosty. Garnish with a few fresh berries.

Bloody Caesar

A Canadian invention: Rub rim of a tall glass with a cut lime, then dip in a saucer of celery salt. Fill glass with ice. Add a couple dashes of hot sauce and Worcestershire sauce, and vodka. Top with Clamato, season to taste with salt and pepper, and stir well. Garnish with a celery stalk and a lime wedge.

Ginger Beer with a Kick

Non-alcoholic ginger beer has a more gingery flavour than ginger ale, but you can use either. Known as a "Moscow Mule" when it's made with vodka (because of vodka's Russian origins), this drink is popular in the Caribbean made with rum: Fill a tall, well-chilled glass with ice. Add lime juice and rum or vodka, then top with ginger beer or ginger ale and stir well. Garnish with a lime wedge.

QUICK TRICK:

Old-Fashioned Lemonade: Combine 1 cup (250 ml) sugar, 1 cup (250 ml) water, and 2 strips of lemon zest in a small saucepan and bring to a boil for 1 minute, or until sugar dissolves. Remove sugar syrup from heat and cool. Remove zest. In a large pitcher, combine sugar syrup with the juice of 4 lemons (about 1 cup/250 ml of juice) and 4 cups (1 L) water. Pour into glasses filled with ice and garnish with fresh mint. Makes 6 cups (1.5 L).

Overleaf: Watermelon Daiquiri, Ginger Beer with a Kick, Mai Tai, Gin Fizz, Bloody Caesar, and Mojito.

Devilish Cheese Twists

2 cups	all-purpose flour	500 ml
½ tsp	salt	2 ml
½ tsp	cayenne	2 ml
½ cup	cold butter, *cut in chunks*	125 ml
3 cups	old Cheddar cheese, *grated*	750 ml
¼ cup	Parmesan cheese, *grated*	60 ml
4–5 tbsp	cold water	60–75 ml
1	egg	
	coarse sea salt, sesame seeds, poppy seeds, *and/or* additional cheese *(for topping)*	

TIPS:

• The pastry can be made several days ahead and kept, well wrapped, in the refrigerator.

• Baked cheese twists can be frozen; reheat in a hot oven just before serving.

You won't believe how quickly these spicy, melt-in-the-mouth twists will disappear at cocktail hour. The pastry is easy to make – especially with a food processor, but two knives or a pastry blender will also do the job.

1. Combine flour, salt, and cayenne in food processor, add butter, and pulse machine on and off until mixture forms coarse crumbs. Add both cheeses to mixture, using same on/off technique.

2. Gradually sprinkle 4 tbsp (60 ml) of ice-cold water over mixture and pulse until pastry comes together. If it isn't holding together, add 1 tbsp (15 ml) more water. Do not overprocess.

3. On a lightly floured surface roll out pastry until it's about ⅛" (3 mm) thick. Cut into strips about ½" (1 cm) wide and 6" (15 cm) long. Twist each strip once or twice, and place on greased and floured or parchment-lined baking sheets.

4. Beat egg lightly with 1 tbsp (15 ml) water and brush twists with the egg wash. Sprinkle with the toppings as desired.

5. Bake in preheated 400°F (200°C) oven for 10–15 minutes until cheese twists are golden-brown. Remove to racks and serve warm.

Makes about 30 twists.

(Devilish Cheese Twists are shown in the photo opposite p. 226.)

Cottage Tapenade

1 cup	black olives, *pitted*	250 ml
1 cup	pimento-stuffed green olives	250 ml
1 clove	garlic	
¼ cup	fresh flat-leaf parsley	60 ml
1 tbsp	red wine vinegar	15 ml
1 tsp	fresh lemon juice	5 ml
¼ cup	extra-virgin olive oil	60 ml
	salt and freshly ground black pepper	

TIPS:

• The tapenade can be made ahead and stored in the fridge for 3–5 days.

• If you don't have a food processor, finely chop the ingredients by hand.

Although prepared tapenade is available, you can quickly create your own version of this Mediterranean olive spread. Serve with garlic toasts, or spread on grilled slices of crusty bread to make crostini.

1. Combine olives, garlic, parsley, vinegar, and lemon juice in the bowl of a food processor. Pulse until mixture is evenly chopped.

2. Add half the olive oil and pulse to combine. Add remaining oil and pulse again until mixture is a fine paste but with some texture remaining. Taste and adjust seasoning.

Makes about 1 cup (250 ml).

QUICK TRICK:

Cheater's Devilish Cheese Twists: Start with store-bought puff pastry instead of making your own pastry. Roll the puff pastry out to a thickness of about ⅛" (3 mm), sprinkle half of it with grated Cheddar and Parmesan cheese and a pinch or two of cayenne, and fold over the other half. Roll again to a thickness of about ⅛" (3 mm). Following directions on facing page, cut into strips and twist, brush with egg wash, and sprinkle with toppings as desired. Bake in preheated 400°F (200°C) oven for 10–15 minutes until twists are golden-brown. Serve warm.

Pesto Duo
Roasted Pepper Pesto & Sun-Dried Tomato Pesto

These two spreads are extremely versatile. Serve them as is accompanied by slices of toasted baguette, plain bagel crisps, or whole-wheat crispbread. Or spoon the pesto on top of creamy goat cheese or deli-style cream cheese, and let guests spread a little of each on baguette toasts or crispbread. The pestos are also delicious tossed with pasta for a quick dinner.

Roasted Pepper Pesto

1. Peel, seed, and chop peppers. Combine with remaining ingedients. Add salt and freshly ground black pepper to taste. *Makes about 1¹/₂ cups (375 ml).*

Sun-Dried Tomato Pesto

1. Combine tomatoes, almonds, garlic, lemon zest, and herbs in the bowl of a food processor. Pulse until mixture is evenly chopped.

2. Add half the olive oil and pulse to combine. Add remaining oil and pulse again until mixture is a paste but with some texture remaining. Season to taste. *Makes about 1 cup (250 ml).*

Roasted Pepper Pesto

4	**roasted peppers,** *2 yellow, 2 red*	
1 clove	**garlic,** *minced*	
¹/₄ cup	**red onion,** *finely minced*	60 ml
1 tsp	**balsamic vinegar**	5 ml
2 tbsp	**fresh parsley,** *finely chopped*	30 ml
1 tbsp	**fresh basil,** *finely chopped*	15 ml
1 tsp	**extra-virgin olive oil**	5 ml

Sun-Dried Tomato Pesto

1 cup	**sun-dried tomatoes in oil**	250 ml
¹/₄ cup	**blanched almonds**	60 ml
1 clove	**garlic**	
1 strip	**lemon zest** *(approx. 3"/8 cm)*	
¹/₂ cup	**fresh basil**	125 ml
¹/₄ cup	**fresh parsley**	60 ml
¹/₃ cup	**extra-virgin olive oil**	75 ml

*both recipes require salt and freshly ground black pepper to taste

TIPS:

• The spreads can be prepared ahead and stored in the refrigerator for about 3–5 days.

• You can substitute 1 tbsp (15 ml) fresh lemon juice for the balsamic vinegar in the pepper pesto.

• Directions for roasting peppers are on p. 126.

Front to back: Sun-Dried Tomato Pesto, Better-than-Bought Hummus (p. 26), and Roasted Pepper Pesto.

Better-than-Bought Hummus
and a Trio of Variations

2 cloves	**garlic,** *chopped*	
1 tbsp	**olive oil**	**15 ml**
3 tbsp	**fresh lemon juice**	**45 ml**
¼ cup	**tahini**	**60 ml**
1 tsp	**salt**	**5 ml**
2–3 tbsp	**water**	**30-45 ml**
½ tsp	**cayenne**	**2 ml**
1½ cups	**cooked chickpeas,** *rinsed and drained (1 19-oz/540-ml can)*	**375 ml**
	aromatic olive oil *(for garnish; optional)*	

VARIATIONS:

• **Red Pepper Hummus:** Roast or grill 1 red pepper. Remove blackened skin and seeds. Add to above mixture and blend until smooth.

• **Roasted Garlic Hummus:** Omit fresh garlic. Add 4–6 cloves of freshly roasted garlic (p. 126) and blend until smooth.

• **Fresh Herb Hummus:** Add 1 tsp (5 ml) ground cumin, ¼ cup (60 ml) chopped fresh coriander, and ¼ cup (60 ml) chopped fresh mint or flat-leaf parsley.

You can find ready-made versions of this popular Middle Eastern chickpea dip in the supermarket, but when you need a quick munchie, it's very easy to make your own – especially if you keep a can of chickpeas and a jar of tahini in the cupboard. The fresh flavour of homemade hummus is far superior to the storebought variety. Serve with wedges of warm pita bread, Moroccan olives, and slices of fresh lemon.

1. In a blender or food processor blend together garlic, 1 tbsp (15 ml) olive oil, lemon juice, tahini, salt, water, and cayenne.

2. Shake the chickpeas in a sieve and quickly pick out as many of the tough little skins as are easily removed. Add the chickpeas to the garlic mixture and blend until smooth. (Or mash all the ingredients together by hand.)

3. Taste and add more salt and/or lemon juice if necessary. Add a little more water if mixture is too thick. (It will thicken as it sits.)

4. Spoon the hummus into a shallow bowl, make an indentation in the centre, and add a spoonful of an aromatic olive oil if desired.

Makes 2 cups (500 ml).

TIP:

• Tahini, a paste made from crushed sesame seeds, is an ingredient in many Middle Eastern dishes. It's readily available now in large supermarkets (in jars) and in bulk-food stores (where it's sold like bulk peanut butter).

(Better-than-Bought Hummus is shown in the photo on previous page.)

Tzatziki

2 cups	plain natural yogurt	500 ml
½	English cucumber, *peeled and grated*	
	salt	
2–3 cloves	garlic, *finely chopped*	
1 tbsp	extra-virgin olive oil	15 ml
1 tbsp	fresh dill, *finely chopped*	15 ml
1 tbsp	fresh mint, *finely chopped*	15 ml
	fresh lemon juice, *to taste*	

*I*t's hard to beat the fresh, creamy taste of this easy homemade version of the classic Greek yogurt-cucumber-garlic dip. Serve as part of a meze selection (see Quick Trick, p. 30), or on its own with black olives and warm pita bread. It's also the perfect accompaniment to grilled lamb kebabs or lamb koftas (pp. 104, 105).

1. Line a sieve with a basket coffee filter or a double layer of cheesecloth and set it over a bowl. Spoon the yogurt in. Leave to drain for several hours, or place in the refrigerator to drain overnight.

2. Toss grated cucumber with 1 tsp (5 ml) of salt and set aside for an hour. Squeeze out and discard the excess liquid.

3. Combine the drained yogurt, cucumber, garlic, oil, and herbs. Add lemon juice and additional salt to taste, and set aside in the refrigerator for an hour or so for flavours to develop.

Makes 2 cups (500 ml).

TIPS:
• The tzatziki is best made on the day of serving, but it will keep, refrigerated, for 2–3 days. Pour away any liquid that accumulates on the surface.

• If you don't have time to drain the yogurt, you can use ¾ cup (175 ml) yogurt and ¾ cup (175 ml) sour cream to achieve the desired creamy consistency.

Red Pepper & Feta Spread

4	**sweet red peppers,** *roasted, peeled, seeded, and chopped*	
½–1	**fresh hot red pepper,** *seeded and chopped (or to taste)*	
2 cloves	**garlic,** *minced*	
2 tbsp	**extra-virgin olive oil**	30 ml
1 lb	**feta cheese,** *crumbled*	500 g
	freshly ground black pepper	
	squeeze of fresh lemon juice	

TIPS:

• The spread can be made ahead and will keep in the refrigerator for up to 3 days.

• To convert the spread into a creamy dip to serve with fresh vegetables, stir in 2 tbsp (30 ml) of yogurt after blending in the feta.

• For how to roast peppers, see p. 126.

Delicious at cocktail hour on plain toasted pita triangles or Spicy Pita Wedges (Quick Trick, below), as a sandwich spread (with grilled lamb on top), or as the base of a wrap stuffed with grilled veggies.

1. Place peppers, garlic, and olive oil in a food processor and blend to a paste.

2. Add feta cheese and pulse to combine just until smooth. Do not over-process or the cheese will become too runny.

3. Taste and adjust seasoning. Depending on the quality of the feta, you may need to add a squeeze of lemon juice or a few grindings of black pepper. (Since the feta is salty, it's unlikely you'll need additional salt.)

Makes 2 cups (500 ml).

QUICK TRICK:

Spicy Pita Wedges: Season ½ cup (125 ml) olive oil with a few shakes of hot sauce and a couple of cloves of minced garlic. Brush on both sides of 6–8 pita rounds. Grill on a medium-hot barbecue for about 10 minutes, turning once, taking care not to let pitas burn. (Or bake in a 400°F/200°C oven.) Cut each pita into 8 wedges and serve warm. If pita bread has a pocket, you can make pita crisps: Cut each round into 8 wedges and split the wedges apart. Brush with the seasoned oil, place on a baking sheet and bake in the oven as above.

Roast the red peppers and make the spread ahead of time, then serve it at cocktail hour with toasted pita bread and olives mixed with hot pepper flakes.

Herbed Feta

½ lb	feta cheese, *cut in small cubes*	250 g
1 tbsp	extra-virgin olive oil	15 ml
2 tsp	fresh oregano, *finely chopped* or	10 ml
1 tsp	dried oregano	5 ml
1 tsp	fresh thyme, *finely chopped* or	5 ml
½ tsp	dried thyme	2 ml
1 tbsp	fresh flat-leaf parsley, *finely chopped*	15 ml
pinch	cayenne *or* hot red pepper flakes	
	freshly ground black pepper	

TIPS:

• Select firm Greek, Bulgarian, or Canadian feta for this recipe; Macedonian feta will be too creamy.

• The version made with dried herbs will keep in the refrigerator for up to a week. Add the fresh parsley and fresh pepper at serving time.

*S*erve this herbed cheese as part of a meze platter (Quick Trick, below) or, for a very simple snack, pile it into a radicchio leaf or onto a bed of romaine or watercress, and accompany it with black olives and roasted pepper strips sprinkled with olive oil and fresh herbs. Serve with slices of grilled garlic bread.

1. Toss feta with oil, herbs, and spices.

2. Refrigerate for a couple of hours before serving to give flavours a chance to blend.

Makes 1¼ cups (300 ml).

QUICK TRICK:

Meze Platter: Meze, the name given to the assortment of tasty morsels that appears on your table in Greece whenever you sit down to enjoy a glass of wine, is my favourite summer pre-dinner offering. A meze platter can be as simple or substantial as you please. Include homemade or store-bought versions of dips such as tzatziki (p. 27), hummus (p. 26), baba ghanouj (a smoky puréed eggplant dip), and taramasalata (a pink-hued dip made with carp roe). Add a bowl of brine-cured kalamata or sun-dried Moroccan olives and warm pita bread or chunky slices of a crusty white loaf.

Other meze possibilities include Lemon Rosemary Almonds (p. 33); Herbed Feta (above); a plate of grilled vegetables (p. 124) sprinkled with a little olive oil, lemon zest, and rosemary; and Simple Sizzling Shrimp (facing page).

Simple Sizzling Shrimp

2 tsp	olive oil	10 ml
8	**jumbo shrimp,** *shell removed except for about ¹/₂" (1 cm) at the tail*	
¹/₄ tsp	salt	1 ml
1	**small garlic clove,** *finely chopped*	
2 tsp	**fresh parsley,** *chopped*	10 ml
	freshly ground black pepper	
1	**lemon,** *cut in wedges*	

TIP:

• This same technique can be used with other seafood, such as scallops or squid, or with bite-size chunks of chorizo or other spicy sausage.

Always popular, extremely delicious, and very easy, this recipe adds an instant hot bite to a pre-dinner snack selection. The shrimp go well with a meze platter or other Mediterranean appetizer selection; use the variation below for a Mexican-themed happy hour. Serve the sizzling shrimp straight from the pan or the griddle.

1. Heat an iron griddle or heavy iron skillet on the top of the stove or on the barbecue until it is very hot. Brush griddle or skillet lightly with olive oil.

2. Toss shrimp with salt and set on the hot griddle or in the hot pan for 2 minutes. Turn shrimp and cook for another 1 or 2 minutes until done. (The shrimp should be just turning pink and still tender and juicy.)

3. Add garlic, parsley, and black pepper to the pan, and serve the shrimp at once, garnished with lemon wedges.

Serves 2–4 as a snack.

VARIATION:

• Replace the parsley with fresh coriander and the lemon with lime to move the flavour from Mediterranean to south-of-the-border.

Curried Nuts & Chili Nuts

2 cups	pecan halves	500 ml
2 cups	cashews	500 ml
2 cups	unblanched whole almonds	500 ml
¼ cup	butter, *melted*	60 ml
	salt	

Curried Nuts

1 tsp	hot sauce	5 ml
4 tsp	curry powder	20 ml
2 cups	raisins	500 ml

Chili Nuts

½ tsp	hot sauce	2 ml
½ tsp	ground coriander	2 ml
½ tsp	paprika	2 ml
½ tsp	ground cumin	2 ml
½ tsp	cayenne	2 ml
½ tsp	freshly ground black pepper	2 ml
1½ tsp	chili powder	7 ml

These twists on standard salted nuts will appeal to people with a hot spot instead of a sweet tooth. Although the recipe calls for mixed nuts, of course you can stick to one type if you have a particular favourite.

1. Preheat oven to 300°F (150°C). Place nuts in a large bowl.

2. Combine butter with hot sauce and spices for either Curried Nuts or Chili Nuts. Pour mixture over nuts and toss to coat on all sides.

3. Spread nuts in a single layer on large baking sheets and bake for about 30 minutes, stirring now and again.

4. Sprinkle nuts with salt and transfer to trays lined with paper towel to cool. Add raisins to Curried Nuts. Store mixture in plastic bags or airtight containers. Allow flavours to develop overnight before serving.

Makes 8 cups (2 L) of Curried Nuts, 6 cups (1.5 L) of Chili Nuts.

TIP:
• Best eaten within a few days. If nuts are kept longer, warm them in a low oven for a few minutes before serving so they regain their crispness.

Lemon-Rosemary and Sweet & Spicy
Cocktail Almonds

Lemon-Rosemary Almonds

2 cups	unblanched whole almonds	500 ml
¼ cup	fresh lemon juice	60 ml
½ tsp	dried rosemary	2 ml
2 tbsp	coarse kosher *or* sea salt	30 ml

Sweet & Spicy Almonds

2 tbsp	peanut oil	30 ml
2 cups	blanched whole almonds	500 ml
2 tsp	sugar	10 ml
½ tsp	ground cumin	2 ml
1 tsp	cayenne *or* **hot sauce**	5 ml
	salt	

QUICK TRICK:
Popcorn with Pizzazz: Freshly popped popcorn is always popular, but if plain popcorn seems ho-hum for cocktail hour, try tossing it with melted butter, a couple of shakes of grated Parmesan cheese, a spoonful of dried mixed herbs, and a couple of dashes of hot sauce.

Make up a batch or two of these almonds to have on hand for cocktail hour. They're best when freshly toasted, although they'll stay fresh in an airtight container for a week or two. (To keep them that long, though, you'll definitely have to hide the containers at the back of the cupboard.)

Lemon-Rosemary Almonds

1. In a bowl, toss almonds with lemon juice and rosemary; let sit for 10 minutes.

2. Spread almonds in a single layer on a baking sheet and sprinkle with salt.

3. Bake in 325°F (160°C) oven for about 20 minutes, stirring occasionally.

4. Set aside to cool, then store in airtight containers. *Makes 2 cups (500 ml).*

Sweet & Spicy Almonds

1. Heat oil in a large, heavy skillet. Add almonds, sprinkle with sugar, and toss over medium-high heat until nuts are a light, even brown, 5–10 minutes.

2. Turn out into a bowl and toss with cumin, cayenne or hot sauce, and salt.

3. Spread nuts on paper towel to cool and crisp. Store in airtight containers. *Makes 2 cups (500 ml).*

Barbecued Marinated Brie

1 tbsp	lemon juice	15 ml
1 tbsp	vegetable oil	15 ml
½	red pepper, *finely chopped*	
1 tbsp	fresh parsley, *finely chopped*	15 ml
1 clove	garlic, *minced*	
1 tsp	Dijon mustard	5 ml
¼ tsp	freshly ground black pepper	1 ml
8-oz wheel	Brie *or* Camembert	250 g
	crackers *or* French bread	

*P*eople continue to tell me how much they love this appetizer. Not only is it delicious, it looks fabulous too. And it's an ideal starter when you have the barbecue going anyway to cook the main course.

1. Combine all ingredients except cheese and crackers or bread. Mix well.

2. Place cheese wheel in a small, shallow glass dish and poke it full of holes with a fork. Pour marinade over cheese. Cover and let sit in refrigerator at least 2 hours, or overnight.

3. Preheat barbecue to medium (350°F/180°C). Place a piece of foil on grill and poke holes in foil with a skewer. Place cheese on foil.

4. Heat just until cheese starts to bulge around the edges and centre is soft, about 15 minutes. Serve warm with crackers or French bread.

Makes about 8 servings.

TIPS:

• For a colourful presentation, use a combination of red and green peppers. (Or just substitute half a green pepper, if that's what you've got on hand.)

• The Brie can also be heated in the oven: Bake at 350°F (180°C) for 10–15 minutes, until cheese just starts to bulge around edges.

Marinate the Brie the day before serving. Then you just have to heat the cheese on the grill and put out a basket of crackers when you're ready to serve.

Artichoke Dip

1 clove	**garlic,** *finely minced*	
1 tbsp	**onion,** *grated*	**15 ml**
1 cup	**mayonnaise**	**250 ml**
¼ tsp	**cayenne**	**1 ml**
2 tbsp	**Parmesan cheese,** *grated*	**30 ml**
	salt and white pepper	
1 can	**artichoke hearts** *(14 oz/398 ml)*	
	paprika	
	pita bread, *cut into triangles and toasted*	

This decadent dip has made an appearance at many gatherings. Friends will gasp and say it's too rich and they shouldn't have any more – and then it will be all gone!

1. Thoroughly blend the first 5 ingredients together. Season to taste.

2. Rinse and drain the artichokes and chop into small pieces. Stir into mayonnaise mixture.

3. Spoon into an ovenproof bowl or gratin dish of about 2-cup (500-ml) capacity, sprinkle with paprika, and bake at 350°F (180°C) for 15–20 minutes, until the dip is bubbling and the top is beginning to brown. Serve hot with toasted pita bread triangles.

Makes 2 cups (500 ml).

QUICK TRICK:
Easy Antipasto Salad: Cut canned artichoke hearts into quarters and combine with chopped red onion, celery, and black olives. Toss with a dressing made from olive oil, wine vinegar, garlic, and hot red pepper flakes. Sprinkle with lots of chopped fresh parsley and paprika. Serve with crisp toasts.

TIPS:

• The flavour of canned artichokes improves greatly if you drain them, rinse them under cold water, and drain them again.

• Be sure to use plain canned artichoke hearts in this recipe – not the marinated ones that come in jars.

2	butternut squash *(approx. 2 lbs/1 kg in total)*	
6 tbsp	olive oil	90 ml
	salt and freshly ground black pepper	
1 head	garlic	
3 tbsp	tahini	45 ml
2 tbsp	lemon juice	30 ml
¼ tsp	cayenne	1 ml

TIPS:

• The squash and garlic can be roasted on the barbecue. Toss with olive oil, season, and wrap in foil. Cook with the lid closed for about 20 minutes, or until tender.

• The dip can be made 1–2 days ahead and stored, covered, in the refrigerator.

• Tahini, a smooth paste of sesame seeds, is found in most supermarkets, but cream or cream cheese make tasty substitutes in this recipe.

Roasted Squash & Garlic Dip

This variation on the traditional Middle Eastern dip baba ghanouj uses squash instead of eggplant as the main ingredient, and roasted garlic (which is sweeter and milder) instead of raw. Serve with Spicy Pita Wedges (Quick Trick, p. 28), pita triangles, bread sticks, bagel crisps, or raw vegetables.

1. Cut, peel, and seed squash and cut into chunks or slice into wedges. Toss with about 2 tbsp (30 ml) olive oil and season with salt and pepper. Spread squash on a baking sheet and roast in a 400°F (200°C) oven for 15 minutes. Turn pieces over and continue to roast until squash is tender and nicely browned on all sides, about 15 minutes longer.

2. Slice about ½" (1 cm) off the top of the head of garlic, wrap head in foil, and roast in the oven with the squash.

3. Squeeze garlic out of skin and blend with roasted squash, tahini, remaining olive oil, and lemon juice in a food processor until smooth. Adjust seasoning with cayenne, salt, and more lemon juice to taste.

Makes 4 cups (1 L).

Stuffed Tortilla Wedges

6	**medium flour tortillas** *(8"/20 cm)*	
½ cup	**salsa**	125 ml
1	**large tomato,** *seeded and chopped*	
2	**green onions,** *finely chopped*	
1 tbsp	**jalapeño peppers,** *finely chopped (fresh or from a jar)*	15 ml
1 cup	**Cheddar cheese,** *grated*	250 ml
1 cup	**feta cheese,** *crumbled*	250 ml
1	**egg,** *lightly beaten*	
¼ cup	**black olives,** *pitted and chopped*	60 ml

These easy-to-make gourmet grilled cheese sandwiches cook on the barbecue in minutes and are always a hit, especially with the teenagers in the group.

1. Place 3 tortillas flat on work surface. Cover each of these tortillas with a thin layer of salsa.

2. Combine remaining ingredients and mix well. Spread ⅓ of the mixture on top of the salsa on each tortilla. Top each with one of the remaining tortillas to cover filling.

3. Grill over medium-high heat for 6–8 minutes, turning halfway through (you'll need 2 spatulas), until tortillas are lightly browned and cheese has melted. Remove and cut into wedges.

Makes 18–24 pieces.

TIPS:

• Keep a package or two of tortillas in your freezer – they're a good base for many snacks. (Also see recipes on pages 48, 222, and 242.)

• These tortilla sandwiches can also be baked in the oven. Place on baking sheets and bake at 350°F (180°C) for about 10 minutes, until the cheese melts.

• You can make the fillings as simple or elaborate as you like. For instance, you can just put grated Monterey Jack or Cheddar cheese and chopped green onions between the tortillas, then dip the grilled wedges in salsa or guacamole. Or fill with grated cheese and chopped grilled veggies. Or try a more exotic combo such as Brie and roasted garlic.

The filling for these tortillas can be assembled quickly, and they cook in minutes on the barbecue or in the oven. Serve with plenty of napkins.

Salsa from the Cupboard

1 tbsp	vegetable oil	15 ml
1	small onion, *chopped*	
1 can	plum tomatoes, *drained, seeded, and roughly chopped* (28 oz/796 ml)	
3	green onions, *chopped*	
2 cloves	garlic, *minced*	
1–2 tbsp	jalapeño peppers, *finely chopped*	15–30 ml
½ tsp	dried oregano	2 ml
½ tsp	ground cumin	2 ml
dash	hot sauce	
2 tbsp	wine vinegar	30 ml
	salt and freshly ground black pepper	
1 tbsp	fresh coriander, *chopped (optional)*	15 ml

*T*here are many good prepared salsas on the market, but if you find yourself without one, this version is not only tasty but it can be whipped up from ingredients you're likely to have in the cupboard. Served with corn chips, it makes a great snack all by itself. But don't sell it short: It's an extremely useful condiment to have on hand, essential with Mexican and Tex-Mex recipes such as Huevos Rancheros (p. 252), Chicken Quesadillas (p. 222), and Steak Fajitas (p. 74). It's also delicious tucked into an omelette or served alongside grilled fish.

1. Heat oil and gently soften onion. Add tomatoes and remaining ingredients. Simmer, stirring now and again, for 15 minutes.

2. Taste and adjust seasoning, making it a little hotter if you like. Transfer to a serving bowl and chill.

Makes about 2½ cups (625 ml).

TIPS:

• If fresh coriander is unavailable, substitute fresh parsley for a different taste or omit it altogether. (Don't substitute ground coriander, as the flavour is unlike that of fresh.)

• The salsa will keep in the refrigerator for about a week.

Guacamole

2	large ripe avocados	
	juice of 1 lime *or* ½ lemon	
1–2 cloves	garlic, *finely chopped*	
2 tbsp	onion, *finely chopped*	30 ml
1	ripe tomato, *seeded and chopped*	
1–2	fresh jalapeño peppers, *seeded and chopped*	
1 tbsp	fresh coriander, *finely chopped*	15 ml
pinch	cayenne *or* a few drops of hot sauce	
	salt	

A popular dip by itself with corn chips, guacamole is also an essential topping for Steak Fajitas (p. 74), Mexican Burgers (p. 101), and Cool Lime Pork Skewers (p. 78). It can be turned into a delicious spread for crackers by blending it with deli-style cream cheese.

1. Halve avocados, remove pits, and scoop flesh from the skins. Sprinkle with lemon or lime juice (peeled avocado quickly turns brown when exposed to air, and lemon or lime juice retards this process) and mash with a fork; don't make the mixture too smooth.

2. Combine remaining ingredients in a small bowl. Stir half of this mixture into the mashed avocado. Taste and adjust seasoning, adding a dash more lemon or lime juice if necessary. Spread the remainder of the tomato mixture on top.

Makes about 1½ cups (375 ml).

TIPS:

• If you don't have any fresh jalapeños on hand, you can substitute ones from a jar, or a couple more healthy dashes of hot sauce.

• You can omit the coriander – the taste will be somewhat different, but delicious nonetheless.

• Guacamole tastes best when freshly made, so serve within an hour or two of making; an occasional stir keeps the colour fresh.

• To test an avocado for ripeness, gently stick a toothpick in the stem end; it should slip smoothly in and out.

Cottage Canoes

12	large fresh jalapeño peppers	
1½ cups	old Cheddar cheese, *finely grated*	375 ml
¼ cup	mayonnaise	60 ml
1	green onion, *finely chopped*	
1 stalk	celery, *finely chopped*	
½ tsp	Worcestershire sauce	2 ml
1	egg, *beaten*	
1 cup	seasoned dry bread crumbs	250 ml

𝒯his spicy appetizer got its name because the pepper halves look like the ubiquitous green canoes you see all over Ontario's cottage country.

1. Cut peppers in half lengthwise and remove ribs and seeds.

2. Mix cheese, mayonnaise, onion, celery, and Worcestershire sauce. Fill peppers with cheese mixture, pressing down on top to flatten. Chill for 20 minutes.

3. Roll each pepper in beaten egg, then dredge in bread crumbs to coat thoroughly. Place on baking sheet.

4. Bake in preheated 350°F (180°C) oven for 10–12 minutes, or until canoe tops are slightly crisp.

Makes 24 pieces.

QUICK TRICK:

Three-Pepper Chip Dip: Combine 1 cup (250 ml) sour cream, or half sour cream and half yogurt, with ½ cup (125 ml) finely chopped sweet red pepper, 1 tsp (5 ml) finely chopped jalapeño pepper, and 1 tsp (5 ml) chili powder. Add a dash of hot sauce for good measure, and a little salt. Allow the dip to sit a while before serving so the flavours will blend – the longer it sits, the hotter it gets.

TIPS:

• Leave the stems on the peppers. They make a nice handle for easy dipping and eating.

• If your skin is sensitive, wear rubber gloves while handling the peppers.

Bet you can't stop at one: These Cottage Canoes have real bite and go extremely well with a glass of cold beer.

Layered Mexican Dip

2 cups	cooked black beans *(1 19-oz/540-ml can)*	500 ml
8 oz	cream cheese	250 g
2 cloves	garlic, *minced*	
2 tbsp	lime juice	30 ml
1 tsp	lime zest, *grated*	5 ml
dash	hot sauce, *or to taste*	
	salt	
2	large tomatoes, *seeded and chopped*	
1 cup	old Cheddar cheese, *grated*	250 ml
4	green onions, *finely chopped*	
¼ cup	black olives, *pitted and chopped*	60 ml
1 tbsp	jalapeño peppers, *finely chopped*	15 ml
½ cup	sour cream	125 ml

This Mexican-inspired dish is such an old favourite I couldn't leave it out of this collection. It's a great party plate – wonderfully easy, makes a lot, and open to variation. If you don't have one of the ingredients on hand, you can omit it or substitute something else. (See Tips, below.) The trick is simply to have several layers/rings of contrasting flavours, colours, and textures. Serve with baskets of tortilla chips for dipping.

1. Blend together black beans, cream cheese, garlic, lime juice and zest, hot sauce, and salt to taste. A blender or food processor does the job in seconds, but an old-fashioned potato masher works too.

2. Spread black bean mixture on a large platter. Arrange a wide ring of chopped tomatoes on top around the edge; spread grated cheese in a ring inside that, followed by a ring of the green onions, followed by the olives and jalapeños combined. Put sour cream in the centre.

Serves a bunch.

TIPS:

• Canned black beans are available in large supermarkets, or you can cook your own. (Directions on p. 156.)

• Instead of the base of black beans, use Spicy Black Bean Dip (p. 46), or a can (14 oz/398 ml) of refried beans that have been heated.

• Add a ring of chopped avocado or a layer of guacamole. (Recipe on p. 41.)

White Bean Dip
with Roasted Garlic

1 head	roasted garlic *(p. 37)*	
1 can	white kidney beans, *rinsed and drained (19 oz/540 ml)*	
2 tbsp	fresh lemon juice	30 ml
2 tbsp	extra-virgin olive oil	30 ml
1 tsp	ground cumin	5 ml
pinch	cayenne	
2 tbsp	fresh flat-leaf parsley *or* mint, *chopped*	30 ml
½ tsp	salt	2 ml

I usually keep a few kinds of dried and canned beans and legumes in my pantry to use in soups, salads, stews, and dips. This simple dip uses canned white kidney beans for convenience, combined with aromatic roasted garlic.

1. Squeeze the soft roasted garlic pulp from each clove and combine with the remaining ingredients in the bowl of a food processor. Process mixture until smooth. Taste and adjust flavour with additional salt and lemon juice if necessary.

2. Cover and set aside in the refrigerator for an hour for flavours to develop before serving.

Makes 1½ cups (375 ml).

TIPS:

• The dip will keep, covered, in the refrigerator for 2–3 days.

• You can also use other bean varieties, such as cannellini or pinto, in this dip.

Spicy Black Bean Dip

2 tbsp	**vegetable oil**	30 ml
1	**small onion,** *chopped*	
2 cloves	**garlic,** *chopped*	
½	**green pepper,** *chopped*	
1	**fresh jalapeño pepper,** *seeded and chopped*	
1 can	**black beans,** *rinsed and drained* (19 oz/540 ml)	
1 tsp	**ground cumin**	5 ml
1 tsp	**chili powder**	5 ml
1 cup	**tomato purée** *or* **drained plum tomatoes,** *roughly chopped*	250 ml
	salt and freshly ground black pepper	
1 tbsp	**red wine vinegar** *or* **lime juice**	15 ml
	fresh coriander *or* **parsley,** *chopped* (*for garnish*)	

*T*his easy dip can be made ahead and will keep for a week stored in a covered container in the refrigerator. It can be enjoyed on its own with corn chips, or used to make nachos and other snacks (such as Black Bean & Pepper Spirals, p. 48). Adjust the amount of jalapeño pepper to your taste.

1. Heat vegetable oil in a large frying pan. Add onion, garlic, green pepper, and jalapeño pepper and cook over medium heat until the vegetables are tender – about 10 minutes.

2. Stir in black beans, cumin, chili powder, tomatoes or purée, and a little seasoning and continue cooking for about 5 minutes. Remove from the heat. Set aside for a couple of minutes to cool.

3. Spoon bean mixture into a food processor and pulse briefly to make a smooth purée, or mash by hand using a potato masher. Adjust flavour with vinegar or lime juice and salt and pepper. Transfer to a serving bowl and garnish with chopped coriander or parsley.

Makes 2½ cups (625 ml).

TIP:

• Include a chipotle pepper (which is a smoked jalapeño) in the dip along with, or instead of, the fresh jalapeño pepper, depending on your tolerance for heat. It will add a rich, smoky flavour. Canned chipotle peppers in adobo sauce (a thick tomato sauce) are found in the Mexican food section of some supermarkets.

Chile con Queso

3 tbsp	olive oil	45 ml
1	medium onion, *finely chopped*	
4	green onions, *finely chopped*	
1–3	jalapeño peppers, *finely chopped*	
½	sweet red pepper, *finely chopped*	
2	large ripe tomatoes, *peeled, seeded, and chopped* or	
1½ cups	canned tomatoes, *well drained and chopped*	375 ml
2 cloves	garlic, *finely chopped*	
	salt and freshly ground black pepper	
¼ cup	35% cream	60 ml
1 lb	Cheddar cheese, *grated (use half mild, half sharp)*	500 g
2 tbsp	flour	30 ml
1 tsp	ground cumin	5 ml

A hot Mexican-style cheese dip for dunking corn chips, pieces of grilled sausage, or crunchy fresh vegetables. Adjust the quantity of hot peppers to your taste.

1. Heat oil in a heavy pot over moderate heat, add onions and peppers, and cook until soft.

2. Stir in tomatoes, garlic, and salt and pepper; simmer for about 5 minutes, until liquid is evaporated. Add cream.

3. Toss grated cheese with flour and cumin. Gradually add to the hot tomato-cream mixture, stirring constantly over moderate heat until sauce is smooth. Serve warm and surround with corn chips and other interesting things for dipping.

Makes about 3 cups (750 ml).

QUICK TRICK:

Spiced Olives: If plain olives seem too ordinary for cocktail hour, toss them with a teaspoon or so of hot red pepper flakes, a couple of cloves of sliced garlic, a little olive oil, dried oregano, and a chopped roasted red pepper. Set aside for an hour or so for flavours to blend. Olives will keep for a week or more in the refrigerator.

Black Bean & Pepper Spirals

4	**large flour tortillas** (*10"/25 cm*)	
1 cup	**Spicy Black Bean Dip** (*p. 46*)	250 ml
¼ cup	**red onion,** *finely chopped*	60 ml
¼ cup	**fresh coriander,** *finely chopped (optional)*	60 ml
1	**green pepper,** *seeded and thinly sliced*	
1	**red pepper,** *seeded and thinly sliced*	
1 cup	**Cheddar cheese,** *grated*	250 ml

These colourful spirals look like you've fussed, but they are simple to make. The rolls can be prepared early in the day and then sliced just before serving.

1. Spread each of the tortillas with an even layer of about ¼ cup (60 ml) Spicy Black Bean Dip, leaving about ½" (1 cm) uncovered around the edge. Sprinkle with red onion and coriander (if using).

2. Arrange ¼ of the pepper slices and ¼ of the grated cheese in an even layer across the lower two-thirds of each tortilla.

3. Roll up the filled tortillas to make neat spirals. Trim off ends, then cut each roll into 6 equal pieces.

Makes 24 spirals.

TIP:

• For a more substantial snack, add sliced grilled chicken to the middle of each tortilla along with the other ingredients. Fold the lower part of the tortilla over the filling, fold in each side, and roll up burrito style. Place on a baking sheet and bake in a preheated 350°F (180°C) oven for 15 minutes. Serve warm with salsa, guacamole, and sour cream.

VARIATIONS:

This basic "tortilla spiral" technique can be used with a variety of fillings. Start by spreading the tortillas with a base to hold everything together – cream cheese, pesto, tapenade, or salsa. Add a tasty filling and a crisp, crunchy vegetable topping. Then roll and slice. Some of my favourite combos include:

• Slices of smoked salmon on a cream cheese base, topped with chopped dill, a few grindings of black pepper, and Boston lettuce or fresh spinach.

• Finely chopped cooked shrimp on a cream cheese base, topped with chopped dill and thinly sliced cucumber.

• Finely chopped grilled vegetables on a tapenade or pesto base, topped with arugula.

Keep a package or two of tortillas on hand to turn into tortilla spirals for quick snacks. Shown here: Black Bean & Pepper Spirals.

Grilled Polenta & Portobellos

Polenta

6 cups	water	1.5 L
1½ tsp	salt	7 ml
2 cups	cornmeal	500 ml
2–4 tbsp	butter *(optional)*	30–60 ml

Portobello Topping

6	portobello mushrooms, *stems removed*	
½ cup	extra-virgin olive oil	125 ml
2 cloves	garlic, *finely chopped*	
2 tbsp	balsamic vinegar	30 ml
½ cup	flat-leaf parsley, *finely chopped*	125 ml
	salt and freshly ground black pepper	

*P*olenta, a kind of cornmeal porridge, is as popular in northern Italy as pasta is in southern, and is frequently served hot as a side dish. It can also be cooled, sliced, browned on the grill, and used as a tasty base for a variety of appetizer toppings – such as grilled portobello mushrooms. Instant and ready-made polenta (see Quick Trick, facing page) can shorten the prep time dramatically.

1. Bring water and salt to a boil in a large deep pot. Add cornmeal in a slow steady stream, whisking vigorously to avoid lumps.

2. Lower the heat and stir, almost constantly, until cornmeal is cooked, about 30 minutes. (The polenta is done when it becomes smooth and pulls away from the sides of the pot.) Stir in butter if desired.

3. Spread the cooked polenta in a smooth, even layer about ⅜" (1 cm) thick on baking sheets. Cover with plastic wrap and leave to cool.

4. Clean the mushroom caps carefully so as not to damage them.

5. Combine oil and garlic. Brush mushroom caps on both sides with the garlic oil, reserving a few tablespoons of the oil. Set mushrooms aside for an hour or so.

6. Preheat the barbecue and lightly oil the rack. Grill the mushrooms over medium heat for 5–7 minutes a side until tender and nicely browned.

7. Using a cookie cutter or glass, cut the cooled polenta into small circles, or slice into small squares or triangles. Brush on both sides with the reserved garlic oil and grill over medium heat until nicely marked and hot.

8. Slice grilled mushrooms into narrow strips, toss with balsamic vinegar, parsley, and seasoning. (If mushrooms are large, cut strips in half.) Pile a spoonful of the warm mushrooms on each piece of polenta. Serve hot.

Makes about 20 appetizer pieces.

QUICK TRICK:

Instant Polenta: Packages of instant cornmeal, imported from Italy, are a terrific shortcut, requiring only 5 minutes to prepare, and they make excellent polenta. (Beretta is one brand.) Follow the cooking directions on the package.

• Quicker still: In some markets you will find premade polenta in a sausage-shaped roll, which is ready to use, right out of the package. Cut the roll into ⅜" (1-cm) slices, brush both sides of the circles with olive oil, and grill.

VARIATIONS:

• Top the grilled polenta pieces with caramelized onions and Asiago shavings (p. 57), or a spoonful of your favourite salsa. (The flavour of Roasted Tomato Corn Salsa, p. 54, works well with the grilled polenta.) Or try Ripe Tomato Wedges with Garlic (Quick Trick, p. 135) on top; just chop the wedges into smaller pieces.

• The Portobello Topping also makes a splendid appetizer piled on grilled Italian-style bread.

TIPS:

• Portobellos – a big brown variety of the common mushroom – have a wonderful meaty texture and great flavour. The stems are tougher than the tops, but still flavourful. Cut off the earthy end and discard. Rinse the stem, then chop or thinly slice and add to soups or stews.

• For a creamier polenta, cook the cornmeal in half water and half milk.

Mussels on the Half Shell
with Roasted Tomato Corn Salsa

24	**large mussels**	
1 cup	**dry white wine**	**250 ml**
¼ cup	**shallots** *or* **onion,** *finely chopped*	**60 ml**
2–3 cloves	**garlic,** *finely chopped*	
1 tbsp	**olive oil**	**15 ml**
1	**small bay leaf**	
2–3 sprigs	**coriander** *or* **parsley**	
pinch	**hot red pepper flakes**	
	freshly ground black pepper	
½ cup	**Roasted Tomato Corn Salsa** *(p. 54)*	**125 ml**

VARIATION:

• The mussels can be served, steaming hot from the pan, in deep bowls with some of the cooking broth, freshly ground pepper, a garnish of chopped fresh parsley, and a loaf of warm crusty bread to mop up the good juices.

There was a time when preparing mussels for cooking was quite a chore. Now, however, you can buy wonderful cultivated mussels, which are raised in controlled conditions and usually so clean they require only a quick rinse — no scrubbing or soaking. Here, the mussels are steamed in a fragrant wine broth and used to create a colourful eat-out-of-your-hand appetizer.

1. Clean mussels thoroughly, trimming away beards if necessary.

2. In a large frying pan, combine wine, shallots or onion, garlic, olive oil, herbs, and spices. Bring to a boil and simmer for 2–3 minutes.

3. Add mussels to the pan, cover, and boil for 5 minutes, shaking the pan occasionally so the mussels cook evenly. Remove open mussels to a platter with tongs. Replace lid and cook any unopened mussels for a minute or two longer. Discard any that stubbornly refuse to open.

4. Discard the top shells, season the mussels lightly, and top each one with a spoonful of Roasted Tomato Corn Salsa.

Makes 24.

TIPS:

• The appetizers can be prepared a few hours ahead, wrapped in plastic, and refrigerated until serving.

• Be sure to purchase your mussels at a market where you can rely on freshness. Mussels must be alive and have their shells clamped shut; discard any that are open or have cracked shells. Keep refrigerated and prepare on the day of purchase.

Mussels steamed in a fragrant wine broth are delicious on their own — but top them with Roasted Tomato Corn Salsa and they become a spectacular appetizer.

Roasted Tomato Corn Salsa

1 ear	**corn,** husk and silk removed	
6	**plum tomatoes**	
1 tbsp	**olive oil**	15 ml
¼ cup	**red onion,** finely chopped	60 ml
¼ cup	**fresh** or **roasted red pepper,** finely chopped	60 ml
½	**jalapeño pepper,** seeded and finely chopped	
2 tbsp	**fresh coriander,** chopped	30 ml
1 tbsp	**lime juice**	15 ml
	salt and freshly ground black pepper	

TIP:

• You can make the salsa 2–3 days ahead (keep it refrigerated), but add the coriander on the day of serving.

*N*ot just a topping for mussels (p. 52). Serve it in a bowl to be scooped up with tortilla chips, or alongside fried fish (p. 273) or grilled chicken. Save time by cooking the vegetables a night ahead, while you have the barbecue on for supper.

1. Blanch corn for 2 minutes in boiling salted water. Drain.

2. Rub corn and tomatoes with olive oil and set on the grill over medium-high heat. Roll the corn over the fire for 4–6 minutes until it is nicely browned. Cut off the kernels.

3. Continue to grill the tomatoes for another few minutes until they are soft and the skins are nicely charred. Chop coarsely.

4. Combine all ingredients and let stand at least an hour for flavours to blend. Adjust seasoning to taste.

Makes 1½ cups (375 ml).

QUICK TRICK:

Lemon Marinated Mussels: For another great appetizer, steam mussels as described on p. 52. Discard shells. Prepare a vinaigrette by whisking together ¼ cup (60 ml) olive oil, 1 tbsp (15 ml) lemon juice, salt, and freshly ground black pepper. Toss mussels with the vinaigrette and add 1 tsp (5 ml) grated lemon zest, 2 finely chopped green onions, and ¼ cup (60 ml) freshly chopped parsley. Serve with hot grilled garlic bread as part of an antipasto selection.

Smoked Fish Spread

6 oz	deli-style cream cheese	170 g
2 tbsp	fresh dill, *chopped*	30 ml
½–1 tbsp	fresh lemon juice, *to taste*	10–15 ml
1 tbsp	capers, *chopped*	15 ml
1 tsp	prepared horseradish	5 ml
pinch	sugar	
8 oz	smoked trout, salmon, *or* mackerel	250 g
	salt and freshly ground black pepper	

The area around my cottage is dotted with trout farms, many with their own smokehouses. Smoked trout or other smoked fish is a treat for a special brunch, lunch, or happy-hour snack. This recipe turns the fish into a tasty spread. Serve with melba toast, slices of fresh pumpernickel bread, crisp cucumber rounds, or spears of Belgian endive.

1. In a food processor, blend the cream cheese with the dill, lemon juice, capers, horseradish, sugar, and half the smoked fish until smooth. (Or mash the ingredients together with a fork.)

2. Add the remaining fish and process (or mash) lightly to combine. Season to taste. (The spread may only need a little pepper.)

Makes about 2 cups (500 ml).

QUICK TRICK:
Homemade Melba Toasts and Pita Chips: Don't panic if you run out of crackers. Cut good stale bread – rye, pumpernickel, whole wheat, walnut, sourdough, challah, or even raisin bread – into thin slices. Spread on cookie sheets and bake at 300°F (150°C) until crisp (about 10 minutes). Or cut pita bread into triangles and toast in the oven. These pita chips are delicious brushed with garlic-flavoured olive oil and sprinkled with grated Parmesan cheese before toasting.

1 loaf	**Italian-style bread** or **French baguette**	
	olive oil	
1 clove	**garlic,** halved	
	fresh basil, chopped (optional)	

Marinated Mozzarella

½ lb	**mozzarella**	250 g
3 tbsp	**olive oil**	45 ml
1	**sun-dried tomato,** cut in slivers	
1 tbsp	**Herbes de Provence** or **a mix of equal parts dried basil, oregano, and thyme**	15 ml
1 tsp	**garlic,** finely chopped	5 ml
¼ tsp	**hot red pepper flakes**	1 ml
	salt and freshly ground black pepper	

TIP:

• For a different flavour, substitute bocconcini (young, fresh mozzarella) or mild goat cheese.

Mozzarella Bruschetta

There are endless variations on the theme of bruschetta, essentially hearty slabs of hot grilled bread with flavourful toppings. Even at its simplest – with chopped fresh tomato and onion, Parmesan cheese, and a scattering of herbs, as pictured here – bruschetta makes a popular snack. But for something different, try it with a topping of Marinated Mozzarella.

1. Cut mozzarella into small cubes and toss with oil, sun-dried tomato, and seasonings. Although the cheese may be used right away, the flavour will improve if you let it stand at least an hour in the refrigerator.

2. Cut the baguette in half lengthwise, or cut chunky slices of Italian-style bread. Brush slices with olive oil and rub with the cut garlic clove. Season with salt and pepper, and toast lightly on the grill.

3. Top with cubes of Marinated Mozzarella and sprinkle with chopped basil if you like. Place slices on a metal tray and return to the grill or oven (375°F/190°C) for a few minutes until the cheese begins to melt. Serve hot, cut in serving-size pieces.

Serves 6.

TIP:

• Marinated Mozzarella also makes a good savoury snack all by itself, or it can be tossed in a salad or used on top of pizza. It will keep 2–3 days in the fridge.

Caramelized Onion Crostini
with Asiago Shavings

1	baguette	
½ cup	olive oil *(approx.)*	125 ml
1 clove	garlic, *sliced*	
2	medium red onions	
	salt and freshly ground black pepper	
1 tbsp	balsamic vinegar	15 ml
1 tsp	dried thyme	5 ml
16–20	shavings of Asiago cheese	

TIPS:

• The onions can be prepared ahead and kept in a covered container in the refrigerator for 1–2 days. The crostini are best made the day of serving.

• A swivel-bladed potato peeler is the perfect tool to make fine shavings of hard cheeses such as Asiago.

• You can caramelize the onions on the stove: Slice thinly and cook slowly over medium-low heat in 2 tbsp (30 ml) olive oil, stirring now and again, until onions are soft and well browned.

• Instead of assembling the crostini, put out a basket of the toasts and bowls of the caramelized onions and cheese shavings and let guests help themselves.

Homemade Italian-style crostini – small slices of crisp toasted bread with a savoury topping (from the Italian for "little crust") – form the base of many wonderful snacks and appetizers. Here, they are topped with sweet, meltingly soft red onions and a sliver of sharp cheese.

1. Cut baguette into ½" (1-cm) slices on the diagonal. Let garlic sit in ¼ cup (60 ml) of the olive oil for about 15 minutes, then brush each slice lightly on both sides with the flavoured oil.

2. Place bread slices on baking trays and bake at 350°F (180°C) for about 5–7 minutes, turning once. Or grill the slices on the barbecue until they are nicely marked on both sides. Set aside.

3. Peel onions and slice into ½" (1-cm) rounds. To keep the rings together, spear horizontally through the slices with one or two metal poultry skewers or bamboo skewers that have been soaked in water for about an hour. Brush each slice with remaining olive oil and season with a little salt and pepper.

4. Grill slowly over medium heat, turning now and again, until evenly browned and very soft, about 15 minutes. Remove the skewers and toss the grilled onion rings with the balsamic vinegar and the thyme. If the rings are too large, chop them into manageable pieces.

5. At serving time, pile a spoonful of warm or room-temperature caramelized onions on each of the crostini and top each with a shaving of Asiago cheese.

Makes 16–20 crostini.

Caponata

6 tbsp	**olive oil**	90 ml
2	**young globe eggplants,** *about 1½ lbs (750 g) in total, cut in ¾" (2 cm) cubes*	
3 stalks	**celery,** *trimmed and thinly sliced*	
1	**medium onion,** *thinly sliced*	
1½ cups	**tomato sauce** *or* **canned plum tomatoes,** *puréed*	375 ml
	salt and freshly ground black pepper	
dash	**sugar** *(if necessary)*	
2 tbsp	**capers,** *rinsed and drained*	30 ml
½ cup	**black olives,** *halved and pitted*	125 ml
3 tbsp	**balsamic** *or* **red wine vinegar** *(or to taste)*	45 ml
	fresh flat-leaf parsley, *chopped*	

The rich, earthy flavours of eggplant and olives combine with sharp capers in this robust Sicilian dish. Serve with crisp toasts on its own, or make it part of an antipasto platter. It also makes a good side dish served with grilled fish or meat.

1. Heat 3 tbsp (45 ml) of the oil in a large, heavy skillet. Add eggplant and cook over medium heat until lightly browned (about 7 minutes), turning often. (Cook in 2 batches if necessary.) Set aside on paper towel to drain.

2. Heat 1½ tbsp (20 ml) of the oil in the skillet; add celery and cook until tender. Set aside on paper towel.

3. Heat remaining oil, add onion, and cook until soft. Stir in tomato sauce or tomatoes. Season with salt, pepper, and a dash of sugar (if needed), and simmer for 5 minutes. Return celery to pan, and add capers, olives, and vinegar. Simmer for 15 minutes. Return eggplant to pan, and simmer for 10 minutes.

4. Turn out into a bowl, cover, and set aside to cool and for flavours to develop. Taste and adjust seasoning before serving. Serve at room temperature with a garnish of fresh parsley.

Makes about 4 cups (1 L).

TIPS:

• This is a great make-ahead appetizer, as it tastes even better after it has had a chance to sit overnight. It will keep about a week in the fridge.

• Young, small eggplants and Japanese eggplants have tender skin, so it's not necessary to peel them. Large eggplants should be peeled and the cubes sprinkled with a teaspoon of salt and allowed to drain in a colander for an hour to draw out the bitter juices. Rinse and pat dry before cooking.

Roasted Eggplant Caviar

1	**globe eggplant,** *(about 1 lb/500 g)*	
3 tbsp	**olive oil**	45 ml
4 cloves	**garlic,** *unpeeled*	
½	**small red onion,** *sliced but unpeeled*	
1 tsp	**balsamic vinegar**	5 ml
squeeze	**lemon juice**	
	salt and freshly ground black pepper	
	fresh parsley and ripe olives, *chopped (for garnish)*	

TIP:

• The eggplant, garlic, and onion can also be roasted on the barbecue. See p. 126 for directions.

A simple purée of roasted or grilled eggplant makes a wonderful snack with sesame crackers or wedges of pita bread.

1. Slice eggplant in half lengthwise and brush cut surfaces with olive oil. Place cut side down on a lightly oiled baking sheet.

2. Arrange garlic cloves and onion slices on the sheet, and brush with oil. Bake in a preheated 375°F (190°C) oven for about 35 minutes until vegetables are tender.

3. Place eggplant in a colander to drain and, when cool enough to handle, peel away the skin in strips starting at the stem end. Snip the tips from the garlic cloves and squeeze out the roasted garlic. Remove outer skin from roasted onion slices.

4. Using a food processor or a potato masher, purée the eggplant, garlic, and onion, adding the rest of the oil (1 tbsp/15 ml or so), the balsamic vinegar, a squeeze of lemon juice, and salt and pepper to taste. Set aside, covered, for an hour or so to let the flavour develop. Garnish with parsley and olives before serving.

Makes about 1½ cups (375 ml).

Easy Thai Shrimp Rolls

½ lb	**shrimp,** *cooked and chopped*	250 g
½ cup	**bean sprouts**	125 ml
½ cup	**carrot,** *grated*	125 ml
¼ cup	**water chestnuts,** *rinsed, drained, and chopped*	60 ml
3	**green onions,** *finely chopped*	
¼ cup	**fresh coriander,** *chopped*	60 ml
2 tbsp	**Peanut Dipping Sauce** *(next page)*	30 ml
	salt and freshly ground black pepper	
10–12	**round rice-paper wrappers**	

TIP:

• The filling is flexible, and could include other vegetables, such as finely shredded napa cabbage, grated celery, or finely slivered mushrooms. You could also include a little fresh chopped mint and basil in the mix if you have them. (Substituting dried herbs in this recipe is not recommended.)

*C*risp, fresh, healthy, and fun to eat, these rice-paper-wrapped parcels are guaranteed to be a hit. And they can be made several hours ahead, requiring no work at the last minute. The dried rice-paper wrappers can be found in the oriental/Thai section of many supermarkets and will keep for months in the cupboard, ready to make tasty little bites.

1. Combine shrimp with vegetables, herbs, and Peanut Dipping Sauce. Season to taste.

2. To assemble the shrimp rolls: Have a bowl of hot water beside you and spread out a clean tea towel on your counter. One at a time, dip the rice-paper wrappers in water for 10 seconds, then place on the towel. Put about 2–3 tbsp (30–45 ml) of filling in a small log shape across the middle third of the wrapper. Fold the bottom third of the wrapper over the filling, then turn in each side. Dip your finger in water and lightly moisten the rim of the upper part of the wrapper and roll it up.

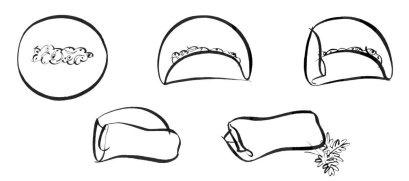

Please turn to next page

Easy Thai Shrimp Rolls: A little practice may be required to get the hang of working with the rice-paper wrappers, but it's worth it.

Easy Thai Shrimp Rolls, *continued*

Peanut Dipping Sauce

½ cup	natural chunky peanut butter	125 ml
2 tbsp	rice vinegar	30 ml
2 tbsp	fresh lime juice	30 ml
2 tbsp	soy sauce	30 ml
2 tsp	brown sugar	10 ml
2 cloves	garlic, *finely chopped*	
½ tsp	red chili paste or	2 ml
pinch	hot red pepper flakes	
	salt	

Light Thai Dipping Sauce

2 tbsp	soy sauce	30 ml
2 tbsp	rice vinegar	30 ml
1 tsp	sesame oil	5 ml
pinch	sugar	
1	green onion, *finely chopped*	
pinch	hot red pepper flakes *(optional)*	

3. Place the assembled shrimp rolls seam side down on a platter, cover securely with plastic wrap, and set in the refrigerator until serving time. Serve with Peanut Dipping Sauce and Light Thai Dipping Sauce, if you like.

Makes 10–12.

Peanut Dipping Sauce

1. Combine ingredients thoroughly. Add warm water a spoonful at a time to obtain a light creamy texture. Taste and adjust seasoning with added lime juice or salt. *Makes about 1 cup (250 ml).*

Light Thai Dipping Sauce

1. Combine all ingredients thoroughly. If you like heat, add a few hot red pepper flakes. *Makes about ⅓ cup (75 ml).*

TIPS:

• At an informal gathering, get guests involved in making the rolls. (Producing a neat roll without tearing the rice paper takes some practice, so count on a few imperfect rolls being devoured in the kitchen along the way.)

• As a time-saver, buy small precooked "salad" shrimp. Since you're chopping them anyway, there's no need to spend more on larger sizes.

Herbed Cheese Coins

1 cup	flour	250 ml
½ tsp	salt	2 ml
3 tbsp	cold unsalted butter, *cut in small pieces*	45 ml
1 cup	Gruyère cheese, *grated*	250 ml
¼ cup	fresh dill, *chopped*	60 ml
1 tbsp	grainy mustard	15 ml
5-6 tbsp	35% cream	75-90 ml

VARIATIONS:

Instead of dill and mustard, try one of these combinations of seasonings, combining them with the flour and salt in Step 1:

• 2 tsp (10 ml) dried rosemary, 1 tsp (5 ml) dried oregano, and 1 tsp (5 ml) dried thyme

• 1 tbsp (15 ml) roughly crushed mixed peppercorns and 1 tsp (5 ml) dried thyme

These are great to have on hand in your freezer for those times you need to produce a quick tasty bite.

1. In a food processor or large bowl, combine flour and salt. Cut in butter until mixture resembles coarse crumbs. Toss in cheese and dill.

2. Stir mustard into 5 tbsp (75 ml) cream and sprinkle over flour mixture. Combine until dough comes together, adding remaining cream if necessary.

3. Form dough into 2 equal balls, then roll each ball gently on your counter to form a small log about 1½" (3.5 cm) in diameter and 5"–6" (12–15 cm) long. Wrap securely in plastic and refrigerate for 2–3 hours or overnight, or freeze for longer storage.

4. When ready to bake, cut the log into slices just under ¼" (6 mm) thick. Arrange on parchment-lined cookie sheets and bake in a preheated 325°F (170°C) oven for about 15–20 minutes, until golden around the edges and quite firm to the touch. (Be watchful during the last few minutes – the cheese coins can become too dark in a flash.) Remove to racks to cool, then store in sealed containers.

Makes about 50.

TIPS:

• Wrapped well, the logs of dough will keep in the freezer for a month. You don't need to thaw them completely before using; just remove from the freezer a few minutes ahead of time.

• The baked Cheese Coins are best when eaten within a couple of days.

Baked Goat Cheese
with Blueberry Balsamic Glaze

6 oz	**goat cheese,** *sliced into 4 rounds*	170 g
½ cup	**walnuts,** *toasted and crushed*	125 ml
4 cups	**fresh baby greens** *(spinach, mâche, Boston lettuce)*	1 L

Blueberry Balsamic Glaze

¼ cup	**Blueberry Syrup** *(p. 305)*	60 ml
2 tbsp	**balsamic vinegar**	30 ml
1 clove	**garlic,** *minced*	
2 tbsp	**mild extra-virgin olive oil**	30 ml
¼ tsp	**salt**	1 ml
¼ tsp	**freshly ground black pepper**	1 ml

The warm, nut-coated goat cheese makes a lovely starter for a summer dinner. Or serve it as the main event for a light lunch, accompanied by crusty bread. You'll find many other uses for the Blueberry Syrup called for in the glaze. (See p. 305 for the recipe and other serving suggestions.)

1. To make the glaze, combine Blueberry Syrup with balsamic vinegar and garlic. Whisk in olive oil and season to taste with salt and pepper.

2. Coat goat cheese rounds on all sides with nuts. Refrigerate until ready to serve.

3. Place cheese on a baking sheet and set in a 350°F (180°C) oven for 10 minutes.

4. Divide greens between 4 plates and top each with a round of cheese. Drizzle with the glaze.

Serves 4.

TIPS:

• Substitute toasted pine nuts, hazelnuts, or pecans for the walnuts.

• For a side salad, omit the goat cheese, toss the greens with the glaze, and garnish with candied pecans.

Make the glaze and get the goat cheese ready for baking early in the day; it will only take a few minutes to complete the salad at serving time.

Gorgonzola Pâté

10 oz	Gorgonzola	300 g
4 oz	deli-style cream cheese, *at room temperature*	125 g
1 tbsp	port	15 ml
¼ tsp	freshly ground black pepper	1 ml
3 heads	Belgian endive, *trimmed and separated into leaves*	
	apples *and/or* pears, *sliced*	
½ cup	walnuts *or* pecans *toasted and chopped*	125 ml
	wheatmeal *or* other crackers	

A convenient, tasty spread to have on hand. Serve it spread on apple or pear slices, dolloped onto endive leaves, or simply mounded in a bowl surrounded by crackers.

1. Mash Gorgonzola and cream cheese together with a wooden spoon (or combine with a few pulses of your food processor). Stir in the port and pepper.

2. Cover and chill for an hour or so to allow flavours to blend.

3. To serve, place a teaspoon of the mixture on each endive leaf or fruit slice and sprinkle with nuts. Mound the remaining pâté in a small bowl, sprinkle with the remaining nuts, and surround with crackers.

Serves 8.

TIP:
• You can make the pâté 2–3 days ahead of serving time and store it, covered, in the refrigerator.

II. GREAT GRILLING

Marinades, Rubs, & Bastes

Most of the marinades, spice rubs, pastes, and bastes you'll find in this chapter taste great with more than one type of grilled food. Here's a handy guide to what works particularly well with what.

	Beef	Chicken	Fish, Seafood	Lamb	Pork	Vegetables	Notes
Asian Spice Rub (p. 82)	●	●		●			*Combine with Hoisin Baste for ribs and Beer Can Chicken*
Balsamic Marinade (p. 111)	●	●	●	●	●	●	*Very versatile; make it ahead using dried herbs*
Basic Herb Marinade (p. 69)	●	●	●	●	●	●	*Just vary the herbs to suit your menu*
Beer & Smoked Chile Baste (p. 70)	●	●		●	●		*Its gutsy flavour works with veggies such as onions, corn, and sweet potatoes*
Caribbean Spice Paste (p. 115)		●			●		*Try on a whole chicken or a pork roast*
Cool Lime Marinade (p. 78)		●	●		●	●	*Perfect for skewers of chicken, shrimp, scallops, or pork*
Garlic Seafood Butter (p. 91)	●	●	●	●	●	●	*Make ahead and have on hand to add instant flavour*
Hoisin Baste (p. 82)	●	●			●		*Use with Asian Spice Rub to create a sweet-spicy oriental taste*
Honey-Garlic Marinade (p. 120)	●	●			●		*A favourite for wings or spare ribs*
Jerk Marinade (p. 77)		●	●		●		*Makes an aromatic baste for a pork loin, bone-in chicken pieces, or a whole fish*
Lemon Garlic Baste (p. 97)		●	●	●	●	●	*Add different herbs according to your menu*
Lemon Grass Marinade (p. 119)		●	●		●		*Try with whole or butterflied chicken, or skewered chicken, pork, shrimp, scallops*
Malaysian Spice Mix & Paste (p. 128)		●			●		*Use it for skewers of chicken or pork, or a whole pork loin*
Mexicali Spice Rub (p. 83)		●			●		*A spicy rub for ribs or rotisserie chicken*
Moroccan Flavour Paste (p. 122)		●		●	●		*Especially good with chicken – either whole pieces or skewers*
Oriental Marinade (p. 73)	●	●	●		●		*Try it with flank steak and tofu*
Red Wine Marinade (p. 72)	●			●			*Excellent for steak and lamb kebabs*
Smoky Red Barbecue Sauce (p. 130)	●	●			●		*The family favourite – make ahead to have on hand for burgers, steaks, ribs, wings*
Spicy Chile Rub (p. 108)		●			●		*Use on chicken or pork for a great fajita filling*
Teriyaki Marinade & Basting Sauce (p. 86)	●	●	●		●	●	*Very popular for flank steak, chicken wings, salmon fillets, or shrimp*
Thai Green Curry Marinade (p. 121)		●	●		●		*A quick baste for chicken, pork, and seafood*
Tikka Curry Paste (p. 112)		●		●	●		*Great on skewers of chicken or a butterflied leg of lamb*

Basic Herb Marinade

½ cup	olive oil	125 ml
¼ cup	fresh lemon juice	60 ml
	freshly ground black pepper	
1 tbsp	fresh herbs, *chopped* or	15 ml
1 tsp	dried herbs *(see Tips)*	5 ml
1	shallot *or* green onion, *chopped (optional)*	
1 clove	garlic, *minced (optional)*	

This simple marinade can be used with meats, poultry, fish, seafood, or vegetables. It makes an excellent base to which you can add your own favourite herbs. If you're cooking meat or fish with a high natural fat content, simply reduce the amount of oil in the marinade so the ratio of oil to acid is 1:1.

1. Combine ingredients thoroughly with a whisk.

Makes ¾ cup (175 ml).

TIPS:

• For the herbs in this marinade, try tarragon or thyme, especially fresh lemon thyme, when marinating chicken, veal, fish, steak, or vegetables.

• With lamb, use mint, rosemary, or oregano.

• For fish, shellfish, and vegetables, add tarragon, fresh dill, or parsley.

• To make an excellent marinade for tuna, replace half the lemon juice in the basic marinade with balsamic vinegar, and add chopped fresh flat-leaf parsley.

• For steak or lamb, replace half the lemon juice with red wine or balsamic vinegar, and add a sliced onion, minced garlic, cracked peppercorns, and rosemary or thyme.

• Try a good-quality balsamic vinegar on its own as a marinade for steak.

• Replace lemon juice with lime juice and use chopped fresh coriander in a marinade for tuna, trout, chicken, pork, or vegetables.

Beer & Smoked Chile Baste
for Grilled Steak

2–2½ lbs	**sirloin steak**	**1 kg**

Beer & Smoked Chile Baste

1 tbsp	**chipotle chiles in adobo sauce,** *puréed (see Tips, below)*	15 ml
2 tbsp	**soy sauce**	30 ml
2 tbsp	**ketchup**	30 ml
2 tbsp	**brown sugar** *or* **maple syrup**	30 ml
1 tsp	**salt**	5 ml
1 tsp	**black peppercorns,** *crushed*	5 ml
1 bottle	**beer** *(approx. 12 oz/341 ml)*	
1 cup	**beef** *or* **vegetable stock**	250 ml
4 cloves	**garlic,** *crushed*	
1	**onion,** *chopped*	
1	**carrot,** *chopped*	
1 stalk	**celery,** *chopped*	
1	**bay leaf**	
½ tsp	**celery salt** *(optional)*	2 ml

Every barbecuemeister worth his salt needs a gutsy marinade for steak in his repertoire. The inspiration for this beer and chipotle baste came from renowned Toronto chef Susur Lee.

1. In a saucepan, combine all the ingredients for the baste. Bring to a boil, reduce heat, and simmer 45 minutes. Allow to cool, remove bay leaf, and push through a sieve.

2. Marinate the steak in ½ cup (125 ml) of the mixture overnight in the refrigerator. Refrigerate the rest of the baste to use while grilling.

3. Remove steak from marinade and bring meat to room temperature. Place steak on preheated barbecue over medium-high heat and brush with fresh Beer & Smoked Chile Baste. Grill 4–5 minutes, turn, brush again, and continue cooking until desired doneness.

4. Remove steak and let it rest for a couple of minutes, then cut into thin slices across the grain.

Serves 6.

TIPS:
• Look for chipotle chiles in adobo sauce (a rich tomato sauce) in small cans in the Mexican food section of large supermarkets.

• Grill thick slices of onions (p. 126), brushing them with the Beer & Smoked Chile Baste, then garnish the steak with them.

• You can prepare the baste ahead – it will keep about a week in a covered container in the refrigerator. Make a double batch if you like, but keep the quantity of chipotle purée the same – unless you like your baste devilishly hot.

A perfectly grilled Beer & Smoked Chile-basted steak, topped with a pile of grilled onions: Summer doesn't get any better.

Wine-Marinated Steak Kebabs

2 lbs	sirloin steak	1 kg

Red Wine Marinade

1½ cups	dry red wine	375 ml
½ cup	olive oil	125 ml
¼ cup	red wine vinegar	60 ml
1	onion, *sliced*	
4 cloves	garlic, *chopped*	
2	bay leaves	
1 tbsp	fresh rosemary, *chopped*	15 ml
	or	
1 tsp	dried rosemary	5 ml
	salt and freshly ground black pepper	

*B*eef melts in the mouth after a few hours in this gutsy marinade. Serve with *Grilled Vegetable Kebabs (p. 127) and garlic or olive mashed potatoes (p. 182).*

1. Trim steak and cut into uniform chunks of about 1½" (4 cm).

2. Combine remaining ingredients and toss the steak in the marinade. Leave for several hours or as long as overnight in a covered dish in the refrigerator.

3. Soak 10" (25-cm) bamboo skewers in water for about an hour.

4. When ready to cook, remove beef from marinade and pat dry. Reserve ¼ cup (60 ml) of the marinade for basting and strain the remainder into a small saucepan. Bring to a boil and simmer for 8–10 minutes to reduce by half and create a sauce. Taste and adjust seasoning.

5. Thread 6 pieces of steak on each skewer, and place on a hot, lightly oiled grill over high heat. Turn and baste with marinade until nicely browned and grilled to your taste – 8–10 minutes for medium rare. Remove from grill.

6. Season with salt and freshly ground black pepper and coat with a spoonful of sauce.

Serves 4.

VARIATIONS:
- Use Red Wine Marinade for a whole steak and grill as for Peppered Sirloin (p. 79).
- The marinade is also delicious with lamb – kebabs, chops, or a whole leg.

Grilled Oriental Tofu or Steak

2 lbs	**steak** (*sirloin, sirlon tip, blade, cross rib, inside round*) **and/or**	**1 kg**
1 block	**firm tofu** (*1 lb/454 g*)	
	vegetable oil	

Oriental Marinade

1 tsp	**garlic,** *finely minced*	**5 ml**
1 tbsp	**fresh ginger root,** *finely minced*	**15 ml**
2 tbsp	**sesame oil**	**30 ml**
3 tbsp	**soy sauce**	**45 ml**
1 tbsp	**brown sugar**	**15 ml**
dash	**red chili paste (sambal oelek)** *or* **hot red pepper flakes**	

TIPS:

• Tofu, a satisfying high-protein food made from soy milk, is sold packed in water in sealed plastic containers. Look for it on the refrigerated green-grocery shelves of your supermarket.

• Freshness is crucial for tofu. Check the date on the container when buying and store in the refrigerator. Once the tofu is opened, change the water daily and use within a day or two. (The smell should always be fresh and sweet.)

If your dinner table includes a mix of vegetarians and meat-eaters, you can easily please both groups by marinating and grilling both tofu and steak. Serve them (separately, of course) sliced on top of Sesame Soba Noodles (p. 203) or as an Oriental Beef or Tofu Salad (p. 137).

1. Combine all ingredients for marinade, doubling the recipe if you are preparing both tofu and steak.

For tofu:

1. Drain tofu and pat dry with paper towel. Cut into slices about ½" (1 cm) thick and cover with marinade. Refrigerate for at least 24 hours, or preferably longer, to allow the marinade to penetrate the tofu.

2. When ready to serve, remove from marinade and pat dry. Brush lightly with vegetable oil. Grill over medium heat, basting now and again with marinade, 5–7 minutes per side. Slice and serve with noodles. *Serves 3–4.*

For steak:

1. Trim excess fat from meat. Cover with marinade and refrigerate for several hours or overnight.

2. When ready to serve, bring meat to room temperature, remove from marinade, pat dry, and place on barbecue over medium-high heat. Grill for 4–5 minutes, brush with marinade, turn, and continue cooking until desired doneness. Allow to rest for a couple of minutes, then cut into thin slices across the grain. *Serves 6.*

Steak Fajitas

3 lbs	flank steak	1.5 kg
2 tbsp	olive oil	30 ml
¼ cup	fresh lime juice	60 ml
½–1 tbsp	chili powder	10–15 ml
1 tsp	ground cumin	5 ml
1 tsp	garlic, *finely minced*	5 ml

TIPS:

• The basic fajita toppings are guacamole (p. 41), pico de gallo (a tomato relish, p. 95), and salsa (p. 40). (Have several types of salsa on hand with different degrees of heat.) You can also put out bowls of chopped jalapeño peppers, sour cream, chopped onions, and grated mild Cheddar or Monterey Jack cheese.

• Plan on two 8"–10" (20–25 cm) tortillas per person, but have an extra package or two on hand, just in case. Warm tortillas before serving: Either wrap a stack in a tea towel and set on a rack over a large pot of boiling water for a couple of minutes, or wrap in foil and warm in a 325°F (170°C) oven or on the top rack of the barbecue for 5–10 minutes. At serving time, keep tortillas wrapped in foil or a warm towel.

Fajitas – thin slices of grilled meat rolled in tortillas with a variety of toppings – make a great informal and easy dinner for a crowd. Set out the platter of sliced meat accompanied by warm tortillas and bowls of toppings, and let guests assemble their own meal. Serve with a salad (the Corn & Black Bean Salad, p. 156, complements the flavour of the fajitas nicely) and cold beer or a pitcher of sangría. Thinly sliced Chile-Rub Chicken (p. 108) also makes an excellent filling for fajitas.

1. Combine oil, lime juice, and seasonings, and rub well into steak on all sides. Leave to marinate in the refrigerator in a covered container or sealed plastic bag for several hours or overnight.

2. About half an hour before meal time, remove meat from the refrigerator. Grill steak over medium-high heat for 5 minutes, then turn and grill 3–5 minutes more, until it is cooked to your liking.

3. Remove to a warm platter and let rest for 5 minutes to allow the juices to be absorbed back into the meat. With a sharp knife, cut thin slices at a 45° angle across the grain and serve with tortillas and toppings.

Serves 6–8.

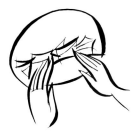

The trick to easy-to-handle fajitas: Fold one end of the tortilla over the filling, fold in the two sides, and then roll up. And don't put too much filling inside!

Barbecued Pork Tenderloin
with 3/3/3 Sauce

2	pork tenderloins *(about ¾ lb/375 g each)*	
⅓ cup	soy sauce	75 ml
⅓ cup	Dijon *or* other prepared mustard	75 ml
⅓ cup	honey	75 ml
1 clove	garlic, *minced*	

VARIATION:

• Try this marinade on chicken pieces.

With only a 15-minute marinating period, this dish is very fast and easy. Serve with rice, Pineapple Salsa (Quick Trick, below), and grilled or stir-fried vegetables.

1. Trim any visible fat and membrane from the meat.

2. Combine remaining ingredients. Pour over meat, turning the pork to coat thoroughly with marinade. Set aside for about 15 minutes.

3. Preheat barbecue to high and lightly oil the grill. Place meat on the grill; adjust heat to medium-high. Turn meat frequently, brushing lavishly with marinade until done, about 10–12 minutes. (The outside will start to caramelize and the inside should be pink.) Let rest for a few minutes, then slice and serve.

Serves 4.

QUICK TRICK:
Pineapple Salsa: For a relish that's excellent with grilled pork, combine a ripe pineapple, peeled, cored, and diced, with 1 finely chopped red onion, ½ jalapeño pepper, seeded and chopped, 2 tbsp (30 ml) finely chopped mint, 2 tbsp (30 ml) lime juice, salt, and freshly ground black pepper.

Jerked Chicken or Pork

3–4 lbs	pork loin	1.5–2 kg
	or	
6	chicken breasts, *bone in (about 3 lbs/1.5 kg)*	

Jerk Marinade

1 tsp	each black pepper, thyme, cayenne, allspice, brown sugar, and salt	5 ml
½ tsp	each nutmeg and cinnamon	2 ml
¼ cup	vegetable oil	60 ml
¼ cup	orange juice	60 ml
2 tbsp	fresh lime juice	30 ml
2 tbsp	soy sauce	30 ml
1	small onion, *finely chopped*	
4 cloves	garlic, *finely chopped*	
1	small fresh hot pepper, *seeded and chopped (or to taste)*	

Jerk refers to a favourite cooking method in the Caribbean. Traditionally, chicken, pork, goat, or fish is rubbed with a variety of spices, and either wrapped in leaves and pit-cooked or slow-grilled over a green-wood fire. This recipe is a simpler way to achieve the same results. Don't be deterred by the long list of spices – you'll find most of them lurking in the cupboard. Jerked food is delicious served with steamed rice, black beans, grilled sweet potatoes (p. 127), and corn.

1. Combine all marinade ingredients to make a paste (by hand or using a blender or food processor).

2. Rub the meat with the marinade, place it in a plastic bag or in a shallow dish, and refrigerate 6 hours or overnight.

3. Bring meat to room temperature while you prepare the barbecue.

4. Using a drip pan, grill pork loin over medium-low indirect heat (see p. 15) until it is cooked through – about 1½ hours. Pork should reach an internal temperature of 160°F (70°C). Or grill chicken breasts for about 30–45 minutes over indirect heat. Chicken should reach an internal temperature of 180°F (82°C). Baste periodically with the marinade.

Serves 6.

Cool Lime Pork Skewers
with Cool Green Dip

2½–3 lbs	pork tenderloin	1–1.5 kg
	salt	
¼ cup	fresh coriander, *chopped*	60 ml

Cool Lime Marinade

2 cloves	garlic, *finely chopped*	
2 tsp	ground cumin	10 ml
1 tsp	lime zest, *grated*	5 ml
¼ cup	fresh lime juice	60 ml
¼ cup	olive oil	60 ml

Cool Green Dip

1 cup	fresh coriander, *finely chopped*	250 ml
½ cup	green onions, *finely chopped*	125 ml
½–1	fresh jalapeño pepper, *seeded and finely chopped*	
1 cup	sour cream	250 ml
½–1 tsp	salt	2–5 ml

*S*trips *of skewered tender pork with a light citrus glaze are delicious hot off the barbecue or grilled ahead and served cold. Serve the pork right on the skewers – the kid-preferred way – or accompany the meat with tortillas so people can make fajita-style sandwiches, topped with guacamole (p. 41), salsa (p. 40), and Cool Green Dip or sour cream. Small skewers make great appetizers or party snacks.*

1. Trim meat and cut into strips approximately ¼" (6 mm) thick, 1½" (4 cm) wide, and 5"–6" (12 cm–15 cm) long.

2. Combine ingredients for marinade. Coat pork strips with marinade, cover, and refrigerate for several hours (or overnight).

3. To make the dip, combine coriander, green onions, and jalapeño in a blender or food processor to make an almost-smooth paste. Stir herb paste into sour cream, season to taste, and refrigerate for an hour or so to allow flavours to blend.

4. Soak bamboo skewers in water for an hour or so. Thread 2 pork strips on each skewer. (Skewers can be prepared to this point up to a day ahead.)

5. Grill over medium-high heat, turning once, until meat is nicely browned on the outside and tender and juicy inside (8–10 minutes). Season lightly and sprinkle with coriander. Serve hot or allow to cool, store in a container with a tight-fitting lid, and refrigerate. Serve at cool room temperature. Accompany with Cool Green Dip and other toppings as desired.

Serves 6.

Peppered Sirloin Steak

2–2½ lbs	**sirloin steak,** *1½" (4 cm) thick*	**1 kg**
1 clove	**garlic,** *halved*	
1 tbsp	**olive oil** *or* **cognac**	**15 ml**
	salt	
2 tbsp	**black** *or* **mixed peppercorns** *(black, white, green, pink), coarsely ground or cracked*	**30 ml**

TIPS:

• The steak can be given its pepper coating up to 24 hours ahead of time. Cover with plastic wrap and refrigerate. Bring the steak to room temperature before you begin cooking.

• An easy way to crack peppercorns is to fold them into a piece of waxed paper or cooking parchment and crush with a rolling pin, bottle, or meat mallet.

A steak grilled to perfection – nicely charred on the outside and tender and juicy within. Ask the butcher to cut a first-class piece of beef for you, and just season it simply (though a pat of Tarragon Butter – see Variation, p. 91 – melting on the grilled steak at serving time would be delicious). Serve the sirloin with grilled vegetables and a baked potato, or sun-ripened field tomatoes and corn on the cob.

1. Rub the steak with the cut clove of garlic and the oil or cognac, and salt lightly. Pat an even coating of pepper on both sides of the meat.

2. Preheat the barbecue and lightly oil the grill rack. Grill the steak about 8 minutes per side over medium-high heat for medium-rare. Remove the steak from the grill when it is just a bit more rare than you like it.

3. Allow to rest for 5 minutes. Serve in slices cut across the grain with all the trimmings.

Serves 6.

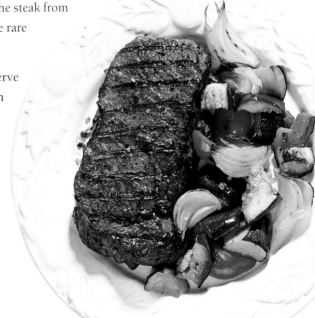

Pepper-Encrusted Loin of Pork

3½ lb	pork loin, *boned*	1.5 kg
¼ cup	fresh cracked black pepper	60 ml
2 cloves	garlic, *finely chopped*	
1 tsp	lemon zest, *grated*	5 ml
1 tsp	salt	5 ml
½ cup	fresh flat-leaf parsley, *finely chopped*	125 ml
2 tbsp	olive oil, *infused with*	30 ml
1 clove	garlic, *chopped*	

TIPS:

• The meat can be prepared for the barbecue (through Step 2) ahead of time and kept covered in the refrigerator for up to 8 hours.

• Replace the pepper/herb seasoning inside the pork loin with tapenade (p. 23), Sun-Dried Tomato Pesto (p. 24), or your favourite commercial variation on the pesto theme.

Delicious prepared on the barbecue and served, hot or cold, with a selection of condiments: your favourite mustard or homemade chili sauce or, for something a little different, grilled fresh pineapple or Pineapple Salsa (p. 76).

1. Open out boned pork loin, boned side up. In a small bowl, combine half the cracked black pepper, the garlic, lemon zest, a little salt, and parsley. Sprinkle mixture evenly over the pork. Roll up the roast and tie in several places to form a compact cylinder.

2. Brush the outside of the pork with a little garlic-infused oil and coat with the remaining pepper and a little salt.

3. Preheat the barbecue, then set the meat on the rack over a foil drip pan; close cover and cook, using indirect heat (see p. 15), at a constant medium temperature (about 350°F/180°C). Baste the meat occasionally with the garlic-infused oil.

4. Cooking time will be approximately 1½ hours, but check with an instant-read thermometer after about an hour. The pork is done when the internal temperature is 160°F (70°C).

5. Remove meat to a warm serving platter, and let rest a few minutes before slicing.

Serves 6.

Pepper-Encrusted Loin of Pork with Pineapple Salsa (p. 76) in pepper cups; also shown: Mexicali Ribs (p. 83), Eggplant & Tomato Salad (p. 127).

Hoisin Ribs

6 lbs	meaty pork back ribs	3 kg
½ cup	sesame seeds, *toasted (optional)*	125 ml

Asian Spice Rub

1 tbsp	coriander seeds	15 ml
1 tbsp	black peppercorns	15 ml
4 tsp	fennel seeds	20 ml
2 tsp	cumin seeds	10 ml
1 tsp	whole cloves	5 ml
1–3	whole dried hot red peppers, *finely chopped*	

Hoisin Baste

1 tsp	Asian Spice Rub	5 ml
1 cup	hoisin sauce	250 ml
2 tbsp	honey	30 ml
¼ cup	rice vinegar	60 ml
2 tbsp	fresh ginger root, *grated*	30 ml
1 tbsp	garlic, *finely chopped*	15 ml
1 tbsp	sesame oil	15 ml

TIP:

• As a timesaver, replace the Asian Spice Rub with a good curry powder.

*O*ne of summer's most popular grilled foods acquires a dynamite Asian twist. The baste gets its sweet-spicy oriental flavour from soybean-based hoisin sauce. Serve individual ribs as finger food at a summer gathering, or racks for dinner accompanied by steamed rice and stir-fried snow and snap peas.

1. Combine spices for Asian Spice Rub in a heavy frying pan and lightly toast over medium heat until aromas are released, about 2–3 minutes. Cool and grind to a fine powder in a spice mill or with a pestle and mortar.

2. Combine 1 tsp (5 ml) of the Asian Spice Rub with the other ingredients for Hoisin Baste in a small saucepan and bring to a simmer over moderate heat. Stir and simmer for a couple of minutes.

3. Cut racks of ribs into manageable lengths (6–8 ribs each), wipe dry, and rub all over with remaining Asian Spice Rub. Set ribs in a single layer in roasting pan(s) and slow-roast in a 200°F (80°C) oven for about 3 hours. (This can be done the day before.) Cool, cover, and refrigerate until needed.

4. When ready to serve, return ribs to room temperature. Place them on a clean, lightly oiled grill over medium-high heat and sear for a few minutes on each side. Brush with Hoisin Baste and close the lid of the barbecue.

5. Turn and baste several times until ribs are tender and nicely charred, but still moist and juicy – about 30 minutes. Serve hot, sprinkled with toasted sesame seeds if desired.

Serves 4–6.

Mexicali Ribs

6 lbs	meaty pork back ribs	3 kg

Mexicali Spice Rub

2 tbsp	chili powder	30 ml
1 tsp	paprika	5 ml
1 tsp	cumin, *ground*	5 ml
1 tsp	cayenne	5 ml
1 tsp	salt	5 ml
1 tbsp	freshly ground black pepper	15 ml
1 tbsp	dried oregano	15 ml
1 tbsp	dried thyme	15 ml
1 tbsp	brown sugar	15 ml

Rib Baste

¼ cup	cider vinegar	60 ml
¼ cup	fresh lemon juice	60 ml
¼ cup	liquid honey	60 ml
2 tbsp	olive oil	30 ml
1 tbsp	hot sauce *(or to taste)*	15 ml

This recipe calls for a long, slow baking of the ribs in a low oven, then a quick finish on the barbecue – and the results are fantastic. (Our tasters rated them the best ribs they ever had.) The oven baking can be done earlier in the day, or even the day before.

1. Thoroughly combine all ingredients for spice rub in a small bowl.

2. Cut racks of ribs in half or keep whole if your pan is big enough; wipe dry and rub all over with Mexicali Spice Rub.

3. Set in a single layer in roasting pan(s) and slow-roast in a 200°F (80°C) oven for about 3 hours. Set aside or refrigerate until needed.

4. Combine ingredients for Rib Baste in a small saucepan. Stir over low heat until honey melts. Cool and refrigerate until needed.

5. When ready to serve, return ribs to room temperature. Place on a clean, lightly oiled grill over medium-high heat and sear for a few minutes on each side. Brush with Rib Baste and close the lid of the barbecue.

6. Turn and baste several times for about 30 minutes until ribs are tender and nicely charred, but still deliciously saucy.

Serves 4–6.

Overleaf: Mexicali Ribs, Teriyaki Salmon (p. 86), and grilled corn (p. 124).

Teriyaki Tuna or Salmon

4	**tuna steaks** *or* **salmon steaks** *or* **fillets** *(about 6 oz/ 170 g each)*	

Teriyaki Marinade & Basting Sauce

½ cup	**soy sauce**	125 ml
¼ cup	**dry sherry**	60 ml
¼ cup	**peanut** *or* **olive oil**	60 ml
¼ cup	**brown sugar**	60 ml
2 cloves	**garlic,** *minced*	
2	**green onions,** *finely chopped*	
1 tsp	**fresh ginger,** *grated*	5 ml

*C*ommercial varieties of teriyaki sauce are available, but your homemade version will taste better. This recipe requires only ¼ cup (60 ml) of marinade, plus some extra for basting, but the rest will keep indefinitely in the fridge. Serve the teriyaki fish with steamed rice and simple vegetables of the season.

1. Combine marinade ingredients in a small saucepan. Set over medium heat and simmer for 5 minutes, stirring to dissolve sugar. Strain and cool before using.

2. Sprinkle ¼ cup (60 ml) marinade over salmon or tuna. (Store the rest of the marinade in a tightly closed bottle in the refrigerator.) Leave fish at room temperature 15–30 minutes, turning once.

3. Set fish on a clean, lightly oiled grill over medium-high heat (or under a preheated broiler) for about 5 minutes. Brush with a little fresh marinade, turn, and grill 3–5 minutes longer, depending on the thickness of the fish. Fish is done when the flesh just flakes when tested.

Serves 4.

TIP:

• Keep Teriyaki Marinade on hand – it's delicious with other firm fish such as halibut, and shellfish such as shrimp and scallops. Also try it on chicken – especially chicken wings – pork, and flank steak.

(The Teriyaki Salmon is shown in the photo on the previous page.)

Oriental-Style Steamed Fish

1	**whole fish** *(2 lbs/1 kg),* *(pickerel, bass,* *red snapper)*	
	salt and freshly **ground black pepper**	
2 tbsp	**fresh ginger root,** *slivered*	30 ml
1	**fresh hot green pepper,** *seeded and slivered*	
2	**green onions,** *slivered*	
2–3 sprigs	**fresh coriander** *(plus additional,* *chopped, for garnish)*	
1 tbsp	**rice wine** *or* **dry sherry**	15 ml
1 tbsp	**soy sauce**	15 ml
2 tbsp	**vegetable oil**	30 ml
1 tsp	**sesame oil**	5 ml

Cooked on the barbecue or in the oven, fish prepared this way is splendid either hot or cold in a salad.

1. Thoroughly clean fish and pat dry. Make 2–4 slashes in the flesh on each side. Lay fish on a large square of heavy-duty foil and rub on both sides with salt and pepper.

2. Sprinkle remaining ingredients on both sides of fish. Fold the foil to make a sealed package.

3. Lay the foil-wrapped fish on a preheated grill and cook, with the grill closed, over moderately high indirect heat (see p. 15) for approximately 30 minutes – allowing 10 minutes for each 1" (2.5 cm) of fish measured at its thickest part, plus 5 minutes for the heat to penetrate the foil. Open foil and test for doneness by making a small slit in the thickest part. The fish should be opaque and separate into moist flakes.

4. Serve hot with the cooking juices poured over top, garnished with a sprinkling of chopped coriander.

Serves 4.

TIPS:

• To serve chilled, allow fish to cool slightly. While it is still warm, carefully scrape away skin and lift the flesh from the bones. Wrap well and refrigerate until serving. Serve accompanied by Asian Rice Salad (p. 168) or Thai Noodle Salad (p. 140) and a green salad with a light vinaigrette.

• Fish can also be cooked in a 450°F (230°C) oven.

Grilled Fish with Crispy Caper Sauce

2 tbsp	melted butter *or* vegetable oil	30 ml
2 tbsp	fresh lemon juice	30 ml
	salt and freshly ground black pepper	
2 lbs	fresh fish fillets	1 kg

Crispy Caper Sauce

2 tbsp	unsalted butter	30 ml
2 tbsp	extra-virgin olive oil	30 ml
2 tbsp	small capers, *rinsed and drained*	30 ml
2 tbsp	fresh lemon juice	30 ml
¼ cup	fresh flat-leaf parsley, *finely chopped*	60 ml
	salt and freshly ground black pepper	

TIP:

• If the family angler delivers small bass or perch, you may need to use a fish-grilling basket. Or cook the fillets in a frying pan on the stove instead.

Freshly caught (or bought) fillets of trout, bass, salmon, or halibut work well in this dish. Serve with grilled asparagus and tiny new potatoes, steamed with chopped fresh dill until just tender. Capers, the flower buds of the caper bush, have a spicy tartness that is a wonderful match with fish.

1. Combine melted butter or oil, lemon juice, and seasoning. Brush mixture lightly over fish fillets.

2. Lay fish on a lightly oiled grill over medium heat and cook for 4–5 minutes for ¼"–½" (about 1 cm) fillets. For thicker fillets (½"–1"/1–2.5 cm) or steaks, turn carefully and continue cooking until the fish is opaque and flakes easily when tested with a fork, about another 4 minutes. (Timing will depend on the thickness of the fish.)

3. Remove to a platter. Drizzle with Crispy Caper Sauce and serve at once.

Serves 4.

Crispy Caper Sauce

1. In a small frying pan, heat the butter and oil. Add the capers and cook until they are just beginning to get crispy, about 5 minutes.

2. Remove from heat, stir in lemon juice and parsley, and season to taste. Pour hot over the fish.

Makes about ⅓ cup (75 ml).

The simplicity of grilled asparagus (p. 124) and steamed new potatoes makes them good accompaniments to the Grilled Fish with tangy Crispy Caper Sauce.

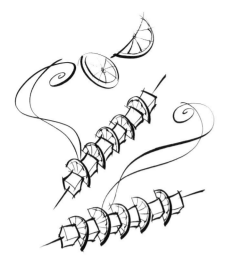

¾ lb	**salmon**	375 g
¾ lb	**grouper, tuna,** *or* **other firm-fleshed fish**	375 g
2	**lemons**	
4	**green onions,** *trimmed*	
½ cup	**Garlic Seafood Butter** *(facing page)*, *melted*	125 ml

TIP:

• If you're alternating different elements or colours on skewers, as with this recipe, lay them out in order on your cutting board first. This "dry run" helps ensure you get the right number of pieces in the right sequence on each skewer, and makes the job of threading them on the sticks faster.

VARIATION:

• **Garlicky Shrimp Kebabs:** Remove shells from large shrimp but leave the tails intact. Thread on skewers with lemon and green onion pieces as above, adding a cherry tomato or two if you like. Brush with Garlic Seafood Butter and place on oiled grill. Cook about 2–3 minutes a side, turning and basting, until shrimp are just opaque.

Garlicky Fish Kebabs

*F*irm-fleshed fish is well suited to grilling. The only trick is to be sure not to overcook it – take it off the barbecue as soon as it turns opaque. Serve with *Roasted Vegetable Couscous (p. 144)* or *Mediterranean Potato Salad (p. 152)*.

1. Soak bamboo skewers in water for about an hour.

2. Trim the fish, removing any skin and stray bones, and cut each fish into 12 equal pieces.

3. Slice the lemons thinly crosswise, and cut each slice in half. Cut each green onion into 3 pieces.

4. Thread fish (6 pieces per skewer), lemon, and green onion pieces alternately onto the skewers, sandwiching the lemon slices tightly between the pieces of fish.

5. Brush the skewers with a light coating of the melted garlic butter and set on a clean, lightly oiled grill over medium heat. After about 4 minutes, turn and baste lightly.

6. Continue grilling until the fish is opaque and just cooked, about 3–4 minutes more. Serve hot with fresh lemon slices on the side and the remaining melted butter for those who would like it.

Serves 4.

(A Garlicky Shrimp Kebab is shown on the cover.)

Garlic Seafood Butter

½ lb	**unsalted butter,** *softened*	250 g
4	**green onions,** *finely chopped*	
3 cloves	**garlic,** *minced*	
2 tsp	**lemon zest,** *grated*	10 ml
1 tbsp	**fresh thyme,** *chopped* **or**	15 ml
1 tsp	**dried thyme**	5 ml
1 tbsp	**Worcestershire sauce**	15 ml
good pinch	**cayenne** **or**	
dash	**hot sauce**	
½ tsp	**salt**	2 ml
½ tsp	**freshly ground black pepper**	2 ml

*U*se this spicy butter as a baste for seafood and lamb, or to top a baked potato.

1. Thoroughly combine all ingredients using a food processor, a mortar and pestle, or a fork and a shallow bowl. Spoon the flavoured butter onto a sheet of wax paper or foil and form into a log.

2. Wrap securely and refrigerate or freeze.

Makes about 1 cup (250 ml).

TIPS:

• You can make the flavoured butter ahead and store it for a couple of days in the refrigerator or for a month or so in the freezer.

• For a party snack or appetizer, use the Garlic Seafood Butter to baste skewers with a large shrimp curled around a sea scallop on each. Grill for about 2–3 minutes per side, turning and basting, until the seafood is opaque.

VARIATION:

• Tarragon Butter: Use the same technique, except mix the butter with 2 tbsp (30 ml) chopped fresh tarragon (or 2 tsp/10 ml dried), 2 tsp (10 ml) grated lemon zest, 2 tbsp (30 ml) fresh lemon juice, and salt to taste. Slice off pats as needed. Great on top of grilled steak, grilled fish, or a baked potato.

Citrus-Glazed Salmon

2	limes	
2 tbsp	liquid honey	30 ml
1½ tbsp	Dijon mustard	20 ml
¼ tsp	salt	1 ml
4	salmon steaks, *at least 1" (2.5 cm) thick*	

VARIATION

• Try this glaze on other firm fish such as tuna or marlin.

This incredibly easy recipe comes from my friend Monda Rosenberg, a stellar cook and the food/nutrition editor of Chatelaine magazine. The honey-lime glaze gives the fish an island taste. Serve the salmon with Grilled Mango Salsa (p. 94), grilled mini potatoes (p. 127), and steamed or grilled asparagus (p. 124).

1. Grate zest from 1 lime. Squeeze juice from both limes to measure about ⅓ cup (75 ml).

2. In a bowl, stir juice with zest, honey, mustard, and salt until smooth.

3. Oil grill and preheat barbecue to high. Brush salmon with the lime sauce.

4. Grill, basting often, until a knife tip inserted into centre of fish feels warm, about 5 minutes per side.

Serves 4.

For an attractive presentation, garnish the Citrus-Glazed Salmon with green onions torn into strips (green part only), curls of lime zest, and mesclun salad greens.

Grilled Mango or Peach Salsa

1	**ripe mango**	
	or	
2	**ripe peaches**	
1 clove	**garlic**	
1	**large ripe tomato**	
1	**small red onion,** *peeled and cut in half horizontally*	
1	**jalapeño pepper**	
2 tbsp	**fresh lime juice**	30 ml
¼ cup	**fresh coriander,** *chopped*	60 ml
	salt and freshly ground black pepper	

TIP:

• Mangoes have a long, flattish pit in the centre, and the flesh doesn't pull away from it (as it does, say, from a peach pit). Follow the drawings for easy cutting – and to eat the sweet juicy mango chunks right off the peel.

VARIATION:

• Fresh Mango or Peach Salsa: Omit tomato and prepare salsa as above without grilling the fruit and vegetables.

𝒯his grilled fruit salsa will complement a variety of food cooked on the barbecue. Try it with grilled pork, fish, and chicken.

1. Slice the flat sides off the mango pit (see Tip, below) or cut peaches in half and remove pits. Wrap garlic clove in foil.

2. Grill mango slabs or peach halves, cut side down, whole tomato, onion, jalapeño, and garlic until just tender and nicely browned, 5–15 minutes.

3. Peel and dice the mango or peaches. Finely chop the garlic. Peel the tomato and jalapeño, and dice all the vegetables. Toss all together with lime juice and coriander and season to taste.

Makes about 2 cups (500 ml).

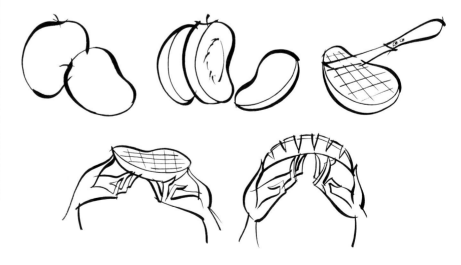

Pico de Gallo

4	**large, ripe tomatoes,** *diced*	
1	**small onion,** *diced*	
2 cloves	**garlic,** *minced*	
2–3	**fresh jalapeño peppers,** *finely chopped, veins and seeds removed*	
3 tbsp	**fresh coriander** *or* **flat-leaf parsley,** *finely chopped*	45 ml
1 tbsp	**fresh basil,** *chopped* **or**	15 ml
½ tsp	**dried basil**	2 ml
2 tbsp	**fresh lime juice**	30 ml
2 tbsp	**safflower** *or* **olive oil**	30 ml
	salt	

*P*ico de Gallo is a refreshing Mexican-style uncooked salsa that tastes best when made just before serving. (Luckily, it takes only minutes to prepare.) It's an essential topping for fajitas (p. 74) and a good accompaniment to grilled fish, but it's also great on burgers or served on its own as a dip with corn chips.

1. Combine all ingredients. Toss lightly.

Makes 2 cups (500 ml).

TIP:

• Some field tomatoes have thin skins, and peeling them is a matter of choice. Others, like the plum varieties, have tough skins that require peeling. A proven technique is to have a pot of water boiling on the stove. Drop in a tomato and count to 10. Lift the tomato out, and drop into cold water or hold under the tap. Cut a cross on the smooth end and the skin will slip off in large sections. Cut out the core at the stem end. The process takes about 10 seconds, so slip another tomato into the pot as you take one out.

Lazy Summer Paella

1½ lbs	**large raw shrimp,** *peeled and deveined (leave tails attached if you like)*	750 g
	Saffron Rice Pilaf *(p. 169)*	
12–24	**mussels** *and/or* **clams,** *cleaned (optional)*	
2–3	**chorizo** *or* **other spicy sausages** *(optional)*	
	salt and freshly ground black pepper	
	lemon slices and fresh parsley, *chopped (for garnish)*	

Lemon Garlic Baste

2 tbsp	**olive oil**	30 ml
squeeze	**fresh lemon juice**	
2–4 cloves	**garlic,** *finely chopped*	
1 tsp	**dried oregano**	5 ml
½ tsp	**lemon zest,** *grated*	2 ml

TIP:

• The mussels and clams can also be cooked on the barbecue in a grilling basket. Close lid and cook for 2–3 minutes until the shells open.

*T*he shrimp are cooked on skewers on the barbecue and served on top of a fragrant, golden rice pilaf. If you want to be more elaborate (and closer to an authentic paella), you can also steam some fresh mussels or clams in the rice and/or grill some spicy sausage to add to the dish.

1. Combine ingredients for baste and set aside for 10 minutes or so to allow flavours to blend.

2. Toss the shrimp with the baste. Set aside in the refrigerator for an hour for the shrimp to marinate. Put bamboo skewers in cold water to soak.

3. Prepare the rice pilaf. Tuck the mussels and clams (if including) into the rice during the last 5 minutes of cooking time, and continue to cook until they open.

4. Meanwhile, preheat barbecue and lightly oil the grill rack. Prick sausages (if including), brush lightly with oil, and set on preheated grill. Turn to brown evenly and cook thoroughly, about 20 minutes.

5. Thread the shrimp on skewers, and grill over medium-high heat for about 2–3 minutes a side, being careful not to overcook. (Shrimp should be pink on the outside, tender and opaque within.) Season with salt and pepper.

6. Fluff the rice with a fork, season, and turn out onto a warm platter. Discard any unopened shellfish. Add the sausages, cut in pieces, and top with skewers of shrimp. Serve at once, garnished with parsley and lemon.

Serves 6.

While the pilaf is cooking, grill the skewered shrimp. If you like, add some mussels to the rice close to the end of the cooking time.

Cedar-Smoked Salmon & Trout

1	**untreated cedar plank,** *approx. ³/₄" x 8" x 16"*	
3 tbsp	**olive oil**	45 ml
1	**skin-on salmon fillet,** *about 2–2¹/₂ lbs (1 kg)* **or**	
2–2¹/₂ lbs	**trout fillets**	1 kg
	salt	
1	**small onion,** *finely chopped*	
2 cloves	**garlic,** *minced*	
2 tbsp	**black peppercorns,** *coarsely ground*	30 ml
4 tbsp	**fresh dill,** *finely chopped (plus additional for garnish)*	60 ml
2	**lemons,** *sliced (for garnish)*	

TIP:

• Check a few times to make sure the plank is not catching fire. Douse flare-ups with water from a spray bottle. If necessary, elevate the plank on small "logs" of crumpled-up aluminum foil to get it farther from the fire.

*P*lank cooking is a technique of Native origins that imparts a subtle smoky flavour to fish. It's also a fabulous, easy way to cook fish for a crowd. Be prepared for the amount of smoke you create!

1. Soak the untreated cedar plank in water for at least an hour. Drain and rub one side with a little of the olive oil.

2. Brush the flesh side of the fish with the rest of the olive oil and sprinkle with salt. Combine onion, garlic, peppercorns, and dill, and pat the mixture onto the flesh to form a crust.

3. Preheat the barbecue. Place the fish skin side down on the side of the cedar plank that was rubbed with oil, tent it with aluminum foil, and place it on the grill over medium-high heat.

4. Cook with the lid down for about 20–30 minutes for 1 large fillet, 10 minutes for smaller ones, or until fish is just opaque at the thickest part. (Time will vary with size of fillet.) Remove plank and fish from grill, and brush fillet with a little more olive oil. Transfer fish to a platter and serve immediately, garnished with lemon slices and chopped fresh dill.

Serves 6–8.

Cedar-smoked fish is moist and flavourful. (Don't overcook it!) Just be sure to use cedar that hasn't been treated.

Italian Burgers

1½ lbs	**ground beef**	750 g
1	**sweet** *or* **hot Italian sausage,** *casing removed*	
1	**small onion,** *grated*	
¼ cup	**Parmesan cheese,** *grated*	60 ml
1 tsp	**dried oregano**	5 ml
pinch	**hot red pepper flakes** *(optional)*	
	salt and freshly ground black pepper	
6 slices	**mozzarella cheese**	
6	**kaiser buns**	
½ cup	**tomato sauce,** *warmed*	125 ml
	grilled *or* **sautéed peppers, onions, and mushrooms** *(optional, for topping burgers)*	

*L*et the kids have their favourite plastic-wrapped cheese on top of their burgers, but the grown-ups will enjoy this tasty version. Delicious topped with grilled or sautéed hot and sweet peppers, onion slices, and white or portobello mushrooms.

1. Toss first 7 ingredients together lightly.

2. Form into 6 patties, ¾" (2 cm) thick.

3. Set burgers on a preheated grill, close the lid, and cook over high heat, 3–4 minutes on the first side; then turn and cook for 2–3 minutes longer. Top each burger with a slice of mozzarella and cook for a minute more to melt the cheese.

4. Serve each burger on a warm kaiser bun brushed on the inside with tomato sauce. Top with grilled or sautéed peppers, onions, and mushrooms to taste.

Serves 6.

VARIATION:

• For a make-ahead supper: Add ½ cup (125 ml) soft breadcrumbs and some chopped parsley to the meat mixture and form into meatballs. Cook in your favourite tomato sauce and serve over pasta.

Mexican Burgers

1 lb	lean ground beef	500 g
2 tbsp	onion, *finely chopped*	30 ml
1 clove	garlic, *minced*	
1 tsp	dried oregano	5 ml
1 tbsp	fresh coriander, *chopped*	15 ml
1 tsp	jalapeño pepper, *finely chopped,* **or** hot sauce, *to taste*	5 ml
	salt and freshly ground black pepper	
dash	water *or* milk	
4 slices	Monterey Jack cheese *or* mild Cheddar cheese	
4	sesame buns, *lightly grilled*	
	lettuce, guacamole, salsa, and sour cream *(optional, for topping burgers)*	

*S*erve these tasty burgers on lightly grilled sesame buns lined with leaf lettuce, and then pile on guacamole (p. 41), salsa (p. 40) or Pico de Gallo (p. 95), and sour cream.

1. Combine meat, onion, garlic, herbs, jalapeño or hot sauce, and seasoning. Mix lightly and moisten with just enough water or milk so that the mixture can be formed into 8 thin patties.

2. Top 4 of the patties with a cheese slice. Top each with another patty and pinch the edges to seal.

3. Grill over medium heat with the lid closed for about 8 minutes, turning once about halfway through. Serve on sesame buns topped with lettuce, guacamole, and other condiments as desired.

Serves 4.

VARIATION:

• **Mexican Mini-Meatballs:** For a great party snack, double the above recipe, cutting the cheese into ½" (1-cm) cubes. Pat about 1 tbsp (15 ml) of meat mixture around each cube to form small meatballs. Thread meatballs on skewers and grill until nicely browned and cooked through, about 8–10 minutes, turning frequently. Or place in a shallow roasting pan and cook in a covered grill over medium heat for about 30 minutes. Serve hot, with salsa and sour cream for dipping. Makes about 35 small meatballs.

Overleaf: Mexican Burgers, Indian-Style Lamb Kebabs (p. 105), and Spicy Grilled Corn (p. 124).

Lamb Koftas

2 lbs	ground lamb	1 kg
1	medium onion, *finely chopped*	
4 cloves	garlic, *minced*	
2 tbsp	fresh dill, *chopped*	30 ml
1/4 cup	fresh mint, *chopped*	60 ml
2 tsp	lemon zest, *grated*	10 ml
1 1/2 tsp	salt	7 ml
1 tsp	cumin	5 ml
	freshly ground black pepper	

VARIATION:

• **Greek Burgers:** Form the Lamb Kofta mixture into patties and grill. Tuck the patties into the pockets of warm pita breads and add roasted peppers, crumbled feta cheese, and tzatziki (p. 27).

These tasty skewers of ground lamb are sweetly spiced with flavours of the Middle East. Serve with baba ghanouj (a grilled eggplant purée that's available in many supermarkets), finely chopped onion and tomato, Taratoor Sauce (Quick Trick, below) or tzatziki (p. 27), and warm pita breads.

1. Soak 32 bamboo skewers in water for about an hour.

2. Combine meat, onion, garlic, herbs, lemon zest, and seasonings. Squeeze mixture with your hands until well blended and smooth.

3. Wet hands lightly, divide mixture into 32 equal portions, and form into uniform cylinder shapes. Thread each cylinder onto a damp bamboo skewer and set on a baking sheet. Cover with plastic wrap and refrigerate several hours or as long as overnight.

4. Remove from the refrigerator 30 minutes before cooking. Place skewers on a hot, lightly oiled grill over high heat. Grill for 8–10 minutes, turning until nicely browned and cooked through.

Serves 4–6.

QUICK TRICK:

Taratoor Sauce is a traditional Middle Eastern accompaniment to Lamb Koftas: Combine 1/2 cup (125 ml) tahini, 1/3 cup (75 ml) fresh lemon juice, and 2 cloves finely minced garlic with enough warm water (4–5 tbsp/60–75 ml) to make a sauce of pouring consistency. Season to taste. The sauce is also delicious with other grilled lamb dishes, beef, and vegetables. (Use it as a dip for grilled asparagus.)

Indian-Style Lamb Kebabs

1 tsp	cumin	5 ml
1 tsp	garam masala *or* **good curry powder**	5 ml
¼ tsp	turmeric	2 ml
½ cup	plain yogurt	125 ml
2 tbsp	fresh ginger root, *finely chopped*	30 ml
2 cloves	garlic, *finely chopped*	
½	small onion, *finely chopped*	
	salt and freshly ground black pepper	
2 lbs	lamb, *boned, trimmed, and cut into 1½" (3-cm) cubes*	1 kg

TIPS:

• Garam masala is a fragrant spice blend available in Indian markets. If you can't find it, substitute a good-quality curry powder.

• You can also use this marinade with a boned and butterflied leg of lamb. Marinate as above; see p. 107 for grilling instructions.

*M*arinated chunks of lean lamb from a boneless leg make wonderful kebabs. Serve the kebabs with basmati rice, grilled corn with spicy butter (p. 124), the cooling Indian yogurt dip called raita (Quick Tricks, below), and a fruit chutney.

1. Combine all ingredients except lamb.

2. Coat lamb pieces with marinade mixture and seal in a plastic bag or set in a shallow, covered dish; refrigerate for 6 hours or overnight.

3. Soak bamboo skewers in cold water for about an hour. Bring lamb to room temperature and thread on skewers.

4. Grill over medium-high heat until kebabs are nicely browned on the outside and tender and juicy inside (8–10 minutes).

Serves 4–6.

QUICK TRICKS:

Raita: Combine 1 cup (250 ml) peeled and grated cucumber (squeeze out and discard excess liquid) with 1½ cups (375 ml) plain yogurt, ½ tsp (2 ml) salt, 1 tbsp (15 ml) fresh chopped mint (or 1 tsp/5 ml dried), 1 tsp (5 ml) toasted cumin seeds, and a pinch of paprika and freshly ground black pepper. Chill before serving. Serve with Indian curries and grilled food.

For variety, make a spinach raita: Prepare as above, omitting the cucumber, salt, and mint; just before serving, stir in about 1 cup (250 ml) chopped cooked spinach and salt to taste.

(The Indian-Style Lamb Kebabs are shown in the photo preceding p. 104.)

Cumin-Scented Leg of Lamb

2–3 lbs	boneless leg of lamb	1–1.5 kg
1 tsp	ground cumin	5 ml
½ tsp	cayenne	2 ml
1 tsp	coarsely ground black pepper	5 ml
1 tsp	salt	5 ml
4 cloves	garlic, *minced*	
1 tbsp	olive oil	15 ml

TIPS:

• This spice paste is also great on lamb kebabs. Cut the meat into cubes, toss them with the paste, and thread on skewers. Grill 8–10 minutes, until the meat is nicely browned outside and tender and juicy within.

• The lemony flavour of cumin comes through best if you lightly toast whole cumin seeds in a heavy skillet for 2–3 minutes over medium heat, just until the aroma is released, then grind them in a spice mill.

*S*erve this boned leg of lamb with its spicy crust cut in thin slices across the grain, with a sprinkle of Cumin Salt on top and a dollop of Mint Yogurt Sauce (Quick Tricks, below) or tzatziki (p. 27) on the side. Rice pilaf, roasted lemon rosemary potatoes, or Mediterranean Potato Salad with Asparagus (p. 152), and lightly steamed carrots are good accompaniments.

1. Spread out boned leg of lamb, trim away excess fat or sinew, and pound lightly to flatten. Slash the thickest parts to make the piece lie flat.

2. Combine remaining ingredients in a small bowl to make a paste, and rub into the lamb on all sides. Place, covered, in a shallow pan or heavy-duty plastic bag and marinate in the refrigerator several hours or overnight.

3. Remove lamb from refrigerator an hour before cooking. Place on a preheated grill over medium-high indirect heat (see p. 15), with a drip pan underneath. Roast 30–40 minutes, turning once, for medium rare. Remove the meat when the internal temperature is just below 140°F (60°C) for rare; 150°F (65°C) for medium. Let rest for 10 minutes before slicing.

Serves 6–8.

QUICK TRICKS:

Cumin Salt: To really bring out the flavour of grilled lamb, combine equal amounts of freshly toasted ground cumin seeds and sea salt and sprinkle on the meat before serving.

Mint Yogurt Sauce: Stir together 1 cup (250 ml) plain yogurt, ½ cup (125 ml) sour cream, 1 tbsp (15 ml) fresh lemon juice, 2 tbsp (30 ml) chopped fresh mint, and ¼ tsp (1 ml) salt. Refrigerate to blend flavours; taste and adjust seasoning before serving.

Grilled Cumin-Scented Leg of Lamb served with Mint Yogurt Sauce and Mediterranean Potato Salad with Asparagus (p. 152).

Chile-Rub Chicken

3 lbs	bone-in chicken pieces	1.5 kg

Spicy Chile Rub

2 tsp	each ground cumin, coriander, and sweet paprika	10 ml
½ tsp	cinnamon	2 ml
¼ tsp	cayenne	1 ml
1 tsp	salt	5 ml
2 tbsp	fresh lime juice	30 ml
3 tbsp	olive oil	45 ml
4 cloves	garlic, *minced*	
1	jalapeño pepper, *seeded and finely chopped*	
1 tsp	fresh ginger root, *grated (optional)*	5 ml

TIPS:

• The spice rub is also excellent on pork. It will keep in a covered jar in the refrigerator for about a week.

• For an easy way to speed up the cooking of bone-in chicken breasts, see p. 129.

𝒯he south-of-the-border flavour of this grilled chicken makes it excellent for fajitas (p. 74). Or you can serve it on the bone, accompanied by a plate of grilled vegetables (p. 124) and garlic roast potatoes (Quick Trick, p. 177).

1. Combine all ingredients for the spice rub in a small bowl.

2. Rub the chicken pieces all over with the mixture. Place in a plastic bag and close securely, or in a covered container, and set in the refrigerator for several hours or overnight.

3. About an hour before serving, remove chicken from refrigerator and preheat the barbecue. Grill chicken with the lid closed using medium, indirect heat (see p. 15) for about 30 minutes or until chicken is done. Remove to a warm platter and let rest for 5 minutes. If serving in tortillas, remove meat from the bone and shred or slice thinly.

Serves 6.

Goat Cheese-Stuffed Chicken

4	plump, boneless, skinless chicken breasts *(about 5–6 oz/150–170 g apiece)*	
5 tbsp	basil pesto *(p. 210)*	75 ml
4 oz	goat cheese	125 g
1	large roasted red pepper, *peeled, seeded, and cut in cubes*	
1	large roasted yellow pepper, *peeled, seeded, and cut in cubes*	
1 tbsp	extra-virgin olive oil	15 ml
	salt and freshly ground black pepper	

VARIATION:

• Try tapenade or sun-dried tomato pesto instead of the basil pesto. Ready-made versions of these popular pastes are available in large supermarkets, or you can make your own. (Recipes on pp. 23–24.)

*S*tuffed chicken breasts are pretty to look at and tasty to eat, and the fussy work can be done ahead. With a simple salad alongside, they make a delicious summer lunch or supper. Serve them warm or at room temperature.

1. Slit the thickest end of each breast with the tip of a paring knife. Then, using the knife and your fingers, carefully make a deep pocket in each breast.

2. Combine 4 tbsp (60 ml) of the pesto with the goat cheese and the roasted peppers. Carefully stuff a quarter of the mixture into each chicken pocket.

3. Season the chicken breasts with the oil and salt and pepper. The chicken can be prepared to this point a few hours ahead and set aside, covered, in the refrigerator.

4. When ready to serve, place the stuffed chicken on a preheated grill and brown lightly on both sides, about 2 minutes per side. Turn off one burner and cook over indirect heat (see p. 15) with the lid closed for 15–20 minutes, or until the chicken is tender and the juices run clear when tested.

5. Brush each breast lightly with a little of the remaining pesto while hot, then slice on the diagonal and serve.

Serves 4.

TIP:

• To serve stuffed chicken breasts cold, set aside to cool, then wrap with plastic wrap and refrigerate until needed. Slice on the diagonal and serve at room temperature. For best flavour, enjoy the same day.

Balsamic-Glazed Chicken
and Portobello Mushrooms

4	**boneless, skinless chicken breasts**	
4	**portobello mushrooms,** *stems removed*	
2	**lemons,** *quartered*	
	fresh basil or thyme, *chopped*	
	freshly ground black pepper	

Balsamic Marinade

3 tbsp	**balsamic vinegar**	45 ml
2 tbsp	**extra-virgin olive oil**	30 ml
1 tbsp	**fresh lemon juice**	15 ml
2 cloves	**garlic,** *minced*	
1 tbsp	**fresh thyme** *or* **basil,** *chopped* **or**	15 ml
1 tsp	**dried thyme** *or* **basil**	5 ml
½ tsp	**freshly ground black pepper**	2 ml
	salt	

*T*his very easy, very flexible recipe can be served as a main course, sliced and turned into a salad, or used as the basis for a dynamite sandwich. If you're serving it as a main course, accompany the chicken and mushrooms with grilled asparagus (p. 124) and creamy polenta (p. 50) or roasted lemon potatoes.

1. Combine all ingredients for marinade. If time permits, set aside, covered, for an hour for flavours to blend.

2. Pour half the marinade over the chicken in one dish and the rest over the mushrooms in another dish. Set aside, covered, for half an hour at room temperature or about 4 hours in the refrigerator.

3. Preheat barbecue to medium-high. With the lid open, grill chicken breasts (skinned side down, so you get nice grill marks on the smooth side) and portobello mushrooms (gill side up) for 2 minutes. Then close barbecue and cook 2–3 minutes more.

4. Place quartered lemons on the grill. Turn chicken breasts and mushrooms. With the barbecue open, brown the other side for 2 minutes. Turn the lemon pieces, then close the barbecue and cook chicken, mushrooms, and lemons for about 2–3 minutes more, or until chicken and mushrooms are tender and cooked through. (Total cooking time will be about 8–10 minutes.)

5. Sprinkle with a squeeze of juice from one of the grilled lemons. Slice mushrooms and serve alongside chicken with the remaining grilled lemon wedges. Garnish with the fresh herbs and freshly ground black pepper.

Serves 4.

Serve the sliced Balsamic-Glazed Chicken and Portobellos on a good country bread spread with mayo (mix in a few chopped basil leaves), or on a bed of greens.

Chicken Tikka

4	boneless, skinless chicken breasts	
	oil *or* melted butter *(for basting)*	

Tikka Curry Paste

1	large onion, *finely chopped*	
4 cloves	garlic, *minced*	
1 piece	fresh ginger root, *minced (1"/2.5 cm)*	
	juice of 1 lemon	
1 tbsp	curry powder	15 ml
¼ tsp	cinnamon	1 ml
¼ tsp	ground cumin	1 ml
pinch	cayenne	
	salt and freshly ground black pepper	
¼ cup	oil	60 ml
1 cup	yogurt	250 ml

*I*f it looks like happy hour may turn into supper, consider marinating small strips of chicken, threading them on bamboo skewers, and grilling them on the barbecue. This fragrant East Indian marinade gives the chicken a lovely colour and taste. Serve the skewered chicken, either straight from the grill or at room temperature, with a fruit chutney dip. The strips can also be wrapped in warm tortillas or tucked into pitas with shredded iceberg lettuce and chutney on top.

1. To make the Tikka Curry Paste, blend onion, garlic, ginger, lemon juice, and spices to form a paste. (A blender does the job in a second, or you can use muscle power and a mortar and pestle or a bowl and a fork.) Add oil and yogurt. Set aside.

2. Pound chicken breasts to flatten and cut into long narrow slices. Coat chicken in the marinade and leave for several hours in the refrigerator.

3. Soak bamboo skewers in cold water for about an hour. (See Tip, below.) Thread the marinated chicken strips on the skewers and grill, turning and basting with a little oil or butter, for about 10 minutes or until nicely browned and cooked through.

Serves 4–6.

TIP:
• If the chicken is being served as party snacks, you'll need 4–6 skewers per breast, with 1 strip of chicken per skewer. If it's being served for dinner, you can make larger skewers and will need only 2–3 per breast.

VARIATION:
• Small pieces of chicken threaded on skewers and grilled are also extremely popular in Indonesia, Thailand, and Malaysia. For a different taste, marinate the chicken in Malaysian Spice Paste (p. 128) or Thai Green Curry Marinade (p. 121). Grill as described above, then serve with Peanut Dipping Sauce or Light Thai Dipping Sauce (both p. 62).

Add Asian Rice Salad (p. 168) and spicy or plain grilled corn (p. 124), and turn the Chicken Tikka appetizers into dinner.

Bus-Stop Chicken

4 cloves	garlic	
1	small onion, *chopped*	
1 bunch	green onions, *chopped*	
1	green pepper, *chopped*	
1 stalk	celery, *chopped*	
1	Scotch bonnet pepper or	
2	jalapeño peppers, *chopped (or to taste)*	
½ tsp	ground allspice	2 ml
2 tbsp	fresh thyme	30 ml
1 tbsp	balsamic vinegar	15 ml
	juice of ½ lime	
2	bay leaves	
½ bunch	parsley	
2 tsp	salt	10 ml
1 tsp	freshly ground black pepper	5 ml
½ cup	olive oil	125 ml
¼ cup	amber rum	60 ml
3½–4 lbs	chicken pieces	1.5–2 kg

This recipe comes from Keely Schierl, owner of The Butcher's Daughters, an excellent specialty food store, butcher shop, and café in Huntsville, Ontario. She invented it to recreate the charcoal-grilled chicken she had at a dusty bus stop in Belmopan, Belize – "the best grilled bird I'd ever eaten," she says. Don't be dissuaded from trying it by the long list of ingredients – everything just gets combined in the food processor.

1. Purée all ingredients except chicken in a food processor. If the mixture is too stiff, add a bit of water.

2. Place chicken and marinade in a heavy-duty plastic bag and shake to coat all pieces. Marinate, refrigerated, for 12–24 hours, the longer the better.

3. Shake excess marinade from chicken and grill directly over medium heat until the outside of the chicken pieces is nicely crisped, about 3 minutes a side. (They will get quite blackened-looking.) When the outsides are grilled to your satisfaction, switch to indirect cooking (see p. 15) and cook with the lid closed until the juices run clear and the dark-meat pieces are quite tender (about 10–15 minutes).

4. Remove chicken from grill and let rest for 10 minutes. Season to taste and serve.

Serves 4–6.

Rotisseried Island Chicken

2	whole chickens	
	(2½ –3 lbs/	
	1–1.5 kg each)	

Caribbean Spice Paste

4 tsp	paprika	20 ml
2 tsp	cumin	10 ml
2 tsp	freshly ground black pepper	10 ml
2 tsp	chili powder	10 ml
1 tsp	sugar	5 ml
1 tsp	ground ginger	5 ml
½ tsp	allspice	2 ml
½ tsp	cayenne	2 ml
4–8 cloves	garlic, *mashed*	
2 tsp	lemon zest, *grated*	10 ml
2 tbsp	fresh lemon juice	30 ml
	Caribbean hot sauce (*optional*)	

TIPS:

• Serve the chickens with barbecue sauce for dipping if you like.

• Make up a double batch of the dry spices for the paste ahead of time and have it on the pantry shelf, ready when needed.

It's well worth getting a rotisserie for your barbecue – if only to roast chickens. The chickens baste themselves as they turn, making the meat moist, succulent, and flavourful, and the skin fabulously crispy.

1. To make the spice paste, combine dry spices and sugar. Just before you're ready to use the paste, add the garlic, lemon zest and juice, and a couple of dashes of hot sauce if desired.

2. Rinse chickens in cold water and pat dry inside and out. Remove any excess fat. Rub some of the spice paste inside the cavity, then spread some evenly under the skin. Rub the rest on the outside of the birds. Truss them to make a compact shape and keep the wings and legs from flopping as the spit turns. (See p. 129 for directions.) Set aside for 15 minutes or so at room temperature, or longer in the refrigerator if you like.

3. Arrange the birds on the spit, and secure with pronged rotisserie forks, two for each bird. If you wish, place a drip pan underneath to reduce flare-ups. Roast in a covered grill for 1¼ hours at 400°F (200°C), or until the chicken juices run clear and the internal temperature registers 180°F (82°C). Let the chickens rest 15 minutes before carving.

Serves 4–6.

Island Beer Can Chicken

1	**whole chicken**	
	(3¹/₂–4-lbs/1.5–2 kg)	
3 tbsp	**Caribbean Spice**	45 ml
	Paste *(p. 115)*	
1 can	**dark beer**	
	(12–16 oz/351–500 ml)	

TIPS:

• Warm some of your favourite barbecue sauce and serve it on the side for dipping.

• If your barbecue is large enough, cook two birds at once so you have some for another meal. The spicy chicken is great cold; shredded, it makes the basis of a very tasty wrap sandwich.

This quirky method for grilling whole chickens without a rotisserie results in moist, flavourful meat and irresistible crispy skin. The Caribbean-style spice paste adds zest, but you can use the same technique with your favourite barbecue rub or sauce.

1. Rinse the chicken under cold running water and dry inside and out with paper towels. Remove any excess fat from around the cavity. Rub some of the Caribbean Spice Paste inside the cavity, then spread some evenly under the skin. Rub a little more over the outside of the bird. Set aside in a covered dish or heavy-duty plastic bag in the refrigerator for several hours or overnight.

2. Put a foil drip pan over one burner of the grill and preheat all burners to medium high. Open the beer and quench your thirst with an inch or so, then make a few more holes in the top of the can.

3. Stuff the open end of the chicken onto the beer can. Set it upright on the rack over the drip pan, spreading the drumsticks apart to keep the bird balanced. Turn off the burner under the chicken, close the lid, and cook using indirect heat (see p. 15) for 1¹/₄–1¹/₂ hours, or until very tender. (The inside temperature of the thigh should reach 180°F (82°C) on an instant-read thermometer.)

4. Carefully, using heavy oven mitts and a strong spatula, remove the chicken and beer can to a nearby wooden board or platter. Let rest for 5 minutes, then lift the chicken from its perch, cut into portions, and serve hot.

Serves 3–4.

Self-basted from its perch on a beer can, the chicken emerges from the grill moist and tender. Do two birds at once – you'll be happy to have any leftovers.

Butterflied
Lemon Grass Chicken

1	**whole chicken (about 3 lbs/1.5 kg)**	
½ cup	**Lemon Grass Marinade** *(facing page)*	125 ml
1 tbsp	**vegetable oil**	15 ml
	slivers of hot red or green peppers *(optional)* **and green onion, chopped fresh coriander, and lime slices,** *for garnish*	

TIP:

• Leftover chicken, cut in slivers, makes a tasty addition to a noodle salad (such as the one on p. 140), or a salad roll or sandwich wrap.

The Lemon Grass Marinade gives this chicken a wonderful Thai flavour. Serve the chicken with Fragrant Coconut Rice (p. 172) and Asian Pickled Cucumber Salad (p. 176) or stir-fried snow and snap peas. Butterflying the chicken (so it lies flat on the grill) helps speed up the cooking.

1. Butterfly the chicken following the directions on p. 129 (or buy the chicken from the butcher already butterflied). Rub the butterflied chicken on all sides with half the marinade, reserving the rest for basting. Cover and refrigerate for several hours or overnight.

2. Remove chicken from refrigerator 30 minutes before cooking. Wipe off excess marinade, and brush surfaces lightly with oil.

3. Lay chicken on a hot, lightly oiled grill, skin side up, and cook for 5 minutes over moderately high direct heat. Baste with reserved marinade, turn the chicken over, and cook skin side down for 5 minutes.

4. Baste and turn again, and continue cooking using indirect heat (see p. 15) until the chicken has a nice crisp, brown skin and the juices run clear – about 30–40 minutes more. Serve the chicken garnished with the slivered peppers (optional), green onion, coriander, and lime slices.

Serves 3–4.

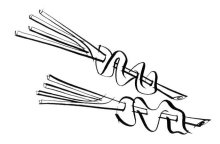

Lemon Grass Marinade

2 cloves	**garlic,** *finely chopped*	
2 tsp	**fresh ginger root,** *finely chopped*	10 ml
2 stalks	**lemon grass,** *trimmed, tough outer layers discarded, and remainder finely chopped (see Tips, below right)*	
3	**green onions,** *white part only, finely chopped*	
1–2	**small hot red peppers,** *seeded and finely chopped* **or**	
½–1 tsp	**red chili paste**	2–5 ml
2 tsp	**brown sugar**	10 ml
1 tbsp	**fresh lime juice**	15 ml
2 tbsp	**rice vinegar**	30 ml
3 tbsp	**fish sauce** *(see Tip, below)*	45 ml
2 tbsp	**vegetable oil**	30 ml

TIP:

• If fish sauce is unavailable, you can substitute 1 tbsp (15 ml) of light soy sauce.

*U*se this Thai-inspired marinade for the butterflied chicken on the facing page, as well as for skewered strips of chicken and pork, or whole scallops and shrimp. For a special presentation, use lemon grass stalks as skewers. (See Tips, p. 15.)

1. Mash together the garlic, ginger root, lemon grass, green onions, hot peppers or chili paste, and brown sugar to make a chunky paste. (A blender does the job in seconds, or you can use a mortar and pestle.)

2. Whisk in remaining ingredients.

Makes a generous ½ cup (125 ml).

TIPS:

• The marinade can be made a day ahead and refrigerated until needed.

• For further convenience, make a paste of the garlic, ginger, lemon grass, green onions, and hot peppers. Store it in small foil packages in the freezer so it's ready when needed to make the marinade.

• A whole chicken should spend at least a few hours and as long as overnight in the marinade. Reduce the marinating time to about an hour for strips of chicken or pork and 30 minutes for seafood.

• Look for lemon grass with the fresh herbs in the produce section of your supermarket. Select firm, pale green stalks; they will keep in the crisper drawer of the refrigerator for several weeks. When using, trim both ends and remove the outside tough layers. Toss lemon grass trimmings or pieces of stalk into a stock or stew to lend a hint of exotic lemon flavour.

• You can substitute a strip of finely chopped lemon zest and a couple of tablespoons of fresh lemon juice for a stalk of lemon grass.

Honey-Garlic Wings

24	chicken wings	
½ cup	sesame seeds	125 ml

Honey-Garlic Marinade

3 tbsp	vegetable oil	45 ml
3 tbsp	liquid honey	45 ml
1 tbsp	fresh lemon juice *or* **wine vinegar**	15 ml
½ cup	soy sauce	125 ml
1 tbsp	fresh ginger root, *grated*	15 ml
2 tsp	garlic, *finely minced*	10 ml
2	green onions, *finely chopped*	

TIPS:

• There are approximately 5 wings – or 10 wing pieces – to the pound (500 g).

• These wings can also be cooked in the oven: Set them on a grill rack over a baking sheet in a 350°F (180°C) oven and proceed as above, increasing the cooking time to about 45 minutes.

• You can cook the wings ahead of time and refrigerate them until ready to serve. Then brush wings with a little fresh marinade and put them under the broiler or back on the grill for about 5 minutes to glaze and reheat them.

These crispy, sweet wings are popular with kids, as well as their parents. (Leave off the sesame seeds for the young set.) If you like a dipping sauce, make up an extra recipe of the marinade. Simmer for 5 minutes, strain, and serve alongside the wings.

1. Combine ingredients for marinade.

2. Cut off and discard tips from wings, and cut wings in two at the joint. Coat well in marinade and refrigerate for several hours.

3. Remove wings from marinade and barbecue over medium heat for 10 minutes. Turn wings, baste with marinade, and sprinkle with half the sesame seeds; cook 10 minutes more. Turn, baste, sprinkle the other side with sesame seeds, and continue to cook until crisp and golden, about 10–15 minutes longer.

Makes 48 pieces.

Thai Green Curry Wings

24   **chicken wings**

Thai Green Curry Marinade

¼–½ cup	green curry paste	60–125 ml
1 can	coconut milk	400 ml
½ tsp	salt	2ml

TIPS:

• Thai green curry paste is a fiery mix of hot peppers, garlic, onion, ginger, and spices that's sold in jars, small cans, and envelopes. (Look for it in the Thai/oriental aisle of the supermarket.) Maesri is a favourite brand in my kitchen.

• Try the marinade on other chicken pieces too.

*S*picy hot, full of flavour – and easy, since they start with a prepared paste. Serve the wings with either of the Thai sauces on p. 62 for dipping.

1. Combine all ingredients for marinade in a small bowl.

2. Cut off and discard tips of wings and divide wings at the joint. In a large dish, cover wings with marinade and refrigerate for about 2 hours.

3. Preheat barbecue and lightly oil grill. Remove wings from marinade and cook over medium heat for 10 minutes. Turn wings, baste with marinade, and cook 10 minutes more. Turn, baste, and continue to cook until wings are crisp, about 10–15 minutes longer.

Makes 48 pieces.

Moroccan Chicken Kebabs

6	**boneless, skinless chicken breasts**	
2	**lemons,** *sliced*	
2 tbsp	**olive oil**	30 ml
2 tbsp	**fresh coriander** *or* **flat-leaf parsley,** *chopped (for garnish)*	30 ml

Moroccan Flavour Paste

2 cloves	**garlic**	
½ tsp	**salt**	2 ml
½ tsp	**saffron,** *dissolved in 1 tbsp (15 ml) water*	2 ml
2 tsp	**paprika**	10 ml
2 tsp	**ground cumin**	10 ml
1 tbsp	**freshly ground black pepper**	15 ml
1 tsp	**ground coriander**	5 ml
1 tsp	**ground cinnamon**	5 ml
pinch	**cayenne**	
1 tsp	**lemon zest,** *grated*	5 ml
2 tbsp	**olive oil**	30 ml

*S*erve these wonderfully aromatic kebabs on Lemon Couscous (p. 178) or Saffron Rice Pilaf (p. 169), with grilled peppers, squash, and sweet potatoes (pp. 126–127) sprinkled with lemon juice and chopped coriander or parsley.

1. To make the flavour paste: In a small sturdy bowl, or with pestle and mortar, pound the garlic together with the salt until smooth, then combine with the remaining ingredients to form a paste.

2. Pound the chicken breasts lightly to flatten and cut into equal-sized cubes. Massage the paste into the chicken to coat on all sides. If time allows, set the chicken, covered, in the refrigerator for several hours or overnight.

3. Soak bamboo skewers in cold water for about an hour. Thread chicken pieces on the skewers, inserting halved lemon slices now and again. (Reserve some of the lemon slices for garnishing.) Grill over medium-high heat, basting with a little oil and turning frequently, until the chicken is nicely browned and cooked through – about 10–15 minutes. Serve hot, garnished with lemon slices and the chopped coriander or parsley.

Serves 6.

TIPS:

• The flavour paste can be stored, tightly covered, in the refrigerator for a day or two, or it can be frozen for about a month.

• It can also be used to flavour chicken for a wonderful make-ahead Moroccan stew: Chicken Tagine (p. 184).

Chicken or Turkey Burgers

1½ lbs	ground turkey *or* chicken	750 g
½ cup	green onions, *finely chopped*	125 ml
1 tsp	dried thyme	5 ml
2 tbsp	flat-leaf parsley, *finely chopped*	30 ml
1	egg yolk	
½ tsp	salt	2 ml
¼ tsp	freshly ground black pepper	1 ml
	olive oil	
6	whole-wheat *or* sesame buns	
	mayonnaise and butter	
	watercress *or* lettuce, cranberry sauce, and grilled onions *(optional, for topping burgers)*	

*B*ecause everyone knows the perils of eating undercooked poultry, there's an unfortunate tendency to cook chicken and turkey burgers to death. Follow these directions for moist, succulent burgers.

1. Toss the first 7 ingredients lightly together.

2. Form into 6 patties about ½" (1 cm or so) thick. Place on a platter and refrigerate for half an hour.

3. Brush burgers lightly with olive oil and place on a preheated grill. Close lid and cook over medium-high heat for 4–5 minutes, then turn and cook 3–4 minutes longer. Test after 7 minutes – burgers are done when the meat has lost its pink colour throughout and the juices run clear. (Depending on your barbecue, burgers may take a couple of minutes longer, but don't overcook them or they'll dry out.)

4. Lightly toast buns. Spread mayonnaise on the bottom half of each bun and lightly butter the top half. Layer on watercress or lettuce, the burger, a spoonful of cranberry sauce, and a grilled onion slice.

Serves 6.

TIPS:

• Handle the mixture lightly, tossing the ingredients together quickly with a fork.

• Lightly oil your hands before forming the burgers, to help keep the mixture from sticking to your fingers.

• Resist the desire to pat, squeeze, or prod the burgers while they are cooking, so the good juices don't end up in the fire.

Grilled Vegetables

𝒯he slightly smoky taste that comes from grilling enhances the flavour of many vegetables. Here are some basic grilling methods, along with serving suggestions.

Asparagus

In a shallow dish, toss asparagus with olive oil (about 1 tbsp/15 ml per 1 lb/500 g asparagus) and season with salt and pepper. Lay spears across the grill rack over medium-high heat. Turn occasionally until nicely marked and just tender – about 6–8 minutes. Remove from heat and sprinkle with a little lemon juice or balsamic vinegar. Serve hot or at room temperature.

Corn

For a mild smoky taste: Carefully pull back the husks and remove the silks. Smooth the husks back into place, tie them with string at the tip and in the middle, and soak in cold water for 30 minutes to saturate the husks. Drain and set on the grill over medium-high heat for 20–30 minutes, turning often.

For more pronounced smokiness: Shuck corn and blanch in boiling water for 2–3 minutes. Drain, then brush generously with melted butter, season with salt and pepper, and grill for 4–6 minutes over medium-high heat, turning often, until nicely browned.

Please turn to next page

QUICK TRICK:

Spicy Corn Butter: Melt ¼ cup (60 ml) butter and mix with 1 tsp (5 ml) curry powder or garam masala spice mix and a pinch of cayenne. Use instead of plain melted butter in the second method above. In the first method, pull back the husks and brush kernels with the spicy butter after 15 minutes of grilling. (Bunch the husks around the stalk to form a handle.) Grill a few minutes more, turning the ears frequently, until lightly charred.

IDEAS FOR USING MIXED GRILLED VEGETABLES:

• Arrange grilled vegetables on a large platter – sliced eggplant, onion, zucchini, peppers, mushrooms, and whole spears of asparagus – season lightly with salt and pepper, and sprinkle with balsamic or red wine vinegar. Scatter a handful of chopped fresh basil and parsley on top. Serve immediately as is, as a side dish with grilled meat, chicken, or fish. Or set aside, covered, for 1 hour at room temperature or as long as overnight in the refrigerator. Bring to room temperature before serving.

• Grilled Vegetable Antipasto: Arrange a platter of vegetables as above, sprinkling with shaved Parmesan cheese and black olives. Serve as part of an antipasto spread with salamis and other meats and cheeses.

Grilled vegetables make a wonderful antipasto platter with salami, olives, and cheese, or a great sandwich when tucked into a pita.

Grilled Vegetables, *continued*

IDEAS FOR USING ROASTED PEPPERS:

• Slice and serve as a salad, tossing the pepper strips with garlic-flavoured olive oil, freshly ground black pepper, chunks of feta cheese, black olives, and chopped green onion.

• Chop and add to corn bread or cornmeal muffins.

• Tuck into a sandwich with meatballs, barbecued sausages, or pork schnitzel.

• Slice into strips and toss with hot pasta and a little garlic-flavoured olive oil; sprinkle with grated Parmesan cheese.

• Slice and serve alongside scrambled eggs and Italian sausage for a special weekend brunch.

• Chop and combine with chopped tomato, onion, coriander, and lime juice, and serve as a sauce with grilled fish.

• Pack sliced or puréed peppers in small containers, add olive oil just to cover, and freeze. Use on pasta, or to flavour soups, sauces, and stews.

IDEAS FOR USING ROASTED GARLIC:

• Combine with mayonnaise for an excellent sandwich spread.

• Add to mashed potatoes.

• Use as a topping for pizza or focaccia.

• Spread on crostini (p. 57).

• Serve as part of a grilled vegetable side dish or antipasto.

• Add to the dressing for Roasted Vegetable Couscous (p. 144).

Eggplant

Slice globe eggplants crosswise into generous 1/4" (6-mm) slices, sprinkle with salt, and brush with plain or garlic-flavoured olive oil. (Thin Asian eggplants can simply be cut in half lengthwise.) Place on an oiled rack over medium-high heat and cook about 8–12 minutes, turning often, until the slices are tender and nicely browned, but still hold their shape. To roast a whole eggplant (for Roasted Eggplant Caviar, p. 59, or baba ghanouj), place on the grill over medium-high heat and cook for 20–30 minutes, turning frequently, until the skin is blackened and the flesh is soft.

Garlic

Slice horizontally across the top of a whole head of garlic about 1/2" (1 cm) down from the top, exposing the ends of each clove. Rub all over with olive oil. Wrap in foil and cook over medium-high heat about 45 minutes until soft, turning occasionally. Squeeze out the roasted cloves.

Onions

Remove skins from red and white onions, and slice 1/2" (1 cm) thick. Spear horizontally through the slices with one or two presoaked bamboo skewers (or metal poultry skewers) to keep the rings together. Brush with olive oil, and place on an oiled grill rack over medium-high heat. Grill for 10–12 minutes, turning several times, until tender and nicely charred. Splash with a little balsamic vinegar if desired and season to taste.

Peppers

Place red, yellow, and green peppers on barbecue rack over high heat. Roast, turning often, until evenly blistered and charred on all sides, about 15–20 minutes. Transfer to a paper bag or put in a large bowl and cover with plastic wrap. Leave to steam for 10 minutes. Peel away charred skin; cut in half, discard stem and seeds, and slice.

GRILLED EGGPLANT & TOMATO SALAD:

Arrange slices of grilled eggplant on a platter and top with chopped grilled plum tomatoes, finely sliced red onion, and slivered fresh basil. Sprinkle with balsamic vinegar, season to taste, and add a handful of dry-cured black olives if you like. Cover and set aside for an hour or so at room temperature for the flavours to develop.

GRILLED VEGETABLE KEBABS:

Skewers of summer vegetables make colourful individual side dishes to serve with grilled food. Toss small whole mushrooms and uniform chunks of red and yellow peppers, small Asian eggplant, zucchini, and red onion in a large bowl with some olive oil, chopped garlic, and fresh or dried herbs (thyme, rosemary, basil, or oregano). Thread onto skewers and place on a hot, lightly oiled grill over high heat. Cook, turning frequently, until vegetables are lightly charred outside and just tender inside – about 10–12 minutes. Season to taste and drizzle with balsamic vinegar.

GRILLED VEGETABLE PIZZA:

Brush pizza crust (see p. 234) with pesto or basil-flavoured olive oil. Top with chopped grilled vegetables and grated Parmesan or crumbled goat cheese. Bake in preheated 400°F (200°C) oven for 15–20 minutes until crust is crisp and cheese is melted.

Portobello Mushrooms

Remove stems. Combine plain or garlic-flavoured olive oil with an equal amount of balsamic vinegar, and season with salt and pepper. Brush mushrooms with the mixture, and allow to sit for 20–30 minutes. Grill cap side down over medium heat for about 5 minutes; turn and grill 3–4 minutes more until the mushrooms just begin to exude their juices.

Potatoes

Toss mini new potatoes (of uniform size) with a little olive oil and thread on lightly oiled metal skewers. Place on a hot, lightly oiled grill over medium heat. Turn regularly until potatoes are tender, 20–40 minutes, depending on size. Toward the end of the cooking time, move skewers to a hot area of the grill to crisp the skin. Gently push potatoes from the skewers into a warm bowl. Toss with melted butter if desired and season to taste. Sprinkle with finely chopped fresh herbs and chives or green onions.

Sweet Potatoes

Peel and slice sweet potatoes. Toss with a little brown sugar (about 1 tsp/5 ml per potato) and a pinch of allspice and salt. Dot with butter and wrap in heavy-duty foil. Grill over medium heat for about 15–20 minutes or until tender, flipping package occasionally.

Tomatoes

Cut out the tough core at the stalk end of each tomato. Cut tomatoes in half and rub with olive oil, salt, and pepper. Set on the grill over low heat for about 10–12 minutes, turning once.

Zucchini

Slice lengthwise into $1/2$" (1-cm) slices. Brush with olive oil and place on a rack over medium heat. Grill 4–6 minutes, turning often.

South Seas Satays
with Malaysian Spice Paste

1½ lbs	**boneless, skinless chicken breasts** *or* **pork tenderloin**	750 g
squeeze	**lemon** *or* **lime juice**	

Malaysian Spice Mix

2 tbsp	**cumin**	30 ml
2 tbsp	**coriander**	30 ml
2 tbsp	**turmeric**	30 ml
2 tsp	**cinnamon**	10 ml
2 tsp	**freshly ground black pepper**	10 ml
2 tsp	**salt**	10 ml
½ tsp	**cayenne** *or* **hot red pepper flakes** *(optional)*	2 ml

Malaysian Spice Paste

2 tbsp	**Malaysian Spice Mix**	30 ml
4	**green onions,** *trimmed*	
1 tbsp	**fresh ginger root,** *chopped*	15 ml
2 strips	**lemon zest**	
2 tbsp	**lemon juice**	30 ml
2 tbsp	**soy sauce**	30 ml
3 tbsp	**vegetable oil**	45 ml

*T*his spice paste starts with a mix of dry spices, which can be made ahead of time. The paste then whirls together in seconds in a blender or food processor (or you can use muscle power and a mortar and pestle) – ready to make chicken or pork satays. Make small satays for appetizers or party snacks, larger ones for dinner. Accompany them with one of the dipping sauces on p. 62.

1. Combine ingredients for Malaysian Spice Mix and store in a covered container.

2. Combine ingredients for Malaysian Spice Paste in a blender or processor and whirl briefly to form a paste. Or finely mince green onions and ginger, chop 2 tsp (10 ml) lemon zest, and pound ingredients together using a mortar and pestle.

3. Cut chicken or pork into strips about $^1/_4$" (6 mm) thick, $1^1/_2$" (4 cm) wide, and 5"–6" (12 cm–15 cm) long. Coat strips with Malaysian Spice Paste and refrigerate, covered, several hours or as long as overnight.

4. Soak bamboo skewers in cold water for about an hour. Thread meat strips on skewers. Grill over medium-high heat for 8–10 minutes, turning occasionally, until nicely browned and cooked through. Serve hot, sprinkled with fresh lemon or lime juice.

Serves 4.

TIP:
• The spice paste should be used within a few hours of preparation. The spice mix will stay fresh for a month or two. (The spice mix recipe makes enough for several batches of the paste.)

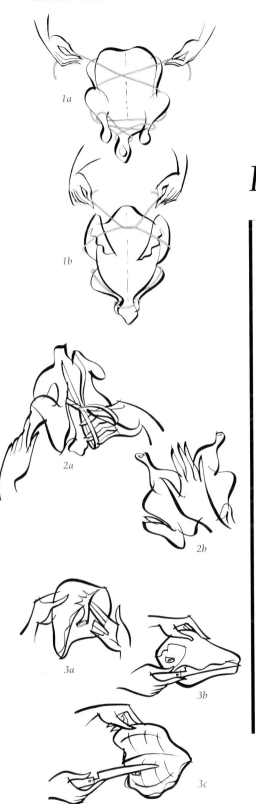

1a.

1b.

2a.

2b.

3a.

3b.

3c.

Preparing Chicken for the Grill

How to truss a chicken for the rotisserie

Trussing a chicken keeps the wings and legs from flopping as the spit turns. *1a.* Place the chicken on its back with a long piece of strong cotton butcher's twine centred under the tail. Bring each end of the string up and around the opposite drumstick. Pull the ends of the string to bring the legs and tail close together. *1b.* Turn the bird on its breast. Bring one end of the string under the thigh, then repeat with the other end. Draw both ends forward and around the opposite wing, tucking in the tip. Turn the chicken, snug up the string, and tie the ends across the breast, making sure the wings are secured.

How to butterfly a chicken

Butterflying a chicken (so it lies flat) helps speed up the cooking, making this a great way to grill a whole bird without a rotisserie. *2a.* Using kitchen shears or a sharp, heavy knife, cut the chicken along each side of the backbone. Remove and discard the backbone. *2b.* Open out the chicken, skin side up, and press quite firmly on the breastbone to flatten.

You can also butterfly bone-in chicken breasts: *3a.* Pull out whatever remains of the heavy breastbone and its soft cartilage continuation. (Run your fingers between the meat and the bone to loosen it.) *3b.* With the breast bone side down, slice through the meat parallel to the rib bones, starting at the thin edge. As you cut, continue to leave roughly the same thickness of meat on both sides of the knife. Stop cutting when you are about $1/4"$ from the thick edge. *3c.* Open up the breast like a butterfly.

Smoky Red Barbecue Sauce

1 tbsp	vegetable oil	15 ml
1	medium onion, *finely chopped*	
2 cloves	garlic, *finely chopped*	
1 can	tomato sauce *(28 oz/796 ml)*	
½ cup	cider vinegar	125 ml
¼ cup	dark brown sugar	60 ml
1 tbsp	molasses	15 ml
½ cup	orange juice	125 ml
1 tsp	paprika	5 ml
2 tsp	chili powder	10 ml
1 tsp	dry mustard	5 ml
	salt and freshly ground black pepper	
½–1	chipotle chile in adobo sauce, *chopped* or hot sauce *(to taste)*	

*M*ake this sauce as spicy as you want by adjusting the amount of chipotle chile. It's a great all-purpose barbecue sauce – fantastic on ribs, chicken (try it on wings), and burgers. Keep a batch on hand in the refrigerator; it will keep about 3–4 weeks.

1. Heat oil in a large pot over medium heat. Add onion and cook until soft and lightly browned. Add garlic and cook for a minute.

2. Stir in remaining ingredients. Bring to a boil, lower heat, and simmer, uncovered, for an hour or so.

3. Using a blender or food processor, purée the sauce in batches or, if you like it very smooth, press it through a sieve. Store in a covered container in the refrigerator.

Makes 2 cups (500 ml).

III. SALADS & SIDE DISHES

Classic Vinaigrette

1 clove	**garlic,** *minced*	
1 tsp	**salt**	5 ml
1 tbsp	**Dijon mustard**	15 ml
1/3 cup	**vinegar** *(see Tips, below)*	75 ml
1 cup	**oil** *(see Tips, below)*	250 ml
	freshly ground black pepper	

TIPS:

• Try different vinegars: red wine, champagne, sherry, balsamic, or rice vinegar, or equal parts fresh lemon juice and vinegar.

• Olive, corn, and safflower oil are all good choices for a vinaigrette.

• If you find your dressing is too acidic for your taste, soften the flavour with a scant teaspoonful of honey or sugar.

*W*ith the addition of different fresh herbs or a little crumbled cheese at serving time, this basic vinaigrette can be used to dress a variety of salads. (Just for starters: It's used in the recipes on pp. 134, 135, 152, 162, and 164.) Mix up a batch and store it in a covered jar in the refrigerator – it will keep for up to 10 days. Use 3–4 tbsp (45–60 ml) of dressing for every 4–5 cups (1–1.2 L) of greens.

1. Mash garlic with salt, then mix with mustard and vinegar.

2. Whisk in oil and season to taste.

Makes 1 1/3 cups (325 ml).

QUICK TRICK:
   Crispy Croutons: Cut homemade-style bread into cubes to make about 6 cups (1.5 L). Toss with salt and pepper, and other seasonings if desired: 2 tsp (10 ml) dried herbs, a clove of minced garlic, a dash of hot sauce or hot red pepper flakes, and/or 2 tbsp (30 ml) Parmesan cheese. Sprinkle with 3 tbsp (45 ml) olive oil – or part oil, part melted butter – and toss again. Spread croutons on a baking sheet and bake at 375°F (190°C) for 10–15 minutes until crisp and golden, shaking a few times during baking. Cool and store in a covered container.

Three Vinaigrette Variations

Grilled Tomato Vinaigrette

1	plum tomato	
½ cup	extra-virgin olive oil	125 ml
½ tsp	ground cumin	2 ml
pinch	cayenne	
¼ cup	balsamic vinegar, *or* half lemon juice half vinegar	60 ml

Balsamic Vinaigrette

¼ cup	extra-virgin olive oil	60 ml
¼ cup	balsamic vinegar	60 ml
1 tsp	Dijon mustard	5 ml

Lemon Cumin Vinaigrette

1 clove	garlic, *minced*	
1 tsp	ground cumin	5 ml
2 tbsp	fresh lemon juice	30 ml
2 tbsp	balsamic *or* red wine vinegar	30 ml
6 tbsp	extra-virgin olive oil	90 ml

* all 3 recipes require about ¼ tsp (1 ml) salt and a few grindings of black pepper

Grilled Tomato Vinaigrette

Use this vinaigrette with Roasted Vegetable Couscous (p. 144).

1. Cut the tomato in half and rub with a little of the olive oil and salt and pepper. Set on the grill over low heat for about 10–12 minutes, turning once.

2. Peel blackened skin off tomato and squeeze out seeds. You should have about 1 tbsp (15 ml) of pulp.

3. Add cumin, cayenne, and salt and pepper to the pulp and pound to a paste. Whisk in vinegar and remaining olive oil. *Makes about ³/₄ cup (175 ml).*

Balsamic Vinaigrette

Use this dressing with Mediterranean Barley Salad (p. 166).

1. Combine all ingredients. Taste and adjust seasoning. *Makes ¹/₂ cup (125 ml).*

Lemon Cumin Vinaigrette

Use this dressing with Corn & Lentil Salad (p. 173).

1. Mash garlic with about ¹/₄ tsp (1 ml) salt. Combine with cumin, lemon juice, and vinegar.

2. Whisk in oil. Taste and adjust seasoning. *Makes ¹/₂ cup (125 ml).*

A Quartet of Green Salads

• To prepare greens ahead, wrap the washed and dried leaves loosely in paper towels or a tea towel and store in a perforated plastic bag in the vegetable crisper.

• Soft-textured, mild-flavoured salad greens, such as bibb lettuce and Boston lettuce, spoil quickly and do not travel or keep well. Crisper varieties, such as romaine, green leaf, and red leaf lettuce, are hardier. So are greens such as endive, escarole, frisée, dandelion, young spinach, arugula, watercress, and radicchio and, of course, the ubiquitous iceberg – which comes in handy for adding cool crunch to sandwiches or shredded on tacos.

• Hydroponically grown greens are sold with their roots still attached. This lengthens their refrigerator life and allows them to travel better.

Each of these salads uses a variation of the Classic Vinaigrette (p. 132). You'll need about 4–5 cups (1–1.2 L) of greens for each, which will serve 4 people.

Arugula-Orange Salad

To a scant ¼ cup (60 ml) Classic Vinaigrette, add 1 tsp (5 ml) walnut oil, 1 tbsp (15 ml) orange juice, and 1 tsp (5 ml) grated orange zest. Toss with young arugula. Add peeled orange segments and toasted walnuts.

Spinach-Mushroom Salad

To a scant ¼ cup (60 ml) Classic Vinaigrette, add 1 tbsp (15 ml) fresh lemon juice, 1 tsp (5 ml) grated lemon zest, and 1 tsp (5 ml) fresh chopped tarragon or ½ tsp (2 ml) dried tarragon. Toss with spinach leaves. Add sliced fresh mushrooms, thinly sliced red onion rings, and crumbled crispy bacon.

Romaine-Blue Cheese Salad

To ¼ cup (60 ml) Classic Vinaigrette, add 2 oz (50 g) mashed blue cheese. Toss with romaine leaves, thinly sliced red onion rings, and a handful of croutons. Top with more crumbled blue cheese, if you like.

Cheater's Caesar Salad

To ¼ cup (60 ml) Classic Vinaigrette made with half lemon juice, half vinegar, add 1 anchovy fillet and 2 tbsp (30 ml) grated Parmesan cheese. Mash anchovy into dressing. Toss with romaine leaves, add a handful of croutons, and sprinkle with more grated Parmesan.

Salade Niçoise

1 lb	**potatoes,** *cooked, cooled, and cut in chunks*	500 g
1 cup	**Classic Vinaigrette** *(p. 132)*	250 ml
1 head	**lettuce**	
1 lb	**green beans,** *blanched and cooled*	500 g
4	**firm, ripe tomatoes,** *quartered*	
1 can	**chunk tuna,** *drained (6.5 oz/184 g)*	
3	**hard-boiled eggs,** *quartered*	
1 can	**anchovy fillets** *(2 oz/50 g)*	
½ cup	**black olives**	125 ml
3	**green onions,** *finely chopped*	
	fresh herbs, *chopped (a combination such as parsley, chives, and thyme)*	

VARIATIONS:

• Substitute slices of fresh grilled tuna for the canned.

• Substitute lightly steamed asparagus spears for the green beans.

T̄his classic salad, served with warm, crusty French bread, is one of my favourite summer meals. The colourful platter is a feast for the eyes, and the combination of flavours and textures is utterly delicious. In addition, the quantity of ingredients is easily adjusted according to the size of the group to be served.

1. Toss potatoes with about ½ cup (125 ml) of the vinaigrette; set aside.

2. Just before serving, line a platter with lettuce. Season beans and tomatoes with a little more vinaigrette. Arrange potatoes in the centre of the platter. Surround with beans and tomatoes and decorate with tuna, eggs, anchovy fillets, and olives. Sprinkle with chopped green onions and herbs, and a little more vinaigrette.

Serves 4 for lunch.

QUICK TRICK:

Ripe Tomato Wedges with Garlic: When tomatoes are at their peak, this simple salad is fantastic. Cut 2 large ripe tomatoes in half, then cut each half into narrow wedges. Discard the seeds. Toss the wedges with 2 cloves of slivered garlic, ¼ cup (60 ml) of chopped fresh flat-leaf parsley, 1 tbsp (15 ml) each of extra-virgin olive oil and red wine vinegar, and salt and freshly ground black pepper. Let the salad sit at room temperature for half an hour for flavours to blend.

If you chop the tomato wedges in smaller pieces, the salad becomes a topping for bruschetta or circles of grilled polenta (p. 50).

Asian Chicken Salad
with Oriental Coleslaw

Chicken poached with oriental flavourings is the star in this main-dish salad. The coleslaw with its crunchy topping can also be served solo as a side dish with Asian-inspired grilled food, such as Hoisin Ribs (p. 82).

1. Combine all the ingredients for the poached chicken except the chicken in a deep frying pan. Add 1 cup (250 ml) water. Bring to a boil, lower heat, and simmer for 5 minutes.

2. Add chicken, cover, and cook gently, turning once, for about 10 minutes – until chicken is tender and cooked through. Remove to a side dish, allow to cool, season with salt and pepper, and slice. Refrigerate until needed.

3. Meanwhile, make the coleslaw: Finely shred the cabbage, julienne the carrots, and cut the peppers into slivers. Halve the baby corn lengthwise and thinly slice the celery on the diagonal. Chop the green onions and parsley.

4. In a large bowl, combine all the vegetables except the parsley and toss with Oriental Dressing. Arrange vegetables on a platter and top with the sliced chicken. Sprinkle with parsley and almonds or crumbled rice crackers.

Serves 6–8.

Asian Poached Chicken

1 cup	dry white wine	250 ml
1 stalk	lemon grass or	
4 strips	lemon zest	
2 slices	fresh ginger root (½" /1 cm thick), *crushed*	
4 cloves	garlic, *crushed*	
4 sprigs	fresh coriander *or* flat-leaf parsley	
10	black peppercorns	
4	boneless chicken breasts	

Oriental Coleslaw

½	small green cabbage	
2	large carrots	
½ each	red and green pepper	
8 ears	canned baby corn	
2 stalks	celery	
6	green onions	
½ cup	fresh parsley	125 ml
½ cup	Oriental Dressing *(facing page)*	125 ml
½ cup	sliced almonds, *toasted, or* rice crackers, *crumbled*	125 ml

TIP:

• Poaching keeps the chicken moist. You can vary the flavourings of the liquid to suit the ingredients you have on hand.

Oriental Beef or Tofu Salad

¼ lb	rice stick noodles *or* **rice vermicelli**	125 g
1 tbsp	vegetable oil	15 ml
¼ lb	snow peas *(about 2 cups/500 ml)*	125 g
6	dried Chinese mushrooms	
¾–1 lb	Grilled Oriental Tofu *or* Steak *(p. 73)*	375–500 g
2	green onions, *chopped*	
1 tsp	lemon zest, *grated*	5 ml
¼ cup	fresh coriander, *or* **flat-leaf parsley,** *chopped (optional)*	60 ml

Oriental Dressing

¼ cup	rice vinegar	60 ml
2 tbsp	soy sauce	30 ml
1 tbsp	each vegetable oil and sesame oil	15 ml
1 clove	garlic, *minced*	
1 tbsp	fresh ginger root, *finely chopped*	15 ml
1 tbsp	sugar	15 ml
½ tsp	red chili paste or	2 ml
¼ tsp	hot red pepper flakes	1 ml
pinch	salt	

*P*repare the components of this salad early in the day, so that all you have to do at dinnertime is arrange them on a platter. In fact, time in the fridge will actually improve the flavour of this dish, giving the dressing a chance to permeate the steak or tofu, noodles, and vegetables.

1. Cook the noodles or vermicelli in a large quantity of boiling salted water until tender, about 3–4 minutes for the noodles and a scant minute for the vermicelli. Drain well and toss with most of the oil.

2. Remove stems and strings from snow peas and blanch in boiling water for about a minute. Drain, toss immediately into ice water, then drain again.

3. Remove stems from mushrooms; discard. Cover caps with boiling water and let sit until softened (about 15 minutes). Drain, slice, and stir-fry 5 minutes in remaining oil. Add to snow peas.

4. Combine all dressing ingredients in a small jar and shake well.

5. Toss snow pea-and-mushroom mixture, noodles, and grilled steak or tofu separately in a spoonful or two of Oriental Dressing apiece.

6. To serve, pile noodles on a platter and arrange steak and vegetables on top. Sprinkle with green onions, lemon zest, and coriander or parsley.

Serves 4.

TIPS:

• Steps 1–5 can be done early in the day and the 3 groups of ingredients refrigerated.

• Add a dash more chili paste or hot red pepper flakes to the dressing if you like the heat.

Raspberry-Spinach Salad

Almond Topping

½ cup	slivered almonds	125 ml
¼ cup	sugar	60 ml
2 tsp	water	10 ml

Dressing

¼ cup	sugar	60 ml
1½ tbsp	poppy seeds	20 ml
¼ tsp	paprika	1 ml
½ cup	vegetable oil	125 ml
¼ cup	raspberry vinegar	60 ml
2 tsp	onion, *finely chopped*	10 ml
¼ tsp	Worcestershire sauce	1 ml

Salad

1 lb	fresh spinach	500 g
2 cups	fresh raspberries	500 ml

*C*runchy *caramelized almonds add the crowning touch to this simple, beautiful-looking, and always-popular summer salad.*

1. Combine topping ingredients in a large frying pan. Cook over medium heat, stirring constantly, until sugar melts to a golden brown and coats almonds, about 5–8 minutes. Turn out onto a square of greased foil. Cool, then break up into small pieces.

2. Combine all dressing ingredients in a container with a tight-fitting lid. Shake well to blend, then shake again before using.

3. Wash and dry spinach, and place in a large bowl with raspberries. Add dressing and toss. Add almonds; toss lightly and serve immediately.

Serves 4.

TIP:
• **Prepare a few batches of almonds and dressing ahead of time and keep on hand. Hide the topping in a safe place, though, or it may disappear.**

Raspberry-Spinach Salad: It looks impressive but is easy to prepare. Make the caramelized almonds ahead of time.

Thai Noodle Salad

6 oz	**rice vermicelli** *or* **rice stick noodles**	170 g
¼ lb	**snow peas** *(about 2 cups/500 ml)*	125 g
½	**red pepper,** *seeded and cut in slivers*	
2 cups	**lettuce,** *shredded*	500 ml
2	**green onions,** *cut in diagonal slivers*	
¼ cup	**peanuts,** *chopped*	60 ml
1	**lime,** *thinly sliced*	

Thai Dressing

1–2	**fresh hot peppers,** *seeded and chopped* **or**	
1–2 tsp	**red chili paste**	5–10 ml
3 tbsp	**fresh lime juice**	45 ml
2 tbsp	**fish sauce** *(see Tips)*	30 ml
2 tbsp	**vegetable oil**	30 ml
1 tbsp	**sesame oil**	15 ml
2 tbsp	**chunky peanut butter** *(optional)*	30 ml
1 tsp	**sugar**	5 ml
2 tbsp	**fresh coriander,** *chopped*	30 ml
2	**green onions,** *finely chopped*	

*T*his is a light, refreshing side dish to serve with food from the grill. Or you can add chicken or seafood and turn it into a main dish. (See Tips, below.) Prepare everything ahead and then toss the salad together just before serving.

1. Combine all ingredients for dressing and refrigerate until needed.

2. Cook the noodles or vermicelli in a large quantity of boiling salted water until tender, about 3–4 minutes for the noodles and a scant minute for the vermicelli. Drain well, toss with a little dressing, and refrigerate until needed.

3. Blanch the snow peas for about a minute in lightly salted boiling water. Drain and immediately put into ice water to stop the cooking. Drain again and slice on the diagonal.

4. Just before serving, toss noodles with snow peas, red pepper, and remaining dressing. Arrange salad on a bed of shredded lettuce and garnish with green onions, chopped peanuts, and lime slices.

Serves 6.

TIPS:
• If you don't have fish sauce, substitute 2 tbsp (30 ml) water.

• The dressing can be made a day ahead and refrigerated, but add the green onions and the coriander to it just before using.

MAIN-DISH VARIATIONS:
• Toss with slices of poached Asian Chicken (p. 136) or shredded grilled Lemon Grass Chicken (p. 118).

• Add warm or cold grilled Lemon Grass Shrimp and/or Scallops (p. 119).

Roquefort & Pear Salad
with Walnuts

1 tbsp	sherry vinegar	15 ml
1 tsp	Dijon mustard	5 ml
¼ tsp	salt	1 ml
3 tbsp	extra-virgin olive oil	45 ml
6 cups	mixed mild and peppery salad greens *(frisée, curly endive, watercress, romaine)* *(heaping cups)*	1.5 L
4 oz	Roquefort or other favourite blue cheese, *crumbled (scant ½ cup/125 ml)*	125 g
12	walnut halves, *toasted and roughly chopped*	
1	firm, ripe pear, *peeled, cored, and thinly sliced*	
	freshly ground black pepper	

A salad with this rich combination of flavours is designed to stand alone as part of a meal, either before or after a light main course. Crisp toasted slices of walnut bread are delicious alongside.

1. In a small bowl, whisk together the sherry vinegar, mustard, and salt. Then slowly whisk in the olive oil.

2. Toss the greens with the dressing. Arrange on a platter, or on individual serving plates. Scatter crumbled cheese and nuts on top, and place a fan of pear slices on the side. Season generously with freshly ground black pepper.

Serves 6.

TIPS:

• Substitute an unpeeled, crisp green Granny Smith apple, thinly sliced and dipped in lemon juice, or peeled orange segments or slices of fresh figs for the pear.

• Aged sherry vinegar brings together all the wonderful tangy, sweet, and salty flavours of this salad. (Also try a dash of it in sauces and marinades.) If you don't have it on hand, you can substitute a full-flavoured red wine vinegar.

Orzo with Shrimp

½ lb	orzo	250 g
¼ cup	olive oil	60 ml
	salt and freshly ground black pepper	
1 lb	large shrimp, *in the shell*	500 g
1 clove	garlic, *minced*	
2 tbsp	fresh lemon juice	30 ml
1 tbsp	Dijon mustard	15 ml
½ cup	fresh flat-leaf parsley, *chopped*	125 ml
¼ cup	fresh dill, *chopped*	60 ml
½	red pepper, *finely chopped*	
½	green pepper, *finely chopped*	
2	green onions, *finely chopped*	
½ cup	mayonnaise	125 ml
¼ cup	sour cream *or* yogurt	60 ml

TIPS:

• Add steamed mussels or poached scallops or monkfish with the shrimp.

• Steps 1–3 can be done early in the day and the components refrigerated.

*O*rzo is a small, rice-shaped pasta that makes a light, pleasant foil for all kinds of summer flavours. This salad looks irresistible arranged on a large platter lined with crisp lettuce and decorated with lemon wedges, ripe olives, and fresh chopped herbs. With a plate of sliced tomatoes and good crusty bread, you've got a great summer meal.

1. Cook orzo in a large quantity of boiling salted water until just tender, about 8 minutes. Drain well, and toss while still warm with a good drizzle of olive oil and freshly ground black pepper. Set aside.

2. Drop shrimp into boiling salted water; when water returns to the boil, simmer 2–5 minutes, depending on size. Test after 2 minutes – the shrimp should be light orange in colour and tender but resilient to the touch. Cool and peel.

3. Make the dressing by combining the remaining olive oil with the garlic, lemon juice, mustard, salt and pepper to taste, and half the parsley and dill.

4. Coat the shrimp (and any other seafood you're including; see Tips, below) in a spoonful or two of the dressing. Toss orzo with peppers, green onions, the rest of the herbs, and enough dressing to coat and flavour the pasta. Fold in the shrimp, mayonnaise, and sour cream or yogurt. The salad can be served immediately, but is even better if refrigerated for an hour or so to allow the flavours to blend.

Serves 4.

Add steamed mussels and poached monkfish to Orzo with Shrimp for a gala presentation.

Roasted Vegetable Couscous

1	**medium eggplant,** *sliced*	
2	**zucchini,** *sliced*	
1	**large red onion,** *sliced or cut in eighths*	
2	**sweet peppers,** *seeded and cut in quarters*	
2 cloves	**garlic,** *finely chopped*	
4 tbsp	**olive oil**	60 ml
	salt and freshly ground black pepper	
¾ cup	**Grilled Tomato Vinaigrette** *(p. 133)*	175 ml
1 cup	**couscous**	250 ml
1 cup	**hot vegetable** *or* **chicken stock**	250 ml
1 tbsp	**lemon juice**	15 ml
4 oz	**feta** *or* **goat cheese,** *crumbled*	125 g
	parsley, *finely chopped*	

TIPS:

• The salad can be made ahead and refrigerated; bring it to room temperature before serving.

• Substitute other vegetables if you like. You should have 4–6 cups (1–1.5 L) of chopped veggies before grilling.

*C*ouscous – *flour-coated semolina – is a handy grain, since it is easily prepared and can be combined with many flavours. Look for it in bulk-food stores and in boxes in the supermarket. (Read the preparation instructions, since some types have been precooked.) This salad is an excellent side dish with any grilled food, and a great main dish for a picnic when piled into pita-bread pockets. Pack it in a container for travelling, then spoon it into the pita breads when it's time to eat.*

1. Toss vegetables with garlic, 3 tbsp (45 ml) of the oil, and a little salt and pepper. Arrange vegetables on a preheated barbecue and grill for about 5–10 minutes per side over medium-high heat until tender and lightly browned. Note: A roasted plum tomato is required for the vinaigrette (see p. 133), so grill it at the same time as the other vegetables.

2. Meanwhile, place couscous in a large bowl, cover with hot stock, and leave for 5 minutes. When all the liquid is absorbed, fluff grains with a fork. Liven flavour with the lemon juice and remaining olive oil.

3. Cut the vegetables into small pieces and toss with couscous and Grilled Tomato Vinaigrette. Season to taste and scatter cheese and parsley on top.

Serves 4–6.

TIPS:

• For a roasted vegetable pasta salad, substitute 2 cups (500 ml) cooked penne for the couscous.

• The vegetables can also be roasted in the oven: Spread in a single layer in a large shallow roasting pan and roast on the top rack of the oven at 400°F (200°C) for 30–40 minutes, turning a few times, until lightly browned and just tender.

White Bean & Sausage Salad

1 clove	garlic, *minced*	
	salt and freshly ground black pepper	
2 tbsp	red wine vinegar	30 ml
1/3 cup	olive oil	75 ml
2 tbsp	fresh mint, *chopped*	30 ml
1 can	white beans, *rinsed and drained (19 oz/540 ml)* **or**	
2 cups	cooked white beans *(directions on p. 156)*	500 ml
1/2	small red onion, *slivered*	
1 lb	hot *or* sweet Italian sausage *or* chorizo	500 g
4	firm, ripe tomatoes	

Traditionally, mint is used to flavour this salad from southern Italy, but if you don't have a supply of fresh mint, use basil or thyme instead. Simply omit the sausage for a lighter, vegetarian salad.

1. Make dressing: Combine garlic with salt and pepper, vinegar, 1/4 cup (60 ml) of the oil, and half the mint.

2. Combine beans and onion, and toss gently with the dressing.

3. Simmer the sausage in 1/2" (1 cm) of water in a covered skillet for 10 minutes. Drain and continue cooking in the skillet, or grill on the barbecue, until nicely browned. Cool, cut into thin slices, and add to the beans. Refrigerate until serving time.

4. Just before serving, seed the tomatoes and and cut them into chunks, then toss with the rest of the oil and the mint, and season to taste.

5. Mound the bean mixture on a platter and circle with tomatoes. Serve at room temperature with hot crusty bread to mop up the good juices.

Serves 4.

TIP:

• To remove seeds from a tomato, cut in half horizontally, loosen seeds with your fingers, and squeeze gently. Or slice into 8 segments and release the seeds from each section.

VARIATION:

• This salad is also delicious with tuna instead of sausage: Reserve some of the dressing before tossing it with the beans and add a squeeze of lemon juice. Toss chunks of grilled fresh tuna or canned tuna with this dressing. Add the tuna to the beans at serving time with a handful of ripe Italian olives.

Tabbouleh with a Twist

1 cup	**fine bulgur**	250 ml
1½ cups	**boiling water**	375 ml
4	**green onions,** *chopped*	
4	**tomatoes,** *seeded and finely chopped*	
1 bunch	**fresh parsley,** *finely chopped*	
½ cup	**fresh mint,** *finely chopped*	125 ml
½	**green pepper,** *chopped*	
½	**English cucumber,** *finely chopped*	
2 cups	**feta cheese,** *cubed*	500 ml
1 can	**chickpeas,** *rinsed and drained (19 oz/540 ml)*	
2	**carrots,** *grated*	
½ cup	**fresh lemon juice**	125 ml
½ cup	**olive oil**	125 ml
2 tsp	**garlic,** *minced*	10 ml
	salt and freshly ground black pepper	

*T*abbouleh, a traditional Middle Eastern salad, is a great summer dish: It can be made ahead, is easily transported, and is even better the second day – if there's any left. This version contains feta cheese, which adds a delicious tangy taste.

1. Cover bulgur with the water and leave for 20 minutes, until water is absorbed and grains are soft. (Press out any excess water.) Fluff with a fork.

2. Add remaining salad ingredients and half the lemon juice to bulgur in a large bowl.

3. Combine olive oil, the rest of the lemon juice, garlic, and salt and pepper in a jar with a tight-fitting lid, and shake to blend. Pour over salad and toss until well mixed.

Serves 6–8.

TIPS:

• Bulgur (a nutty-tasting cracked wheat) is available at bulk-food stores and many supermarkets.

• For traditional tabbouleh, omit the green pepper, feta, chickpeas, and carrots.

• The flavour improves with standing time, so make ahead if possible.

Tabbouleh is great for a picnic or potluck since it travels well. You can leave out the feta cheese and chickpeas if you don't have them on hand.

Lemon Blueberry Tabbouleh

1 cup	fine bulgur	250 ml
1½ cups	boiling water	375 ml
¼ cup	fresh lemon juice	60 ml
	zest of ½ lemon, *grated*	
1 clove	garlic, *minced*	
¼ cup	mild extra-virgin olive oil *or* vegetable oil	60 ml
1 cup	blueberries	250 ml
½ cup	pine nuts *or* slivered almonds, *toasted*	125 ml
½ cup	fresh flat-leaf parsley, *finely chopped*	125 ml
½ cup	green onions, *thinly sliced on the diagonal*	125 ml
¼ cup	fresh mint, *finely chopped*	60 ml
½ tsp	salt	2 ml

Imagine a light, herb-nut variation of tabbouleh with a burst of fruit flavour in every bite. Serve it as a side dish with grilled chicken kebabs or pork tenderloin.

1. Place bulgur in a large shallow bowl and cover with the water. Let sit uncovered for 20 minutes or until all of the water is absorbed and grains are soft. Fluff with a fork.

2. Mix together lemon juice, grated lemon zest, garlic, and oil, and stir into the bulgur.

3. Stir in the rest of the ingredients. Taste and adjust seasoning.

Serves 4.

Couscous-Stuffed Tomatoes

6	**firm, ripe tomatoes**	
1 tbsp	**lemon juice**	15 ml
½ cup	**couscous**	125 ml
1	**small onion,** *finely chopped*	
2 tbsp	**olive oil,** *plus extra for drizzling*	30 ml
1 clove	**garlic,** *minced*	
1 tsp	**ground cumin**	5 ml
½ tsp	**dried oregano**	2 ml
pinch	**cayenne**	
2 tbsp	**currants**	30 ml
¼ cup	**fresh flat-leaf parsley,** *chopped*	60 ml
¼ cup	**pine nuts,** *toasted*	60 ml
	salt and freshly ground black pepper	

TIP:

• The tomatoes can also be baked on the grill: Set them in a foil dish, cover with foil, and cook over medium heat with the lid closed following the directions in Step 6.

Try this recipe when flavourful field-ripened tomatoes are abundant and you want to showcase them in something other than a salad. Serve as a side dish with food from the grill, or as a main dish for a light vegetarian lunch or dinner.

1. Cut the tops off the tomatoes about ½" (1 cm) down. Scoop out the insides with a small spoon. Discard seeds, but save and chop the pulp.

2. Lightly salt the inside of each tomato and set upside down on paper towels to drain.

3. Meanwhile, prepare stuffing: Heat lemon juice with a scant cup (235 ml) water until boiling, and pour over couscous. Leave until liquid is absorbed (about 5 minutes), then fluff with a fork.

4. In a small frying pan, cook the onion in oil until soft; add garlic, reserved tomato pulp, and seasonings. Cook gently for about 10 minutes.

5. Remove from heat, stir in currants, parsley, and pine nuts, and season to taste. Lightly toss mixture into couscous.

6. When ready to bake, season insides of tomatoes, spoon in stuffing, and drizzle a little extra olive oil on top. Set in a baking dish, cover with foil, and bake at 350°F (180°C) for 15 minutes. Remove foil and continue baking until the tomatoes are tender and the stuffing is nicely brown – about 10 minutes more. (Don't overcook.) Serve hot or at room temperature.

Serves 6.

Napa Cabbage Salad

2 pkgs	instant oriental noodles with chicken, beef, *or* mushroom-flavoured soup base *(85–100 g each)*	
1 cup	vegetable oil	250 ml
6 tbsp	rice vinegar *or* balsamic *or* white wine vinegar	90 ml
4 tsp	sugar	20 ml
2 tsp	salt	10 ml
1	large napa cabbage *(10"/25 cm long)*	
8	green onions, *chopped*	
½ cup	fresh parsley, *chopped*	125 ml
1 cup	sliced almonds, *toasted*	250 ml
½ cup	sesame seeds, *toasted*	125 ml

TIPS:

• A small, diced red pepper adds a nice touch of colour.

• If napa cabbage is unavailable, you can substitute finely shredded regular green cabbage.

*N*apa cabbage, also called Chinese cabbage, looks like a long, celery-shaped head of cabbage, and goes well with the oriental flavours in this salad. The recipe is great for a crowd – not only because it makes a lot, but because everyone seems to love it. However, you can easily halve it if you wish.

1. Several hours before using, mix together the soup flavour packets from the noodles, oil, vinegar, sugar, and salt. Stir occasionally.

2. Chop the cabbage. (You should have about 16 cups/4 L.) Add the onions and parsley.

3. Mix dressing thoroughly with salad greens. Just before serving, add almonds, sesame seeds, and dry soup noodles, slightly crushed. Toss to mix.

Serves 15.

TIPS:

• Toast almonds and sesame seeds in shallow baking pan at 375°F (190°C) for 3–6 minutes, stirring often until golden brown.

• Salad can be prepared the day before. Add sesame seeds, almonds, and noodles just before serving.

Lemon Cumin Slaw
with Raisins & Nuts

1	**small red** *or* **green cabbage**	
2	**medium carrots**	
3	**green onions,** *sliced*	
½ cup	**raisins**	125 ml
¼ cup	**fresh parsley,** *chopped*	60 ml
½ cup	**walnuts** *or* **pecans,** *toasted and chopped*	125 ml

Lemony Slaw Dressing

2 tbsp	**fresh lemon juice**	30 ml
2 tsp	**brown sugar**	10 ml
1 tsp	**ground cumin**	5 ml
6 tbsp	**extra-virgin olive oil**	90 ml
	salt and freshly ground black pepper	

*C*abbage salads generally stand up well, and this crisp, nutty one – a change from the usual mayo-based slaw – is no exception. It travels happily to a potluck or picnic; just carry the toasted nuts along separately and toss them with the rest of the salad right before serving.

1. Combine all ingredients for the dressing and shake well.

2. Slice cabbage in quarters and cut away core. Slice into the finest shreds you can, or use a grater. Coarsely grate the carrots. Toss cabbage and carrots together with the green onions and raisins.

3. A few hours before serving, add parsley, toss salad with dressing, and refrigerate. At serving time, bring salad to room temperature and add toasted nuts.

Serves 6–8.

TIP:
• You can make the dressing and prepare the salad ingredients a day or two ahead. Store separately in covered containers in the refrigerator.

Mediterranean Potato Salad

2 lbs	small new potatoes	1 kg
½ cup	dry white wine	125 ml
	salt and freshly ground black pepper	
½	medium red onion, *finely chopped*	
½ cup	ripe black olives, *pitted and chopped*	125 ml
4	green onions, *finely chopped*	
¼ cup	sun-dried tomatoes, *softened and chopped*	60 ml
½ cup	Classic Vinaigrette *(p. 132)*	125 ml
½ cup	fresh flat-leaf, parsley, *chopped*	125 ml

This potato salad, packed with favourite Mediterranean flavours, is great to take along on picnics because it is made without mayonnaise and the flavours intensify at room temperature.

1. Cover potatoes with salted water and boil until just tender. (Test them after 10 minutes; they will continue to cook for a few minutes after they are drained.) Drain, remove skins if desired, and halve or quarter.

2. Sprinkle potatoes with wine and salt and pepper.

3. Add red onion, olives, green onions, and sun-dried tomatoes, and toss with vinaigrette.

4. Set aside at room temperature for about an hour for flavours to blend. Toss again with chopped fresh parsley before serving.

Serves 6.

VARIATIONS:

• Add slivers of roasted red, green, or yellow peppers; capers; quartered marinated artichoke hearts; or a handful of chopped sharp fresh greens such as arugula or endive.

• Potato and Asparagus Salad: Omit the olives and sun-dried tomatoes. Blanch 1 lb (500 g) asparagus in boiling, lightly salted water until just tender, about 3–5 minutes. Blanch 4 oz (125 g) snow peas for a minute or so. Drain well and chill until serving time. Then slice the vegetables on the diagonal and toss with a little of the dressing and ¼ cup (60 ml) chopped dill. Toss the mixture with the rest of the salad.

• To make a main-dish salad: Add grilled tuna or slices of grilled Italian sausage. Or top with skewers of tender grilled shrimp (p. 90).

TIPS:

• Remember this rough guideline: Buy round potatoes for boiling and long oval ones for baking and frying. Round ones have a higher moisture content and hold their shape when boiled. Long, oval potatoes will disintegrate.

• Hot potatoes absorb flavours well; cold ones don't. Therefore, when making a potato salad with a vinaigrette, toss potatoes in some of the dressing while they are still hot.

Green & Yellow Beans
with Honey-Mustard Dressing

½ lb	green beans	250 g
½ lb	yellow wax beans	250 g

Honey-Mustard Dressing

3 tbsp	Dijon mustard	45 ml
3 tbsp	honey	45 ml
	juice of 1 lemon	
3 tbsp	white wine vinegar	45 ml
½ cup	mild olive oil *or* vegetable oil	125 ml
½ cup	fresh dill, *chopped*	125 ml
	salt and freshly ground black pepper	

*B*eans never taste any better than during the summer months, when they are freshly picked. The Honey-Mustard Dressing is guaranteed to become a favourite; try it as a dip with asparagus or other fresh vegetables, or serve alongside cold salmon.

1. Snip the stem ends off the beans and toss in a large pot of lightly salted boiling water. Cook until just tender, tasting after 5 minutes. (Cooking time will vary depending on the size and freshness of the beans.)

2. Dump beans into ice water to stop the cooking, and drain well.

3. Combine all ingredients for Honey-Mustard Dressing.

4. Just before serving, toss beans with enough dressing to coat them lightly. (You won't need all the dressing.)

Serves 4.

TIPS:

• Steps 1 and 2 may be done the day before. Store, covered, in the fridge.

• The Honey-Mustard Dressing will keep 2–3 days in a covered jar in the refrigerator. It will keep for several weeks if you omit the fresh dill and mix it in just before serving.

• Beans lose their fresh colour when left too long in a vinaigrette, so combine them with the dressing just prior to serving.

Green Beans & Feta
with Sun-Dried Tomato Vinaigrette

¾ lb	**green beans,** *trimmed*	375 g
	leaf lettuce leaves	
½ lb	**feta cheese,** *cut in cubes*	250 g
4	**sun-dried tomatoes,** *packed in oil*	
⅓ cup	**kalamata olives**	75 ml
1–2 tbsp	**chives** *or* **green onions,** *chopped*	15–30 ml
	fresh oregano leaves *(for garnish; optional)*	

Sun-Dried Tomato Vinaigrette

2	**sun-dried tomatoes,** *packed in oil*	
3 tbsp	**red wine vinegar**	45 ml
1 clove	**garlic,** *minced*	
1 tbsp	**fresh oregano,** *minced* or	15 ml
1 tsp	**dried oregano**	5 ml
1 tsp	**sugar**	5 ml
	salt and freshly ground black pepper	
⅓ cup	**olive oil**	75 ml

$\mathcal{T}$his Mediterranean-inspired salad makes a good accompaniment to grilled meats. Or it can be served on individual plates as a salad course.

1. To make the vinaigrette, finely chop the 2 sun-dried tomatoes and whisk together with the vinegar, garlic, oregano, sugar and salt and pepper until blended. Slowly drizzle in oil, whisking constantly.

2. Steam or blanch beans until tender-crisp. Plunge into cold water to stop the cooking, then drain and wrap in paper towel. Chill until ready to serve.

3. Line a platter with lettuce leaves. Arrange half the beans on top of the lettuce. Top with feta cubes, then put remaining beans over cheese. Slice remaining 4 sun-dried tomatoes into thin strips and scatter with olives around beans.

4. Drizzle vinaigrette over salad. Sprinkle with chives or green onions and garnish with additional oregano leaves, if you wish.

Serves 4.

TIPS:

• Dressing can be made ahead and stored, covered, in the refrigerator for up to 1 week.

• If oil-packed tomatoes are not available, dried tomatoes that have been rehydrated work equally well.

Feta cheese, olives, and sun-dried tomatoes give this green bean salad zip. It goes together quickly and can be easily doubled if you're serving a larger group.

Corn & Black Bean Salad

2 ears	**corn,** *husk and silk removed*	
1½ tbsp	**olive oil**	20 ml
1 can	**black beans,** *rinsed and drained, (19 oz/540 ml)* **or**	
2 cups	**cooked black beans** *(see below)*	500 ml
1	**large, ripe tomato,** *seeded and chopped*	
1	**red pepper,** *roasted, peeled, seeded, and chopped*	
1 tbsp	**jalapeño pepper,** *chopped (fresh or canned)*	15 ml
1–2 cloves	**garlic,** *finely chopped*	
2	**green onions,** *finely chopped*	
	juice of 1 lime	
dash	**hot sauce**	
	salt and freshly ground black pepper	
¼ cup	**fresh coriander** *or* **flat-leaf parsley,** *chopped*	60 ml

*C*ooking the corn on the grill adds a light smoky taste to this colourful vegetable mixture. Serve it as a before-dinner snack with crisp corn chips, or as a side dish with grilled chicken, pork, or fish.

1. Blanch corn for 2 minutes in boiling salted water. Drain, rub with a little of the olive oil, and set on the grill over medium-high heat. Roll the corn over the fire for 4–6 minutes until it is nicely browned.

2. Remove kernels from the cobs and combine with remaining olive oil and the rest of the ingredients. Let mixture stand an hour or so in the refrigerator for flavours to blend. Taste and adjust seasoning.

Makes 3 cups (750 ml).

TIP:
• The salad will keep 2–3 days in the refrigerator. If you plan to make it ahead, add the green onion and fresh herbs on the day of serving.

HOW TO COOK DRIED BEANS:
• Rinse and pick through the beans to remove any debris. Place beans in a large saucepan and cover with cold water. Cover pan and bring to a boil. Remove from heat and set aside for an hour. (Alternatively, instead of boiling, leave beans in cold water to soak overnight.) Drain, rinse beans, and cover with fresh, cold water. Add some flavourings if you like (an onion studded with 2 cloves and a bay leaf, for example). Gently bring to a boil, lower heat, and cook, covered, until tender – about 1½ hours.

• 1 cup (250 ml) dried beans equals 2–2½ cups (500–625 ml) cooked beans.

Greek Salad

½ head	romaine lettuce	
2	large tomatoes, *sliced* or	
1 pint	cherry tomatoes, *halved*	
1	green pepper, *sliced in thin rings*	
½	red onion, *sliced in thin rings*	
½ cup	feta cheese, *crumbled*	125 ml
3 tbsp	olive oil	45 ml
1 tbsp	red wine vinegar *or* fresh lemon juice	15 ml
	salt and freshly ground black pepper	
1 tsp	dried oregano	5 ml
2 tbsp	fresh flat-leaf parsley, *chopped*	30 ml
½ cup	kalamata olives, *pitted and sliced*	125 ml

*S*un-ripened tomatoes, good-quality Greek feta, and firm, tangy olives combine to make an excellent salad to serve with any Mediterranean-flavoured grilled fish or meat.

1. Tear up lettuce leaves and line a large platter with them.

2. Arrange layers of tomato slices and green pepper and onion rings on the lettuce. Top with crumbled feta cheese.

3. Whisk together olive oil, vinegar or lemon juice, and salt and pepper, and drizzle over salad.

4. Sprinkle oregano, parsley, and olives on top and add a dash more pepper.

Serves 6.

TIPS:

• Store tomatoes in a cool, airy spot. Refrigerators are too cold and cause tomatoes to become "grainy" and lose their flavour.

• You can add a layer of sliced cucumber instead of, or along with, the green pepper if you like.

Very, Very Green Salad

1 head	**broccoli,** *florets only*	
1½ cups	**green beans,** *sliced diagonally*	375 ml
1½ cups	**snow peas**	375 ml
1 bunch	**fresh spinach,** *trimmed, washed, and dried*	
1½ cups	**seedless green grapes**	375 ml
2 tbsp	**green onion,** *chopped*	30 ml
2 tbsp	**chives,** *chopped*	30 ml
½ cup	**golden raisins**	125 ml
2 cups	**Creamy Citrus Dressing** *(p. 160)*	500 ml
½ cup	**pine nuts,** *toasted*	125 ml
½ lb	**bacon,** *cooked crisp and chopped (optional)*	250 g

*B*eautiful colour, great taste – plus, it serves a crowd. This salad goes well with Pepper-Encrusted Loin of Pork (p. 80) or simply grilled chicken.

1. Blanch broccoli, green beans, and snow peas (see Tip, below) and combine in a large bowl with spinach, grapes, green onion, chives, and raisins. Toss to mix well.

2. Add Creamy Citrus Dressing and toss again. Chill for an hour before serving to let flavours blend.

3. Just before serving, add pine nuts and bacon (if desired) and toss again.

Serves 10.

TIP:

• Blanching the broccoli, beans, and snow peas for 1–2 minutes in lightly salted boiling water brings out their flavour and colour. Use the same pot, putting in one type of vegetable at a time. Lift out with a slotted spoon, refresh in ice water to stop the cooking, and drain thoroughly.

Very, Very Green Salad: You can vary the green items to suit your own taste (and the contents of your fridge).

Two Citrus Dressings

Creamy Citrus Dressing

1 cup	mayonnaise	250 ml
½ cup	orange juice	125 ml
2 tsp	honey	10 ml
½ cup	sour cream *or* **yogurt**	125 ml
1 tbsp	rice vinegar	15 ml
1 tsp	dry mustard	5 ml
1 clove	garlic, *minced*	
2	green onions, *chopped*	
¼ cup	fresh parsley, *chopped*	60 ml
	salt and freshly ground black pepper	

Citrus Vinaigrette

1 tbsp	orange juice	15 ml
1 tbsp	fresh lemon juice	15 ml
1 tbsp	balsamic *or* **red wine vinegar**	15 ml
6 tbsp	olive oil	90 ml
	salt and freshly ground black pepper	

*U*se the Creamy Citrus Dressing on the Very, Very Green Salad, p. 158. Dress the Wild Rice Salad on the facing page with the Citrus Vinaigrette.

Creamy Citrus Dressing

1. Combine all ingredients, mixing well, and season to taste. (Dressing can be made in a food processor if desired.) Keep refrigerated until ready to use. If dressing is being made more than a few hours ahead, add green onions and parsley just before serving.

Makes about 2 cups (500 ml).

Citrus Vinaigrette

1. Whisk all the ingredients together and season to taste.

Makes about ½ cup (125 ml).

TIPS:

• Rice vinegar has a mild, sweet taste that is well suited to the creamy dressing. However, you can substitute another white vinegar if desired.

• The Citrus Vinaigrette makes a good marinade for chicken or pork.

QUICK TRICK:

Watercress & Orange Salad: Toss most of the Citrus Vinaigrette with 6 cups (1.5 L) watercress; ½ small red onion, thinly sliced; 2 green onions or 1 shallot, minced; and 1 large orange, peeled and cut into bite-sized pieces. Add a bit more dressing if necessary. A piece of Stilton crumbled on top is a delicious accompaniment.

Wild Rice Salad
with Fruit & Nuts

1 cup	wild rice	250 ml
½ cup	basmati *or* long-grain white rice	125 ml
½ cup	Citrus Vinaigrette *(p. 160)*	125 ml
1	orange	
½ cup	dried cranberries	125 ml
½ cup	orange juice *or* water, *warmed*	125 ml
4	green onions	
½ cup	pecans, *toasted and chopped*	125 ml
¼ cup	fresh parsley, *chopped*	60 ml
	salt and freshly ground black pepper	

TIP:

• Basmati rice should be rinsed before using to remove surface dust. Put the rice in a bowl, pour in cold water, and swirl grains around with your fingers. Pour off the water and repeat till the water runs clear. Before steaming basmati, cover with fresh, cold water, and leave to soak for 15–30 minutes. Drain and cook.

The nutty flavours and satisfying crunch of this salad go well with grilled chicken or pork marinated in the same Citrus Vinaigrette.

1. Place wild rice in a large saucepan, cover with 4 cups (1 L) water, and add a dash of salt. Bring to a boil, lower heat, cover, and simmer until grains are tender but still chewy, about 30 minutes.

2. Bring 4 cups (1 L) water to a boil. Add basmati or white rice. Boil for about 10 minutes, uncovered, until grains are just tender. Drain.

3. While rice is still warm, toss both types together with half the dressing and set aside.

4. Remove the skin and pith from the orange. Slice the orange, then cut each slice into bite-sized pieces. Soak the dried cranberries in warm orange juice or water for 15 minutes to soften. Drain and pat dry.

5. Shortly before serving, add the fruit, green onions, nuts, and parsley to the rice. Toss with more of the dressing and season to taste.

Serves 4–6.

TIPS:

• You can substitute golden raisins for the cranberries, or 1 cup (250 ml) of seedless purple or red grapes, cut in half.

• The rice can be cooked and combined with the dressing (Steps 1–3), and the other ingredients prepared (Step 4), early in the day. Toss all together just before serving.

Wheat Berry Salad
with Wild Rice & Orzo

1½ cups	**wheat berries**	**325 ml**
½ cup	**wild rice**	**125 ml**
1 cup	**orzo**	**250 ml**
½	**medium red onion,** *finely chopped*	
2	**green onions,** *finely chopped*	
2 stalks	**celery,** *finely chopped*	
1	**zucchini,** *grated*	
½ cup	**fresh parsley,** *finely chopped*	**125 ml**
½ cup	**Classic Vinaigrette** *(p. 132), made with extra-virgin olive oil and red wine vinegar*	**125 ml**
	arugula *or* **romaine lettuce leaves**	

*W*heat berries (whole, unprocessed kernels of wheat) and orzo (a rice-shaped pasta) are among the huge selection of interesting grains and pasta varieties now widely available in our markets. They are easy to prepare and add lots of flavour, texture, and goodness to salads.

1. Bring a large pot of lightly salted water to a boil. Add the wheat berries and cook, uncovered, for 10 minutes. Add the wild rice to the same pot and continue cooking for 30 minutes more, or until grains are tender. In another pot, cook the orzo in lightly salted water for 10–15 minutes. Drain grains and orzo well.

2. In a large bowl combine cooked grains and pasta with onions, celery, zucchini, and parsley, and toss with the vinaigrette, reserving a couple of tablespoons of dressing.

3. At serving time, either pile the salad on a platter lined with arugula or romaine, or tear up some of the green leaves and toss with the salad. Taste and adjust seasoning, adding a little more dressing if needed.

Serves 8–10.

TIPS:

• Look for wheat berries – also called "hard wheat kernels" – in bulk-food and natural-food stores. You'll find orzo in boxes in the pasta section of the supermarket, as well as in bulk stores.

• The salad can be made ahead (through Step 2) and will keep in the refrigerator for a couple of days.

Both Wheat Berry Salad with Wild Rice & Orzo and Tuscan Pepper & Tomato Salad (p. 164) are real standouts on a potluck or party table.

Tuscan Pepper & Tomato Salad

2	**red peppers**	
1	**yellow pepper**	
1	**green pepper**	
1	**jalapeño pepper** *(optional)*	
1	**medium red onion,** *thinly sliced*	
1 pint	**cherry tomatoes,** *halved*	500 ml
¼ cup	**black olives,** *pitted*	60 ml
¼ cup	**Classic Vinaigrette** *(p. 132), made with* *red wine or balsamic* *vinegar and extra-virgin* *olive oil*	60 ml
¼ tsp	**hot red pepper flakes**	1 ml
1 tbsp	**fresh basil** *or* **part basil, part** **oregano,** *chopped*	15 ml
	salt and freshly **ground black pepper**	
	fresh greens *(such as arugula,* *romaine, and endive)*	

*E*very bite of this crisp, colourful salad says summer. Serve it alongside Peppered Sirloin (p. 79) or Garlicky Fish or Shrimp Kebabs (p. 90), or on top of Mini-Meatball-Stuffed Pitas (p. 229).

1. Halve all peppers lengthwise. Remove seeds and core, and cut into very fine slices.

2. In a large bowl toss the peppers, onion, tomatoes, and olives with the dressing, red pepper flakes, and herbs. Adjust seasoning.

3. Line a platter with a bed of crisp greens and arrange the salad on top.

Serves 4.

TIP:

• The peppers and onion can be prepared a few hours ahead, but add the tomatoes just before serving, as they tend to become soft and release their juices.

MAIN-DISH VARIATION:

• Add slices of bocconcini (or regular mozzarella) and salami, or chunks of grilled tuna to the platter.

(Tuscan Pepper & Tomato Salad is shown in the photo on the previous page.)

Fresh Herb Rice Salad
with Tomatoes, Olives, & Capers

4 cups	**cooked basmati rice,** *cooled to lukewarm*	1 L
¼ cup	**extra-virgin olive oil**	60 ml
2 tbsp	**sherry vinegar** *or* **red wine vinegar**	30 ml
¼ cup	**cracked green olives,** *rinsed, pitted, and chopped*	60 ml
¼ cup	**dry-cured black olives,** *pitted and chopped*	60 ml
¼ cup	**small capers,** *rinsed and drained*	60 ml
¼ cup	**red onion,** *finely chopped*	60 ml
¼ cup	**fresh basil,** *chopped*	60 ml
¼ cup	**fresh flat-leaf parsley,** *chopped*	60 ml
1 cup	**cherry tomatoes,** *halved, or* **ripe field tomatoes,** *seeded and chopped*	250 ml
1 tsp	**salt**	5 ml
	freshly ground black pepper	

I have always found it difficult to make a rice salad that tastes really good, but this one bursts with sunny flavours. It goes extremely well with grilled tuna or other grilled fish, seafood kebabs, or good-quality canned tuna.

1. In a large bowl, toss the rice lightly with the oil and vinegar, using a fork to separate the grains. Add the rest of the ingredients and season to taste.

2. Pile the salad onto a large platter and serve at room temperature.

Serves 4–6.

TIPS:

• The salad can be made ahead and refrigerated, but return to room temperature and add the basil, parsley, and tomatoes just before serving.

• To get 4 cups (1 L) of cooked basmati rice, start with 1 cup (250 ml) raw rice.

• You can substitute other grains such as couscous, or even orzo (the little rice-shaped pasta) for the rice, or use a combination of grain and pasta.

Mediterranean Barley Salad

2 cups	vegetable *or* chicken stock	500 ml
1 cup	barley	250 ml
¼ cup	sun-dried tomatoes	60 ml
2	medium tomatoes, *seeded and chopped*	
3	green onions, *finely chopped*	
½ each	red and yellow pepper, *seeded and chopped*	
1 tbsp	fresh oregano, *chopped* or	15 ml
1 tsp	dried oregano	5 ml
½ cup	fresh flat-leaf parsley, *chopped*	125 ml
½ cup	Balsamic Vinaigrette *(approx.) (p. 133)*	125 ml
	salt and freshly ground black pepper	
¼ cup	feta cheese, *crumbled*	60 ml
¼ cup	pine nuts, *toasted (optional)*	60 ml

*O*ften overlooked as a salad or pilaf ingredient, barley adds nutty flavour and makes a nice change from other grains. Here it's combined with fresh and sun-dried tomatoes, colourful peppers, and feta cheese to create a salad rich in flavour and substance – suitable as a main dish for vegetarian friends.

1. Bring stock to a boil in a large saucepan. Slowly stir in barley, cover pan, lower heat, and simmer for about 30 minutes, or until the grains are just tender and the liquid is absorbed. Fluff grains with a fork and turn into a large bowl to cool.

2. Soak sun-dried tomatoes in hot water for about 15 minutes to soften. Finely chop and add them to the cooled barley along with the fresh tomatoes, green onions, peppers, oregano, and half the parsley. Toss together gently with about half the Balsamic Vinaigrette, reserving the rest.

3. Before serving, lightly toss the salad, taste, and adjust with salt and pepper and additional vinaigrette as required. Sprinkle with the crumbled feta, pine nuts (if using), and the rest of the parsley.

Serves 6–8.

TIPS:

• The salad can be prepared several hours ahead through Step 2 and kept covered in the refrigerator. Add the cheese and nuts before serving.

• If you like, tear up 2 cups (500 ml) of crisp greens such as watercress, arugula, and endive and fold them into the grain mixture. Or serve the salad on a platter lined with greens.

Serve Mediterranean Barley Salad as a side dish with grilled food or as a vegetarian main dish.

Asian Rice Salad

1½ cups	**brown rice,** *rinsed*	375 ml
½ lb	**green beans, asparagus, snow peas,** *or* **sugar snap peas**	250 g
1	**orange**	
½	**each red and green peppers,** *diced*	
1 can	**water chestnuts,** *rinsed and sliced (8 oz/227 ml)*	
2	**green onions,** *finely chopped*	
1 cup	**roasted peanuts,** *chopped (plus additional for garnish)*	250 ml
2 tbsp	**fresh coriander** *or* **parsley,** *chopped*	30 ml

Dressing

¼ cup	**fresh orange juice**	60 ml
¼ cup	**fresh lemon juice**	60 ml
3 tbsp	**soy sauce**	45 ml
3 tbsp	**brown sugar**	45 ml
½ cup	**vegetable oil**	125 ml
½ tsp	**hot red pepper flakes**	2 ml
	salt and freshly ground black pepper	

*E*njoy this crunchy salad beside chicken or pork satays (p. 128). Since it keeps well for a day or two, you may want to make enough to put aside for a tasty light lunch. Although the recipe calls for brown rice, you can substitute basmati (white or brown) or long-grain white rice.

1. Cook rice in a large pot of lightly salted boiling water, uncovered, until tender, about 20–25 minutes. Drain well.

2. Blanch the green beans, asparagus, or snow or snap peas, and cut on the diagonal into ½" (1-cm) pieces. Grate the orange zest and divide the orange into segments.

3. Mix dressing ingredients together well. Taste and adjust seasoning.

4. While the rice is still warm, toss with a spoonful or two of dressing. Cool, then mix in all the remaining ingredients. Add more dressing as required and season to taste. Garnish with some extra chopped peanuts and chopped coriander or parsley sprinkled on top.

Serves 4–6.

TIPS:

• Salad will keep in a tightly covered container in the refrigerator for about 2 days.

• Rice salad absorbs dressing as it sits in the refrigerator. Toss with extra dressing if needed.

Saffron Rice Pilaf

3 cups	**fish stock** *or* **light chicken stock** *(see Tip, below)*	750 ml
½ tsp	**saffron threads**	2 ml
2 tbsp	**olive oil**	30 ml
1 cup	**Spanish onion,** *finely chopped*	250 ml
2–3 cloves	**garlic,** *minced*	
½	**red pepper,** *seeded and chopped*	
½	**green pepper,** *seeded and chopped*	
2	**ripe plum tomatoes,** *peeled, seeded, and chopped*	
1½ cups	**medium-grain Spanish rice** *or* **arborio rice**	375 ml
	salt and freshly ground black pepper	
	lemon slices, Spanish paprika, and fresh parsley, *chopped (for garnish)*	

TIP:
• Use light chicken stock as the cooking liquid when serving the pilaf with meat.

*S*affron adds its subtle exotic fragrance and lively golden colour to this tasty pilaf. Essential for Lazy Summer Paella (p. 97), the pilaf is also delicious under skewered fish (p. 90) or simply grilled lamb or pork.

1. Heat stock in a small saucepan. Cook saffron in a small dry frying pan over moderate heat for about 30 seconds to bring out the flavour.

2. Pour ½ cup (125 ml) of the stock from the saucepan into a small bowl, crumble the toasted saffron into the hot liquid, and set aside to steep.

3. Heat oil in a large, deep frying pan with a well-fitting lid. Add onion and cook over moderate heat until soft, then add garlic, peppers, and tomatoes, and continue to cook for about 10 minutes. Add rice and stir over the heat for a few minutes until all the grains are coated with the flavoured oil.

4. Pour in the hot stock and the saffron-flavoured liquid and stir gently while mixture comes to a boil. Reduce the heat to low, cover, and leave to cook for about 15 minutes, until liquid is absorbed and rice is tender. Remove from heat and set aside, covered, for about 5 minutes.

5. Fluff the rice with a fork, season, and turn out onto a warm platter. Garnish with lemon slices, paprika, and parsley, and serve.

Serves 6.

White Bean & Spinach Salad

6 tbsp	extra-virgin olive oil	90 ml
½	medium red onion, *thinly sliced*	
1 clove	garlic, *finely chopped*	
1 tsp	ground coriander	5 ml
1 bunch	young spinach *(about 10 oz/300 g), trimmed, washed, and dried*	
2 tbsp	fresh lemon juice	30 ml
	salt and freshly ground black pepper	
1 can	white beans, *rinsed and drained (19 oz/540 ml)*	
3–4 oz	feta cheese, *crumbled (optional)*	100–125 g

MAIN-DISH VARIATION:

• Garnish salad with grilled sliced lamb or lamb kebabs, or slices of grilled sausages.

A simple salad that takes only minutes to prepare and uses the pantry staple of canned beans. Serve at room temperature for the best flavour.

1. Heat 2 tbsp (30 ml) of the olive oil in a large frying pan over moderate heat. Add onion and garlic and cook until soft. Stir in coriander.

2. Add spinach, sprinkle with a little salt, and cover pan. Let spinach steam until just wilted. Set aside.

3. Mix lemon juice with remaining olive oil. Season with salt and pepper to taste.

4. Combine spinach-onion mixture with beans and toss with lemon dressing. Adjust seasoning. Sprinkle crumbled feta cheese on top.

Serves 4.

TIPS:

• If fresh spinach isn't available, use a package of frozen leaf spinach, thawed and thoroughly patted dry.

• You can also replace the spinach with blanched and chopped rapini.

• The salad can be made a few hours before serving.

Spinach Rice

1 lb	**fresh spinach**	**500 g**
3 tbsp	**olive oil**	**45 ml**
1	**large onion,** *finely chopped*	
1 clove	**garlic,** *finely chopped*	
1 cup	**medium-grain** *or* **arborio rice**	**250 ml**
½ cup	**fresh dill,** *chopped*	**125 ml**
½ cup	**fresh parsley,** *chopped*	**125 ml**
1	**lemon,** *juice and grated zest*	
	salt and freshly ground black pepper	
1½ cups	**water** *or* **stock** *(chicken or vegetable)*	**375 ml**

TIP:

• The spinach rice is an ideal stuffing for tomatoes, perhaps with the addition of a little crumbled feta cheese. (See recipe on p. 149 for directions on stuffing and baking tomatoes.)

A side dish with the flavour of the Greek islands. Medium-grain or arborio rice combined with the light, fresh tastes of dill and lemon makes a tasty accompaniment to grilled chicken, skewered Garlicky Shrimp or Fish Kebabs (p. 90), or Cumin-Scented Leg of Lamb (p. 107).

1. Trim tough stalks off spinach and blanch leaves for 2 minutes in a large pot of lightly salted boiling water. Drain. Immerse spinach in ice water to stop the cooking and drain again. Squeeze dry and chop roughly. Set aside.

2. Heat oil in a 3 qt (3 L) heavy-bottomed saucepan. Add onion and cook until soft. Add spinach, garlic, and rice. Stir in about ¾ of the dill, parsley, lemon juice and zest; ½ tsp (2 ml) salt; and a few turns of the pepper mill. Continue stirring for a couple of minutes until rice grains are coated with flavoured oil.

3. Add water or stock, stir gently, and bring to a boil. Cover pot, reduce heat to low, and cook gently for 15 minutes.

4. Remove pan from heat. Set aside, covered, for 10 minutes. Serve warm, sprinkled with remaining dill, parsley, lemon juice, and lemon zest.

Serves 4.

Fragrant Coconut Rice

2 cups	Thai *or* basmati rice	500 ml
1¾ cups	water	425 ml
1 cup	coconut milk	250 ml
1	cinnamon stick (3"/8 cm)	
2	whole cloves	
1 piece	lemon grass stalk (3"/8 cm), smashed or	
1 strip	lemon zest (3"/8 cm)	

TIP:

• Coconut milk is available in cans in many supermarkets. (Look for it with the oriental/Thai foods or the canned milk.) If a recipe only calls for part of a can, you can freeze the rest to use another time.

The addition of herbs and spices raises plain steamed rice above the ordinary, and the coconut milk gives it a rich flavour (though you can use all water if you prefer). Serve with Asian-inspired meals such as Shortcut Seafood Curry (p. 202), Quick Thai Vegetable Curry (p. 198), Hoisin Ribs (p. 82), or Lemon Grass Chicken (p. 118).

1. Rinse rice in several changes of water until the water runs clear; drain well.

2. Place rice in a heavy saucepan. Add water, coconut milk, and flavourings, and bring to a simmer.

3. Stir briefly, then cover tightly and lower heat to lowest temperature. Cook until rice is tender and liquid is absorbed – about 10 minutes.

4. Remove saucepan from heat and set aside, still covered, for 5 minutes.

5. Fluff rice with a fork and remove spices before serving.

Serves 6.

Corn & Lentil Salad

1 cup	**green** *or* **brown lentils**	250 ml
	leaves from 1 celery stalk	
1	**bay leaf**	
3–4 ears	**corn,** *grilled (p. 124) and kernels removed (approx. 2 cups/500ml)* **or**	
2 cups	**frozen corn kernels,** *cooked*	500 ml
½	**medium red onion,** *finely chopped*	
½	**red pepper,** *seeded and finely diced*	
½	**green pepper,** *seeded and finely diced*	
¼ cup	**fresh flat-leaf parsley,** *finely chopped*	60 ml
¼ cup	**fresh coriander,** *finely chopped*	60 ml
½ cup	**Lemon Cumin Vinaigrette** *(p. 133)*	125 ml

*W*hen you are cooking on the barbecue, grill a few extra ears of corn and use them in salads or salsas to add a light, smoky taste. Serve this salad as a side dish with simply grilled meats, or mix chunks of spicy grilled sausage into the salad to make a one-dish meal; accompany it with wedges of fresh country bread.

1. Toss lentils into a large quantity of salted water with celery leaves and bay leaf. Bring to a boil, lower heat to moderate, and cook, uncovered, until just tender. Cooking time varies depending on the variety and quality of the lentils; start testing after 15 minutes. Drain lentils; discard celery leaves and bay leaf.

2. Combine warm lentils with remaining ingredients. Cover and refrigerate for an hour or so for flavours to blend. Allow the salad to return to cool room temperature before serving.

Serves 6.

TIPS:
• Cooking the lentils from scratch takes a few minutes more, but results in a salad with much better texture and flavour. If you're pressed for time, you can substitute 2 cups (500 ml) canned lentils, rinsed and drained.

• If you're making the salad more than a few hours ahead, add the fresh herbs right before serving.

MAIN-DISH VARIATION:
• Grill 3–4 spicy sausages (such as chorizos), cut them into ½" (1-cm) chunks, and combine with the salad.

(The Corn & Lentil Salad is shown in the photo opposite p. 191.)

Pickled Beets with a Bite

1 lb	beets	500 g
1 tsp	creamed horseradish	5 ml
1 tbsp	white wine vinegar	15 ml
2 tbsp	vegetable oil	30 ml
	fresh dill *or* parsley, *chopped* *(optional)*	
	salt and freshly ground black pepper	

TIP:
• The pickled beets will keep for several days in the refrigerator.

*B*eet varieties of many sizes and hues are now a familiar sight at farmers' markets. Small, summer-fresh ones are especially sweet. Try mild golden beets or, for a treat, splurge on an orangey-red variety called Chiogga, whose flesh has dramatic red and white rings.

1. Cut away all but 1" (2.5 cm) of the leafy tops from the beets, leaving the skin and tail intact, and scrub clean. Wrap in foil and bake in a 350°F (180°C) oven until tender. Test after 30 minutes; cooking time will depend on the freshness and size of the beets. Trim away the tops and tails, and remove the skin. Slice beets and cut into $1/2$" (1-cm) cubes.

2. Combine remaining ingredients and toss with beets.

3. Cover and chill for a few hours before serving.

Makes about 2 cups (500 ml).

QUICK TRICK:
Raw Beet and Carrot Salad: For a salad with great colour and flavour, toss equal quantities of grated raw beets and grated raw carrots with a simple dressing of 2 parts oil, 1 part fresh lemon juice, and salt and freshly ground black pepper.

Chickpeas & Roasted Peppers

1 can	**chickpeas,** *rinsed and drained* (19 oz/540 ml)	
2	**red peppers,** *roasted, peeled, seeded, and sliced*	
1	**yellow pepper,** *roasted, peeled, seeded, and sliced*	
½	**small red onion,** *finely chopped*	
¼ cup	**fresh parsley,** *chopped*	**60 ml**
2 stalks	**celery,** *cut into fine matchstick lengths*	
1	**carrot,** *cut into fine matchstick lengths*	

Dressing

1–2 cloves	**garlic,** *minced*	
	salt and freshly ground black pepper	
½ tsp	**dried oregano**	**2 ml**
3 tbsp	**red wine vinegar**	**45 ml**
½ cup	**extra-virgin olive oil**	**125 ml**

*A*nother colourful salad that is one of my summer favourites. It's quick and easy to assemble using ingredients frequently on hand in the pantry, and it travels and keeps well, too.

1. To make the dressing, mash garlic with a little salt and whisk in the remaining ingredients.

2. Combine chickpeas with peppers, onion, and parsley. Toss with the dressing, reserving about 3 tbsp (45 ml). Mound the chickpea mixture on a shallow platter.

3. Toss celery and carrot sticks in the remaining dressing. Arrange on the platter around the chickpeas, or simply combine the two mixtures. Serve the salad at room temperature.

Serves 4.

TIP:

• The salad can be made a day ahead and kept, covered, in the refrigerator. Bring to room temperature before serving.

MAIN-DISH VARIATION:

• For a vegetarian main dish, add crumbled feta cheese, a handful of black olives, and quartered hard-boiled eggs. For non-vegetarians, you can also add slices of grilled steak.

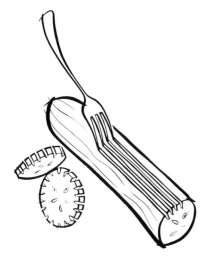

Asian Pickled Cucumber Salad

1	**English cucumber**	
1	**small red onion,** *thinly sliced*	
½	**small, fresh green hot pepper,** *seeded and cut lengthwise into slivers*	
¼ cup	**rice vinegar**	60 ml
2 tbsp	**fresh lime juice**	30 ml
1 tbsp	**fish sauce** *(see Tip, below right)*	15 ml
1 clove	**garlic,** *finely minced*	
	salt and freshly ground black pepper	
pinch	**sugar**	
1 cup	**cherry tomatoes,** *halved*	250 ml
2 tbsp	**fresh coriander,** *chopped*	30 ml
	arugula, watercress, *or* **leaf lettuce**	

TIP:

• The salad will keep for several days in the refrigerator without getting too watery if you drain the cucumbers as suggested above and add the tomatoes and coriander right at serving time.

A tangy make-ahead side dish that goes well with almost any Asian-flavoured grilled food. Try it with Lemon Grass Chicken (p. 118) or Oriental-Style Steamed Fish (p. 87).

1. Score the cucumber lengthwise with the tines of a fork to make long grooves on the skin, and slice into thin rounds. Sprinkle with salt and leave to drain in a sieve for an hour or so.

2. Press moisture out of cucumber slices and pat dry. Combine slices with remaining ingredients, except the cherry tomatoes, coriander, and greens. Set aside for a few hours or overnight for the flavours to blend.

3. Just before serving, add tomatoes and coriander, and pile the salad on a platter on a bed of arugula, watercress, or leaf lettuce.

Serves 4–6.

TIP:

• Look for bottles of fish sauce in the oriental/Asian section of large supermarkets. Although there is no other condiment that provides the same taste, if you can't find it you can substitute 1 tbsp (15 ml) of light soy sauce in this recipe.

Potatoes Savoyard

2 lbs	**potatoes,** *peeled and thinly sliced* ⅛" *(3 mm) thick*	1 kg
	salt and freshly ground black pepper	
3 tbsp	**butter**	45 ml
1 clove	**garlic,** *minced*	
2 cups	**Gruyère cheese,** *grated*	500 ml
1 cup	**beef, chicken,** *or* **vegetable stock**	250 ml

QUICK TRICK:

Garlic Roast Potatoes: Cut potatoes into chunks. For each 1 lb (500 g) potatoes, heat 1½ tbsp (20 ml) garlic-flavoured olive oil in a shallow roasting pan in a 400°F (200°C) oven. When oil is hot, toss in potato chunks, sprinkling with some fresh or dried herbs if you like. Roast for 30 minutes, turning occasionally until brown and crispy. Sprinkle with salt and freshly ground black pepper and serve at once.

This classic recipe comes from the Savoie region of France, where potatoes are baked with stock in place of milk or cream, as in the familiar scalloped-potato dish. It goes well with most main courses, but is especially good with grilled or roasted meats.

1. Lightly butter a shallow 9" x 13" (23 cm x 33 cm) baking dish. Cover the bottom of the dish with a slightly overlapping layer of thin potato slices. Season with salt and pepper, dot with a third of the butter, add a little garlic, and sprinkle with a third of the cheese.

2. Repeat the layers, finishing with butter and cheese.

3. Pour the stock over top. Bake in a 425°F (220°C) oven for 30 minutes. Tilt the dish and spoon the cooking juices over the potatoes.

4. Lower the heat to 350°F (180°C) and continue cooking until potatoes are tender and the top is nicely browned, about 20–30 minutes more.

Serves 6.

TIP:

• Use a mature all-purpose variety of potato such as Yukon Gold; moist, waxy varieties do not absorb the cooking liquid as well and tend to stay too firm.

Lemon Couscous

2 cups	chicken stock *or* **water**	500 ml
2 tbsp	unsalted butter	30 ml
½ tsp	salt	2 ml
1½ cups	couscous	375 ml
1 tbsp	lemon zest, *grated*	15 ml
½ cup	slivered almonds	125 ml
1 tbsp	fresh lemon juice *(approx.)*	15 ml

*C*ouscous has been a staple food in other wheat-growing cultures for centuries and has started to become readily available on North American supermarket shelves. Quick and simple to prepare, it makes an interesting alternative to rice, pasta, or potatoes and is great for soaking up sauce. Try this lemony version with *Chicken Tagine (p. 184), Moroccan Chicken Kebabs (p. 122), or Very Lemon Chicken (p.180).*

1. In a large saucepan, combine stock or water, 1 tbsp (15 ml) of the butter, and the salt and bring to a boil. Stir in couscous, remove from heat, cover, and set aside for 5 minutes.

2. Heat the remaining butter in a small frying pan, add lemon zest and almonds, and cook until nuts are lightly browned.

3. Fluff the couscous with a fork, tossing in the lemony almonds. Taste and adjust flavour with the lemon juice and additional salt, if necessary.

Serves 4–6.

IV. MAKE-AHEAD MAIN DISHES, PASTAS, & ONE-POT MEALS

Very Lemon Chicken

1 clove	garlic, *halved*	
1/4 cup	extra-virgin olive oil	60 ml
1/2 cup	fresh lemon juice	125 ml
1	small onion, *grated*	
1 tsp	dried thyme	5 ml
1	fresh hot pepper, *seeded and chopped*	
2 tbsp	butter *or* olive oil	30 ml
6	boneless, skinless chicken breasts	
	salt and freshly ground black pepper	

TIPS:

• If you plan to make the chicken ahead and reheat it, reduce simmering time to 5 minutes. Cover and refrigerate chicken in the lemon sauce.

• To serve cold (to take on a picnic or serve in a sandwich or salad), simmer as in Step 3, then cover and refrigerate the chicken in its sauce until needed.

*W*hen doubled, this recipe feeds a large group, and there are many ways to use the leftovers. (The chicken is excellent cold, shredded for a wrap or sliced in a sandwich; see p. 232.) The chicken pieces can be cooked ahead of time. Reheat and serve over rice or with crispy roasted potatoes and green beans or asparagus for a complete supper, or with salad and warm biscuits (p. 257) for a lighter evening meal.

1. Combine the garlic, 1/4 cup (60 ml) olive oil, lemon juice, onion, thyme, and hot pepper in a small bowl. Cover and leave in the refrigerator for an hour to allow the flavours to blend.

2. Heat the 2 tbsp (30 ml) butter or oil in a large frying pan. Season the chicken breasts and lightly brown on both sides. (You may have to brown them in 2 batches so as not to crowd the pan.)

3. Pour lemon mixture over the chicken and cover the pan. Lower heat and simmer until chicken is cooked, about 10 minutes, depending on the size of the breasts.

Serves 6.

Rosemary Lemon Chicken

2 tbsp	olive oil	30 ml
1 tbsp	fresh lemon juice	15 ml
1 tbsp	fresh rosemary, *chopped* **or**	15 ml
1 tsp	dried rosemary	5 ml
2	bay leaves	
	salt and freshly ground black pepper	
3½–4 lbs	bone-in chicken pieces	1.5–2 kg
1 tbsp	unsalted butter	15 ml
½	onion, *chopped*	
8–12	mini-potatoes, *scrubbed*	
½ cup	chicken stock	125 ml
¼ cup	red wine vinegar	60 ml
6	ripe plum tomatoes, *peeled, seeded, and chopped* **or**	
1 can	plum tomatoes, *drained and chopped (28 oz/796 ml)*	
1 tsp	liquid honey	5 ml
¼ cup	capers, *drained*	60 ml
1 tbsp	fresh flat-leaf parsley, *chopped*	15 ml
1 tsp	lemon zest, *grated*	5 ml

The flavours of this one-pot supper transport you to the eastern Mediterranean. Serve with warm, crusty bread for mopping up the sauce.

1. Combine olive oil, lemon juice, rosemary, bay leaves, and salt and pepper, and rub chicken pieces on all sides with the mixture. Cover and refrigerate for 2–24 hours.

2. Heat butter in a large frying pan with a lid. Add onion and cook over medium heat until soft, about 5–6 minutes, stirring occasionally. Add chicken with marinade and potatoes. Toss over the heat for a couple of minutes, until chicken and potatoes are well coated with the buttery juices.

3. Add about ¼ cup (60 ml) of the stock, cover, lower heat, and cook gently until chicken and potatoes are tender, 30–35 minutes. Add a bit more of the stock to the pan if the contents get too dry during cooking.

4. Remove chicken and potatoes to a warm platter. Raise heat and add vinegar to the pan. Cook 5–10 minutes, until liquid is reduced to a glaze, then add chopped tomatoes and honey. Cook 2–3 minutes more, then season to taste, return chicken and potatoes to the pan, and stir to coat with the sauce. Serve hot, garnished with capers, parsley, and lemon zest.

Serves 4.

TIP:

• You can prepare this dish a day or two ahead. Gently reheat in a covered pan on the stove or in a conventional or microwave oven. Garnish just before serving.

Slow-Roasted Garlic Chicken

3 lbs	**bone-in chicken pieces**	1.5 kg
1	**large onion,** *cut in eighths*	
2 heads	**garlic,** *separated into cloves (about 20 unpeeled cloves)*	
1 tsp	**dried rosemary** *or* **tarragon**	5 ml
½	**lemon,** *thinly sliced*	
2 tbsp	**olive oil**	30 ml
	salt and freshly ground black pepper	
1 cup	**fruity white wine**	250 ml

TIPS:

• The softened garlic cloves can be squeezed out of their skins and eaten as is with the chicken or spread onto bread. You can also blend some of the garlic into the sauce or mash it with the potatoes.

• The dish can be made a day ahead. Complete through Step 4, cover, and refrigerate. Then simply reheat in a covered casserole in a 350˚F (180˚C) oven.

This dish takes just a few minutes to put together and reheats well. The quantity of garlic may seem outrageous, but slow roasting softens and sweetens its flavour. Serve the chicken with a platter of lightly steamed green beans, Olive-Flavoured Mashed Potatoes (Quick Trick, below), and warm, crusty bread.

1. Toss chicken pieces in a bowl with the onion, garlic, herbs, lemon slices, olive oil, and salt and pepper.

2. Place the chicken in a shallow roasting pan, scatter the onion, garlic, and lemon slices over and around it, and sprinkle with the wine.

3. Cover the pan tightly with foil and place on the centre rack of a preheated 350˚F (180˚C) oven. After about an hour, remove foil, baste chicken with the pan juices and continue to roast, uncovered, until the chicken is lightly browned and cooked through – about 20 minutes more.

4. Transfer chicken and garlic cloves from the pan to a serving dish. Strain the cooking juices into a small saucepan, skim off fat, and simmer for a few minutes to strengthen the flavour. Season to taste and pour over the chicken.

Serves 4.

QUICK TRICK:

Olive-Flavoured Mashed Potatoes: Into mashed potatoes for 4, fold ½ cup (125 ml) coarsely chopped Niçoise olives and ¼–⅓ cup (60–75 ml) warm olive oil. Season to taste.

You'll want to serve this Slow-Roasted Garlic Chicken with warm, crusty Italian bread, so people can smear the sweet cloves of garlic on it like soft butter.

Chicken Tagine

3 lbs	bone-in chicken pieces	1.5 kg
1 recipe	Moroccan Flavour Paste (p. 122)	60 ml
2 tbsp	olive oil	30 ml
2	medium onions, *finely chopped*	
2 cloves	garlic, *minced*	
1 cup	canned plum tomatoes, *drained and chopped*	250 ml
1½ cups	chicken stock *or* water	375 ml
½ cup	dry-cured black olives *(see Tips, below)*	125 ml
	salt	
2 tbsp	fresh lemon juice	30 ml
2 tbsp	fresh coriander *or* flat-leaf parsley, *chopped (for garnish)*	30 ml
1	lemon, *sliced (for garnish)*	

TIPS:

• The tagine tastes even better prepared a day ahead.

•Dry-cured black olives, also called Moroccan olives, are wrinkled and sold dry, not in brine.

A tagine is an aromatic Moroccan stew traditionally made with chicken or lamb and served over couscous. It gets its distinctive taste from a saffron-infused spice paste (p. 122), which can be made ahead and kept in the freezer. Serve the tagine with Lemon Couscous (p. 178) and a simple green salad.

1. Rub chicken pieces with the Moroccan Flavour Paste to coat on all sides. If time allows, refrigerate the chicken, covered, overnight.

2. In a large, heavy pot or skillet with a lid, heat the oil over medium-high heat. Brown chicken pieces on all sides a few at a time. Remove to a side dish.

3. Lower heat to medium, add onions to the pot, and cook until translucent, 5–7 minutes. Add garlic and cook a minute more.

4. Stir in tomatoes and stock or water and return chicken to pot. Lower heat, cover, and simmer until chicken is tender. Test breasts after about 15 minutes; legs and thighs may take 10 minutes or so longer. As chicken is done, lift out and set aside on a warm platter.

5. Return pot to high heat and bring the sauce to a boil, scraping up any good bits stuck to the bottom. Simmer for a few minutes to reduce the sauce, then skim off any excess fat. Toss in the olives. Taste sauce and adjust flavour with a pinch or two of salt and the lemon juice.

6. Pour sauce over the chicken. Garnish with the coriander or parsley and lemon slices, and serve hot on Lemon Couscous.

Serves 4–6.

Chicken & Black-Eyed Peas

12–16	**chicken legs and thighs,** *skin removed*	
	salt and freshly ground black pepper	
2 tbsp	**olive oil**	30 ml
1–2 tsp	**cumin seed**	5–10 ml
2	**large onions,** *chopped*	
4 cloves	**garlic,** *finely chopped*	
1	**green pepper,** *chopped*	
2–3	**fresh jalapeño peppers,** *chopped*	
1 can	**plum tomatoes,** *drained (reserve juice) and chopped* (28 oz/796 ml)	
1 can	**tomato paste** (5½ oz/156 ml)	
1	**bay leaf**	
1 tsp each	**basil and oregano**	5 ml
¼ cup	**parsley,** *chopped*	60 ml
2 cans	**black-eyed peas** (19 oz/540 ml cans), *rinsed and drained* **or**	
4 cups	**cooked black-eyed peas** *(see p. 156)*	1 L
1 cup	**mild Cheddar cheese,** *grated*	250 ml

This hearty main course of chicken simmered in a rich sauce, then baked with black-eyed peas, has a comforting warmth on a cool day.

1. Season chicken pieces with salt and pepper. Heat oil in a large, heavy skillet. Add 1 tsp (5 ml) cumin seed and heat until it pops. Brown chicken on all sides, in batches if necessary. (Heat another teaspoon of cumin seed in the oil before adding the second batch of chicken.) Remove and set aside.

2. In the same pan, brown the onions. Add garlic, green pepper, and jalapeños, and cook for a few minutes.

3. Transfer to a large pot and stir in chopped tomatoes and reserved juice, tomato paste, herbs, and seasonings. Bring sauce to a boil, then lower heat and return chicken pieces to the sauce; cover the pot, and leave to simmer until chicken is almost tender – about 30 minutes. Season to taste.

4. Remove the chicken from the sauce; toss the black-eyed peas with half the sauce and spread in two 8" x 8" (2-L) ovenproof casseroles. Arrange the chicken pieces on top of the peas and cover with the rest of the sauce. Cover the dishes with foil and set in a 350°F (180°C) oven. After about 20 minutes, remove foil and sprinkle with Cheddar cheese. Continue baking, uncovered, until cheese has melted and browned slightly (about 15 minutes longer).

Serves 6–8.

TIP:
• This dish can be assembled (without the cheese) and then frozen before baking. When ready to serve, defrost in refrigerator, then bake for about 30 minutes before topping with cheese and proceeding as above.

(The Chicken & Black-Eyed Peas is shown in the photo opposite p. 186.)

Chicken & Sausage Jambalaya

2 tbsp	vegetable oil	30 ml
1 cup	smoked ham, *diced*	250 ml
½ cup	spicy smoked sausage, *diced*	125 ml
2 cups	boneless chicken breast, *diced*	500 ml
2	large onions, *finely chopped*	
4 stalks	celery, *chopped*	
1	green pepper, *chopped*	
4 cloves	garlic, *finely chopped*	
2	bay leaves	
1 tsp	each oregano, cayenne, freshly ground black pepper, and salt	5 ml
½ tsp	thyme	2 ml
1 tsp	filé *(optional)*	5 ml
2 cups	long-grain converted rice	500 ml
1 cup	tomatoes *(fresh or canned), chopped*	250 ml
3 cups	chicken stock	750 ml

A great one-pot dish originating in Louisiana kitchens. While sometimes difficult to find, filé (powdered sassafras leaves, sold in jars) is often used in Cajun cuisine to flavour and thicken soups and stews. The dish will be just fine, however, if you leave it out.

1. Heat oil in a large heavy pot, add ham and sausage, and brown lightly. Lift out and set aside.

2. Add chicken pieces and brown, then remove and set aside.

3. Add half the onions, celery, and pepper to the pot, cooking until soft and well browned. Toss in the rest of the vegetables and the garlic, and cook over moderate heat until softened.

4. Return meats to pot with all the seasonings and cook for 5 minutes. Add rice and stir for a few minutes, then add tomatoes and stock. Bring mixture to a boil, lower heat, cover pot, and leave to cook gently for 20–25 minutes more until liquid is absorbed and rice is tender yet still has texture. Toss gently, remove from heat, cover, and leave to rest for 5 minutes. Serve hot.

Serves 6.

TIPS:

• If you want to prepare part of the jambalaya ahead, cook the meats and vegetables as described above and add the tomatoes and stock, but do not add the rice. Refrigerate or freeze. When you are ready to serve, bring the mixture to a boil, add rice, and cook for 20–25 minutes as described above.

• Jambalaya often includes seafood, such as shrimp and/or fresh oysters; add them during the last 5 minutes of cooking. Add some hot sauce if you like things spicier.

Both Jambalaya and Chicken & Black-Eyed Peas (p.185) are complete meals in a dish. Just add a green salad and some crusty bread.

Picadillo

2 tbsp	**vegetable oil**	30 ml
2	**onions,** *chopped*	
2 cloves	**garlic,** *minced*	
1	**green pepper,** *seeded and chopped*	
2 tbsp	**jalapeño peppers,** *chopped (or to taste)*	30 ml
1½ lbs	**ground beef**	750 g
3	**tomatoes** *(fresh or canned), peeled and chopped*	
1 tbsp	**tomato paste**	15 ml
½ cup	**water** *or* **stock**	125 ml
1 tsp	**dried oregano**	5 ml
	salt and freshly ground black pepper	
½ cup	**raisins** *(optional)*	125 ml
½ cup	**slivered almonds** *(optional)*	125 ml
¼ cup	**pimento-stuffed green olives,** *sliced (optional)*	60 ml

*P*icadillo, which means "minced meat" in Spanish, is a wonderful spicy mixture of Latin American origins that is traditionally served over rice. This dish is very popular with the younger set, and when turned into a taco feast, it's a great way to feed a teenage group of indeterminate number and unpredictable (though usually huge) appetite. Set out the picadillo accompanied by baskets of warm taco shells, lots of toppings – shredded lettuce, sliced avocado, grated Monterey Jack or Cheddar cheese, chopped fresh tomato and onion, sour cream, and salsa – and piles of napkins. The picadillo is also good piled in a warm, crusty kaiser roll to make a very messy (and very tasty) sandwich.

1. In a large, heavy pan, heat oil and sauté onion and garlic until soft. Add sweet and hot peppers and cook briefly.

2. Add ground beef and brown. Stir in tomatoes, tomato paste, water or stock, oregano, and a dash of salt and pepper.

3. Simmer about 20 minutes. Stir in raisins, almonds, and olives (if using) and heat through. Taste and adjust seasoning.

Serves 4.

TIPS:

• The picadillo can be made ahead. Cool, cover, and refrigerate or freeze until needed.

• The recipe multiplies easily to feed a gang.

• If there are vegetarians in the group, make up a batch of Spicy Black Bean Dip (p. 46) for them to use as the base of their tacos instead of the picadillo.

Curried Vegetables
& Couscous

2 tbsp	olive oil	30 ml
1	large onion, *chopped*	
2 cloves	garlic, *minced*	
1 tsp	curry powder	5 ml
1 tsp	ground cumin	5 ml
½ tsp	ground coriander	2 ml
½ tsp	ground ginger	2 ml
¼ tsp	cayenne	1 ml
2	carrots, *quartered lengthwise and chopped*	
½	red pepper, *seeded and chopped*	
1	zucchini, *halved and sliced*	
1	yellow summer squash, *halved and sliced*	
1 cup	green beans, *trimmed and cut in 2" (5-cm) lengths*	250 ml
	salt and freshly ground black pepper	
1½ cups	vegetable stock	375 ml
½ cup	couscous	125 ml

*U*se whatever vegetables you have on hand in this fragrant and satisfying dish. It's open to many variations. Serve with warm pitas or flatbread.

1. Heat oil in a large, heavy frying pan or flameproof casserole. Add onion and garlic and cook over medium heat, stirring often, for about 5 minutes.

2. Stir in spices and vegetables, season lightly, and cook over medium heat for 2–3 minutes, stirring constantly until the vegetables are coated in the spicy onion mixture.

3. Add stock, bring to a boil, lower heat, cover, and simmer until vegetables are tender, about 10 minutes. Stir in couscous, cover, and cook for about 5 minutes longer. Adjust seasoning. Serve hot.

Serves 4.

VARIATIONS:

• Other vegetables that work well in this recipe include peas, mushrooms, eggplant, and cauliflower. Whatever combination you choose, you should have a total of 4 cups (1 L) of chopped vegetables. So that everything cooks in the same amount of time, harder vegetables should be cut into smaller chunks; delicate ones, larger.

• You could include boneless chicken pieces or cubed pork tenderloin, if you like. Brown the meat lightly before you stir in the spices and vegetables.

• This dish is very good topped with some crumbled feta cheese and a sprinkling of chopped fresh coriander or parsley.

Crispy Corn Drumsticks

1 clove	garlic	
½ cup	milk	125 ml
12	chicken drumsticks	
⅓ cup	cornmeal	75 ml
¼ cup	flour	60 ml
1 tbsp	ground cumin	15 ml
1 tsp	paprika	5 ml
1 tsp	dried oregano	5 ml
1 tsp	salt	5 ml
1 tsp	freshly ground black pepper	5 ml
½–1 tsp	cayenne	2–5 ml
2 tbsp	vegetable oil	30 ml

TIPS:

• The legs can be cooked the day before serving and refrigerated.

• If you have the time, leave the chicken to marinate in the garlic-flavoured milk overnight in the refrigerator. The milk helps make the chicken moist.

Delicious cold or hot, these mildly seasoned chicken legs are great for a quick supper or a picnic. They're easy to eat out of your hand, and kid-friendly. (Use the lesser quantity of cayenne if you're making them for kids.) Serve with Cool Green Dip (p. 78), Mango Salsa (p. 94), or your favourite blue cheese dressing.

1. Crush garlic into the milk. Pour the garlic-flavoured milk over the legs and allow them to marinate for at least 20 minutes in the refrigerator.

2. In a large bowl or plastic bag, combine cornmeal, flour, and spices. Toss legs in cornmeal mixture. Shake off excess.

3. Coat a large, shallow baking pan with the oil. Arrange legs in a single layer in the pan. Set on rack in the upper third of a preheated 400°F (200°C) oven. Roast for 30 minutes, turn pieces, and continue to cook until the coating is crispy and nicely browned and the meat is cooked through, 10–15 minutes longer. Serve legs hot, or place on a rack to cool, then wrap well in foil or plastic, or store in an airtight container. Refrigerate until serving.

Serves 6.

QUICK TRICK:

Crispy Corn Chicken Fingers: A surefire hit with the kids. Pound 2 boneless chicken breasts lightly to flatten and cut into strips (1 breast makes 8 fingers). Marinate strips in garlic-flavoured milk, as above. Combine cornmeal, flour, oregano, salt, and pepper as for drumsticks. Replace other spices with ¼ cup (60 ml) grated Parmesan cheese. Roll the chicken strips in the mixture one at a time. Place in a single layer in a well-oiled roasting pan. Cook for 10 minutes in a preheated 400°F (200°C) oven, then turn and cook 5 minutes longer. Check for doneness, cooking an additional few minutes if necessary. Serve hot with the kids' favourite sauce for dunking. Serves 4.

Both Crispy Corn Drumsticks and Corn & Lentil Salad with spicy sausage (p. 173) make great picnic fare.

Greek-Style Chicken

2 tbsp	olive oil	30 ml
3 lbs	bone-in chicken pieces	1.5 kg
	salt and freshly ground black pepper	
1 tsp	dried oregano	5 ml
2 cups	Roasted Plum Tomato Sauce (p. 199) *or* **other good-quality chunky tomato sauce**	500 ml
½ cup	kalamata olives	125 ml
1 cup	feta cheese, *crumbled*	250 ml

I first tried a version of this dish at a friend's house, where it was prepared by her mother in the traditional Greek fashion. The chicken is wonderfully crispy, yet remains moist because it's roasted surrounded by tomato sauce. Serve it with Garlic Roast Potatoes (p. 177) scented with rosemary.

1. Heat oil in a heavy skillet. Add chicken pieces, a few at a time, and brown well on all sides (about 5 minutes per batch).

2. Place browned chicken pieces in a single layer in a shallow roasting pan. Season with salt and pepper, sprinkle with oregano, and surround with tomato sauce and olives.

3. Set pan in a preheated 375°F (190°C) oven. After 10 minutes, sprinkle with crumbled feta cheese. Continue roasting for 15 minutes more, or until chicken is cooked. (Pierce the thighs with the tip of a sharp knife to see if the juices run clear.)

Serves 4.

TIP:

• To make ahead, prepare chicken through Step 2 and bake for about 10 minutes. Remove from oven, cover with foil, and refrigerate. At serving time, set in preheated 375°F (190°C) oven. Cook for 20 minutes, remove foil, scatter feta cheese on top, and continue baking until chicken is cooked through, about another 10–15 minutes.

Greek-Style Chicken: Crispy outside, moist and tender inside, with tangy feta cheese and kalamata olives.

Black Bean & Vegetable Chili

3 tbsp	**vegetable oil**	45 ml
1	**large onion,** *chopped*	
4 cloves	**garlic,** *finely chopped*	
4 cups	**vegetables** *(red and yellow peppers, carrots, celery, potatoes, pumpkin, butternut squash, etc.), cut into cubes*	1 L
1–2	**jalapeño peppers,** *seeded and chopped*	
1 tbsp	**dried oregano**	15 ml
1 tbsp	**ground cumin**	15 ml
½–1 tsp	**cayenne**	2–5 ml
1–2 tbsp	**chili powder**	15–30 ml
	salt and freshly ground black pepper	
1 can	**plum tomatoes** *chopped, with juice (28 oz/796 ml)*	
½ cup	**bulgur** *(optional)*	125 ml
2 cans	**black beans,** *drained and rinsed (19 oz/540 ml cans)* **or**	
4 cups	**cooked black beans** *(cooking instructions on p. 156; reserve cooking liquid)*	1 L

*S*erve this spicy chili with warm tortillas or corn bread (p. 335) and bowls of grated cheese, additional chopped hot peppers, sour cream, chopped green onions, and chopped coriander.

1. Heat oil over medium heat in a large, heavy pot. Add onion and cook for 5 minutes. Stir in garlic, vegetables, and spices, and toss over medium heat for 5 more minutes.

2. Add tomatoes and their juice, and bulgur (if using), and gently simmer, covered, for 30 minutes.

3. Add beans and about 1 cup (250 ml) of water (or cooking liquid, if you prepared your own beans). Continue simmering, uncovered, until chili is nicely thickened and well flavoured, about 30 minutes longer.

Serves 6.

TIPS:

• Bulgur (available in bulk-food stores and some supermarkets) makes this a more complete main dish, but the chili is still delicious without it.

• If you've got some dry sherry on hand, add a splash or two when you add the beans.

Tex-Mex Chili

10	dried ancho chiles	
4	dried chipotle chiles	
5 tbsp	vegetable oil	75 ml
4	medium onions, *chopped*	
2 tbsp	garlic, *finely chopped*	30 ml
3 lbs	stewing beef, *finely chopped*	1.5 kg
1 tbsp	each ground cumin and paprika	15 ml
1 tsp	each dried oregano and basil	5 ml
2 cups	plum tomatoes *(fresh or canned), peeled, seeded, and chopped*	500 ml
2–4 cups	beef stock or **water**	500 ml–1 L
	salt and freshly ground black pepper	
2–4	jalapeño peppers, *(fresh or canned), seeded and chopped*	
3 cups	cooked red kidney beans *or* pinto beans, *drained*	750 ml

$\mathcal{N}$o two chili devotees agree on what makes a great chili. This version gets its rich taste from a purée of dried chiles rather than chili powder. And, like true Texas-style chili, it starts with chunks of beef, not ground beef. True Texas chili does not contain beans, however, so if you want to be a purist, leave them out.

1. Remove stems and seeds from dried chiles. Cover with boiling water and let stand for 30 minutes. Drain, reserving liquid, and purée with 1 tbsp (15 ml) of the oil and enough of the reserved soaking liquid so that the mixture has about the same consistency as tomato paste. Set the purée aside.

2. In a heavy skillet, heat 2 tbsp (30 ml) of the oil over medium heat. Add onions and cook until soft. Stir in garlic and cook for a few minutes.

3. In a large, heavy pot, heat the remaining oil. Add the chopped beef and brown lightly (in several batches if necessary). Add the onions and garlic, the chile purée, and the spices, and toss briefly over the heat. Stir in the tomatoes and stock, and season to taste. Bring to a boil, lower heat, and simmer, partially covered, for 1^1/$_2$–2 hours, stirring occasionally.

4. Before serving, taste and adjust seasoning; stir in jalapeños and beans, and heat through.

Serves 6–8.

VARIATION:

• **Everyday Chili:** For a faster chili, substitute 1–2 tbsp (15–30 ml) good-quality chili powder for the chile purée. Add to the pan at the end of Step 2. Use ground beef instead of stewing beef, skimming away any excess fat after browning.

East Indian Curry in a Hurry

1	**medium onion**	
2" piece	**fresh ginger,** *peeled and roughly chopped*	5 cm
4–6 cloves	**garlic,** *finely chopped*	
2 tbsp	**vegetable oil**	30 ml
2–3 tsp	**curry powder**	10–15 ml
½ tsp	**cayenne** *(optional)*	2 ml
1½ lbs	**ground beef** *or* **ground lamb**	750 g
2	**tomatoes,** *chopped,* or	
1 cup	**canned tomatoes,** *drained and chopped*	250 ml
	salt	
¼ cup	**yogurt**	60 ml
1 cup	**fresh** *or* **frozen peas**	250 ml

Garnish

1 tsp	**cumin seeds,** *toasted*	5 ml
1	**hot green pepper,** *seeded and chopped*	
1 tbsp	**fresh coriander,** *chopped (optional)*	15 ml

In authentic curry recipes, the sauce includes a long list of spices, which traditional cooks meticulously roast and grind togther. This recipe simplifies and shortens the process by using prepared curry powder. An added bonus is that curries are meant to be prepared ahead – they taste better after they have been sitting in the refrigerator for a day. This recipe also freezes well. Serve with rice, chutney, raita (Quick Trick, p. 105), and pita or Indian breads.

1. Combine onion, ginger, and garlic in a blender or food processor and process briefly to make a paste. (Or chop finely by hand.)

2. Heat oil in a large skillet and stir-fry onion mixture quickly until browned. Sprinkle with curry powder and cayenne, then add meat, breaking up the lumps; cook for a few minutes until nicely browned. Skim off fat.

3. Stir in tomatoes, salt lightly, and simmer for about 20 minutes. Stir in yogurt. If the mixture seems dry, add a little water (or stock) as it simmers.

4. Add peas and cook for about 5 minutes longer. Serve over rice, garnished with cumin, hot pepper, and coriander (if using).

Serves 4.

VARIATIONS:

• **Vegetarian Curry in a Hurry: Replace meat with 4 cups (1 L) of cubed vegetables: butternut squash, carrots, celery, peppers, and eggplant.**

• **Replace the ground meat with cubed beef or lamb: First brown the meat in the oil. Set aside, then proceed with the recipe , returning meat to pan with the curry powder and adding about 1 cup (250 ml) stock or water. Increase simmering time to about 1½ hours.**

Curries make excellent food for a casual party. Shown here: East Indian Curry in a Hurry on rice, with cooling cucumber-yogurt raita and onion relish.

Quick Thai Vegetable Curry

2 tbsp	vegetable oil	30 ml
6 cups	vegetables *(eggplant, zucchini,* *green beans, onions,* *peppers, asparagus, etc.),* *cut in even chunks*	1.5 L
1–2 tbsp	green curry paste *(see Tips,* *p. 121)*	15–30 ml
1 can	coconut milk *(14 oz/400 ml)*	
2 tbsp	fish sauce *(optional)*	30 ml
1 tsp	dried basil	5 ml
	salt and freshly ground black pepper	
squeeze	fresh lime juice	
2 tbsp	fresh coriander, *finely chopped*	30 ml

Fast and flexible, this curry makes an excellent vegetarian main dish or a side dish for grilled meat, tofu, or seafood. (Try it with skewers of grilled shrimp or scallops in Lemon Grass Marinade, p. 119.) Vary the vegetables to take advantage of what you've got on hand and what's in season, and serve the curry with rice.

1. Heat oil in a large, heavy casserole. Add vegetables and toss over medium-high heat for 5 minutes.

2. Add green curry paste and stir-fry all together for a few minutes.

3. Stir in coconut milk, fish sauce, and basil. Lower heat and simmer until vegetables are tender – about 20 minutes.

4. Taste and adjust seasoning, adding fresh lime juice and coriander. Serve hot over rice.

Serves 4.

TIP:

• For a non-vegetarian main dish, you can add slivers of chicken breast, pork tenderloin, or sirloin steak to the curry; stir-fry them in the oil and set aside before cooking the vegetables. Return them to the pot at end of Step 3.

Shrimp with Feta
& Roasted Plum Tomato Sauce

4 cups	Roasted Plum Tomato Sauce *or* **other good tomato sauce**	1 L
1 cup	dry white wine	250 ml
1 lb	large raw shrimp, *peeled and deveined*	500 g
4 oz	feta cheese, *crumbled*	125 g
	salt and freshly ground black pepper	
	fresh parsley, *chopped*	

Roasted Plum Tomato Sauce

4½ lbs	fresh ripe plum tomatoes	2.5 kg
¼ cup	olive oil	60 ml
1	large onion, *thinly sliced*	
2 cloves	garlic, *slivered*	
1 tbsp	fresh thyme sprigs *or*	15 ml
2 tsp	dried thyme *or* **oregano**	10 ml
	salt and freshly ground black pepper	

A simplified version of a favourite Greek dish. The charred tomato skins give the Roasted Plum Tomato Sauce a rich smoky sweetness – though you can use any homemade or good-quality storebought tomato sauce. Serve over Saffron Rice Pilaf (p. 169) with lots of fresh parsley.

1. To make the sauce: Toss tomatoes with half the oil. Set on a very hot grill or under the broiler and cook, turning frequently, until the skins are blistered and charred, about 5 minutes. Purée in the food processor.

2. Heat the remaining oil in a large skillet. Add onion, garlic, and herbs and cook gently until soft. Add the puréed tomatoes and cook, stirring frequently, until sauce is thickened, about 5–10 minutes. Season to taste.

3. Transfer 4 cups (1 L) of the sauce to a large pot. Add the wine and simmer for a few minutes.

4. Add shrimp and simmer 5 minutes, then add crumbled feta and simmer for a few minutes more.

5. Taste and adjust seasoning. Sprinkle with parsley.

Serves 4.

TIP:
• The sauce can be made ahead and frozen.

Fettuccine with
Saffron Cream Sauce

1 tbsp	olive oil	15 ml
1	shallot, *finely chopped*	
2 tbsp	dry white wine	30 ml
1 tbsp	garlic, *minced*	15 ml
1 tbsp	tomato paste	15 ml
1 cup	fish *or* chicken stock	250 ml
½ tsp	saffron	2 ml
1 cup	35% cream	250 ml
pinch	cayenne	
1 tsp	salt *(or to taste)*	5 ml
¾ lb	fettuccine *or* other long, thin pasta, *cooked according to package directions*	375 g
1	tomato, *seeded and diced*	
2 tbsp	fresh flat-leaf parsley, *chopped*	30 ml

*S*erve this pasta as a side dish with seafood. It's amazingly good with grilled or sautéed scallops or shrimp, any simply grilled or sautéed fish, or grilled mixed seafood brochettes.

1. In a small saucepan, heat olive oil over medium-high heat and sauté shallot until softened but not browned, about 3–4 minutes. Add wine and simmer for a minute or two, until liquid is reduced to a glaze. Stir in garlic and tomato paste.

2. Add stock and saffron. Simmer for 10–15 minutes.

3. Add cream and simmer for 15–20 minutes, until sauce is reduced to a generous cup. Season with cayenne and salt.

4. In a warm bowl, toss freshly cooked fettuccine with sauce. Garnish with tomato and parsley.

Serves 4.

TIP:

• The sauce can be prepared a few hours ahead and very gently reheated before tossing with the pasta.

Try the Saffron Cream Sauce on spinach fettuccine to accompany fresh scallops that have been quickly sautéed in a little oil or butter.

Shortcut Seafood Curry

1½–2 lbs	**mixed seafood**	750 g–1 kg
	(*shrimp, scallops, and firm-fleshed fish such as grouper, monkfish, or halibut*)	
1 tsp	**each garlic and fresh ginger root,** *chopped*	5 ml
1	**small hot green pepper,** *seeded and chopped*	
½	**lemon,** *grated zest and juice*	
1 tsp	**ground cumin**	5 ml
	freshly ground black pepper	
4 tbsp	**vegetable oil**	60 ml
1	**medium onion,** *finely chopped*	
1 cup	**tomatoes** (*fresh or canned*), *chopped*	250 ml
1 cup	**coconut milk**	250 ml
	salt	
¼ cup	**fresh coriander** *or* **parsley,** *chopped*	60 ml

TIP:

• Steps 1–3 can be completed early in the day. Refrigerate the seafood and sauce in separate containers until it's time to complete the dish.

*C*oconut milk – available in cans in many supermarkets – gives this curry its richness and Indonesian/Thai flavour. This recipe calls for lemon zest and juice rather than the authentic but harder-to-find lemon grass. The preparation can be done in stages and the quantities doubled to make an excellent party dish. Serve over steamed basmati or Fragrant Coconut Rice (p. 172).

1. Cut fish into 1½" (4-cm) cubes. (Leave shrimp and scallops whole.) Toss seafood with garlic, ginger, hot pepper, lemon juice and zest, cumin, and black pepper. Set aside in the refrigerator for a few hours.

2. In a large frying pan, heat 2 tbsp (30 ml) of the oil, and cook the onion until golden. Add tomatoes. Cook, stirring occasionally, for 10 minutes.

3. Reduce heat to low and gently stir in coconut milk. (Do not overheat, as the coconut milk will curdle.) Simmer about 5 minutes to form a creamy sauce. Add salt to taste.

4. Just before you're ready to serve, heat remaining oil in a clean frying pan, add seafood mixture, and toss over medium heat for about 3–5 minutes, until seafood is almost cooked through. (It is ready when the flesh has barely turned from translucent to opaque.)

5. Combine seafood with sauce and gently heat, about 5 minutes. Season to taste. Serve over rice, garnished with chopped coriander or parsley.

Serves 4.

Sesame Soba Noodles

1 oz	**dried mushrooms** *(such as oyster, shiitake, porcini, or portobello)*	28 g
1 tbsp	**olive oil**	15 ml
1 tbsp	**garlic,** *minced*	15 ml
2 tbsp	**fresh ginger root,** *grated*	30 ml
3	**leeks,** *white part only, cut in fine slivers*	
1 tbsp	**soy sauce**	15 ml
¼ cup	**rice vinegar**	60 ml
2 tbsp	**sesame oil**	30 ml
6–8 oz	**soba noodles,** *cooked according to package directions*	170–250 g
2–3 tbsp	**sesame seeds,** *toasted*	30–45 ml

*S*oba noodles, made from buckwheat with a small amount of gluten-rich wheat flour added, have a nutty taste and are popular in oriental cooking. Serve them to accompany Grilled Oriental Tofu or Steak (p. 73).

1. Place dried mushrooms in 1 cup (250 ml) warm water and set aside to soften, about 30 minutes.

2. In a large frying pan, heat olive oil. Add garlic, ginger, leeks, and drained mushrooms, and cook over medium heat until softened and lightly browned, about 3–4 minutes. Add soy sauce, rice vinegar, and sesame oil.

3. Toss freshly cooked soba noodles with sauce and sprinkle with toasted sesame seeds.

Serves 4.

TIPS:

• Soba noodles are sold in natural-foods stores, specialty stores, and some large supermarkets; look for them in the aisle with other oriental products.

• A package or two of dried mushrooms makes a very handy addition to the cupboard. They're sold in large supermarkets and are usually displayed near the fresh mushrooms. If you like, you can substitute 4 oz (125 g) of sliced fresh mushrooms for the dried ones in this recipe.

Super-Quick Pasta Sauces

TIPS:

• Pasta is always best when served freshly cooked. But if you need to hold it for a short time while people gather at the table or you finish the sauce, keep it in the colander and sprinkle it with some of its cooking water to keep the strands separate.

• If you are combining pasta with sauce, do not rinse it after cooking. Immediately after draining, toss it with sauce in a large warm bowl. Rinse pasta with cold water only if it is being used in a salad.

• Generally, for a main course, allow about 3–4 oz (100–125 g) of pasta per person.

• For tender meatballs, don't fry them – just simmer them in your tomato sauce, where they will soak up the taste of the tomatoes and herbs. (See Variation on p. 100 for a tasty Italian meatball recipe.)

*C*onsider serving a pasta with a simple sauce as a side dish with grilled meats, as well as using it as a main course. These three sauces taste as though you slaved over them for hours, but are extremely fast and easy to prepare. Each recipe makes enough sauce for ³/₄ lb (375 g) of dried pasta.

Red Clam Sauce

Drain a 5 oz (142 g) can of clams, reserving ¹/₄ cup (60 ml) juice. Heat the reserved juice with ¹/₂ cup (125 ml) white wine (optional) and reduce by half. Stir in 2 cups (500 ml) tomato sauce. Warm gently, then add clams, a pinch of thyme, and a dash of hot sauce and simmer for 5 minutes. Toss with hot drained linguine in a warm bowl.

Pimento Pasta

Cook 2 finely chopped cloves of garlic in 2 tbsp (30 ml) hot olive oil until soft. Drain a small jar of pimentos and chop roughly. Add to pan and heat through. Toss with hot, drained pasta in a warm bowl and sprinkle with fresh chopped parsley and freshly ground black pepper.

Black Olive Pasta

Toss hot, drained pasta in a warm bowl with 2 tbsp (30 ml) olive oil, ¹/₄ cup (60 ml) tapenade (black olive paste, sold in jars or make your own, p. 23), and finely chopped fresh parsley. Serve at once.

Clockwise from left: Spaghetti alla Puttanesca (p. 206), Old-Fashioned Mac & Cheese (p. 207), and super-quick Black Olive Pasta.

Spaghetti alla Puttanesca

¼ cup	**olive oil**	60 ml
4 cloves	**garlic,** *finely chopped*	
1 can	**anchovy fillets,** *drained and chopped (2 oz/50 g)*	
1 can	**plum tomatoes,** *drained (reserve juice) and chopped (28 oz/796 ml)*	
pinch	**hot red pepper flakes** *(optional)*	
¼ cup	**capers,** *drained*	60 ml
½ cup	**black olives,** *pitted and chopped*	125 ml
1 lb	**spaghetti**	500 g
	freshly ground black pepper	
	fresh parsley, *chopped*	

This robustly flavoured dish is quickly and easily put together. The story goes that it was named for the puttane, the "ladies of the night," who had little time for shopping or fancy footwork in the kitchen. As its name implies, this dish has earthy "adult" flavours and may not be appreciated by the younger set.

1. Heat oil in a large, heavy pan. Cook garlic and anchovies in oil for a few minutes until softened.

2. Add tomatoes and juice, and the red pepper flakes, if desired. Simmer 10 minutes.

3. Add capers and olives and simmer about 10–15 minutes longer, until sauce is nicely thickened.

4. Cook spaghetti until al dente and drain well. Toss sauce with hot pasta in a warm bowl. Taste, adjust seasoning, sprinkle with parsley, and serve at once.

Serves 4.

TIPS:

• A large pot is essential for preparing good pasta. In a small pot, the water can't circulate around the pasta, which consequently cooks unevenly and sticks together. Each 4 oz (125 g) of pasta requires 1 qt (1 L) of boiling water and at least ¼ tsp (1 ml) of salt.

• With good-quality pasta, it's not necessary to add oil to the water to keep the pasta from sticking.

• If anchovies straight from the can have too dominant a flavour for your taste, simply rinse them under cold water and pat dry before using.

(Spaghetti alla Puttanesca is shown in the photo opposite p. 204.)

Old-Fashioned Mac & Cheese

1½–2 cups	**cheese,** *grated* (see Tips, below)	375–500 ml
¼ cup	**Parmesan cheese,** *grated*	60 ml
1½ tbsp	**flour**	20 ml
¼ cup + 1 tbsp	**butter**	60 ml + 15 ml
1 cup	**milk** *or* **cream**	250 ml
pinch	**grated nutmeg**	
	salt and freshly ground black pepper	
1 lb	**penne** *(or other favourite pasta shape)*	500 g
1 cup	**dry breadcrumbs**	250 ml
	additional grated cheese *(optional, for topping)*	

𝒯his crispy-topped version of the old family favourite is an easy substitute when you've run out of the standby packaged version – and I guarantee the family will like it better.

1. Toss the cheese together with the flour. Set aside.

2. In a large, heavy pan heat ¼ cup (60 ml) butter and milk or cream. Sprinkle in cheese, a small handful at a time, adding the softer cheese just at the end. Stir mixture continuously over gentle heat until it forms a smooth sauce between each addition of cheese. Add nutmeg and season to taste.

3. Meanwhile, cook the pasta in a large quantity of boiling, salted water. Drain thoroughly and combine with the cheese sauce.

4. Transfer the pasta and cheese sauce to a 9" x 12" (3 L) buttered casserole. Melt the remaining butter, toss the breadcrumbs in it, and season to taste. Sprinkle the casserole with the breadcrumbs and a little more grated cheese if you like. Set under the broiler for a few minutes until topping is brown and crispy.

Serves 4.

TIP:

• The breadcrumb mixture – perhaps with a little chopped parsley – also makes a tasty, crunchy topping for stuffed vegetables and gratin dishes.

TIPS:

• You can use up odds and ends of various cheeses, as long as the flavours blend. Finely grate hard cheeses such as Parmesan and aged Cheddar, and add them first. Softer cheeses – fontina, medium Cheddar, mozzarella – can be roughly grated or cut into small pieces.

• When making any cheese sauce, use a low temperature – too high a heat and your sauce will become grainy.

(Old-Fashioned Mac & Cheese is shown in the photo opposite p. 204.)

Fusilli with

Roasted Red Pepper Sauce

2	red peppers	
¼ cup	extra-virgin olive oil	60 ml
3 cloves	garlic, *minced*	
¼ cup	butter	60 ml
	salt and freshly ground black pepper	
2 tbsp	balsamic vinegar	30 ml
¾ lb	fusilli *(or other favourite pasta shape), cooked according to package directions*	375 g
¼ cup	black olives *(such as kalamata or oil-cured), pits removed*	60 ml
	shavings of Parmesan cheese	

TIPS:

• The sauce can be prepared a few hours ahead and very gently reheated before tossing with the pasta.

• For an appetizing presentation, arrange slices of grilled chicken breasts on top of or next to the pasta.

This pasta is delicious served with grilled or sautéed chicken breasts, or grilled or roasted vegetables. It can also be served on its own for lunch with a salad.

1. Roast red peppers on the grill or under the broiler for 10–15 minutes, or until skin is blackened. Put in a bowl, cover with plastic wrap, and let sit for 15 minutes or until cool enough to handle. Peel and seed peppers, reserving juices. Purée one pepper with the reserved juice, and cut the other in fine slices.

2. Heat olive oil in a small saucepan over medium-high heat. Add garlic and cook until fragrant but not browned, about 2 minutes. Add butter and salt and pepper. Remove from heat. Combine sliced and puréed peppers with garlic oil. Stir in balsamic vinegar.

3. In a warm bowl, toss freshly cooked fusilli with the sauce. Top with the olives and Parmesan shavings.

Serves 4.

VARIATION:

• Serve the red pepper sauce or a robust tomato or meat sauce on top of strands of crunchy spaghetti squash instead of pasta. Pierce the squash in several places and bake whole in a 375°F (190°C) oven until soft – about an hour. Cut in half, remove the seeds and, using a fork, gently separate and lift out the strands of flesh. Toss in a large bowl with a little olive oil, salt, pepper, parsley, and Parmesan cheese, and top with sauce. A 2–2½-lb (1-kg) spaghetti squash serves 4–6.

For dinner, serve the Fusilli with Roasted Red Pepper Sauce with slices of grilled chicken – or grilled vegetables if you want a meatless meal.

Pasta with Basil Pesto

Freezer Basil Pesto

1 bunch	**large-leaf basil,** *leaves only, washed well (about 4 cups/1 L, packed)*	
3 cloves	**garlic,** *coarsely chopped*	
½ cup	**extra-virgin olive oil**	125 ml
½ tsp	**salt**	2 ml
	freshly ground black pepper	

Pasta

¾ lb	**linguini** *or* **other pasta,** *cooked according to package directions*	375 g
2 tsp	**pine nuts,** *very finely chopped*	10 ml
3–4 tbsp	**Parmesan** *or* **pecorino Romano cheese,** *grated*	45–60 ml

TIP:

• If you like a lighter, more saucy pesto, toss the warm pasta with another tablespoon of olive oil, butter, or pasta-cooking water.

A taste of summer is at your fingertips all year long with a supply of basil pesto in your freezer. Besides serving the pesto as a pasta sauce, you can use it as a base for pizza or as a sandwich spread, or stir it into vegetable soup (see Summer Minestrone, p. 218). Since this version is meant to be frozen, it does not contain pine nuts and cheese. Add them fresh at serving time for the best taste.

1. Combine the basil and garlic in a food processor, scraping down the sides of the bowl. Pulse until quite finely chopped. (Or chop vigorously by hand.)

2. Add the olive oil, salt, and pepper, and process again until well combined. Don't make the mixture too smooth – you want to keep some texture.

3. Spoon the pesto into small containers or an ice cube tray, using about 1 tbsp (15 ml) pesto per cube, and freeze. (Frozen cubes can be popped out of the tray and stored in a freezer bag.) Makes about 20 cubes.

4. When ready to serve, cook linguini or other pasta according to package directions. Defrost 3–4 cubes of pesto and stir in pine nuts and cheese. Drain pasta, toss with sauce in a warm bowl, and serve.

Serves 4.

TIP:

• Serve the Pasta with Basil Pesto with grilled chicken or grilled mildly spiced Italian sausage. Or top with grilled mixed vegetables and crumbled feta cheese.

Beef Braised in Beer
over Egg Noodles

3–4 tbsp	vegetable oil	45–60 ml
3 lbs	lean stewing beef, *trimmed and cut into cubes*	1.5 kg
½ lb	small mushrooms, *cleaned and trimmed*	250 g
	salt and freshly ground black pepper	
6	medium onions, *sliced*	
4 cloves	garlic, *minced*	
3 tbsp	flour	45 ml
2 cups	beef stock *or* beef bouillon	500 ml
2 cups	dark ale	500 ml
1 tbsp	brown sugar	15 ml
1 tbsp	red wine vinegar	15 ml
1 tsp	dried thyme	5 ml
2	bay leaves	
1 lb	carrots, *quartered lengthwise and cut into pieces*	500 g
1¼ lbs	egg noodles	625 g

This stew is wonderful served over broad egg noodles, which soak up the delicious gravy. Make it a day ahead to allow the flavour to develop; return it to a simmer and cook the noodles just before serving.

1. Heat 2 tbsp (30 ml) oil in a large, heavy pot. Pat beef cubes dry and brown well, in batches. As the meat browns, remove it to a side dish.

2. In the same pot, adding a little more oil if needed, brown mushrooms lightly. Season and set aside. Add onions to pot and lightly brown. Stir in garlic and cook for a few minutes.

3. Return meat to pot, sprinkle with flour, season lightly, and toss over high heat for a couple of minutes. Stir in stock, ale, brown sugar, vinegar, and herbs. Gently bring to a boil, stirring constantly. Lower the heat and cover.

4. Simmer over very low heat or braise in a 325°F (170°C) oven until the meat is tender, about 2 hours. After 1 hour, add carrots. Stir in mushrooms when meat is tender. Taste and adjust seasoning.

5. When ready to serve, cook noodles according to package directions. Spoon stew over noodles.

Serves 6–8.

VARIATION:

• Instead of serving the stew over noodles, top with Buttermilk Biscuits (p. 257). Make the biscuit dough, omitting the ham. Gently reheat the stew and turn it into a shallow ovenproof casserole. Drop mounds of dough on the hot stew and bake, uncovered, in a 400°F (200°C) oven for about 15 minutes until biscuits are nicely browned.

Provençal Lamb Stew
with White Beans & Rosemary

2 tbsp	olive oil	30 ml
1½ lbs	lean lamb, *cubed*	750 g
1 tbsp	flour	15 ml
	salt and freshly ground black pepper	
2	onions, *chopped*	
2 cloves	garlic, *minced*	
1	carrot, *chopped*	
1 stalk	celery, *chopped*	
1 cup	dry white wine	250 ml
1 cup	chicken stock	250 ml
1 can	plum tomatoes, *drained and chopped* (28 oz/796 ml)	
1 tbsp	fresh rosemary, *chopped* or	15 ml
1 tsp	dried rosemary	5 ml
1	bay leaf	
1 can	white beans, *rinsed and drained* (19 oz/540 ml)	
	fresh parsley, *chopped*	

The flavours and aromas of southern France are captured in this wonderful stew. It's a personal favourite, and tastes even better if made a day ahead of serving. Accompany with mounds of mashed potatoes with roasted garlic (p. 126) and a simple steamed green vegetable.

1. Heat oil in a large, heavy frying pan. Add lamb cubes in small batches and brown well on all sides. Use a slotted spoon to transfer the browned lamb to a flameproof casserole. Sprinkle with flour, season lightly, and toss over high heat for a couple of minutes.

2. Meanwhile, add onions, garlic, carrot, and celery to the frying pan (you may need to add a dash more oil) and cook over medium heat, stirring frequently, until onions are soft, about 5 minutes. Add wine and bring to a boil, scraping up all the good bits on the bottom.

3. Transfer vegetable mixture to the casserole and combine with the lamb. Add stock, tomatoes, and herbs.

4. Bring gently to a boil, lower heat, cover, and simmer until lamb is tender, about an hour, adding beans midway through the cooking time. Serve hot, sprinkled with parsley.

Serves 4.

VARIATION:
• Substitute cubes of lean pork or chunks of chicken for the lamb in this dish.

Hearty Provençal Lamb Stew is the perfect antidote to a cool, rainy day. A boned leg of lamb works well in this dish.

Braised Pork Tenderloin Slices
in Tomato Rosemary Cream Sauce

2	pork tenderloins, *approx. ¾ lb/375 g each*	
¼ cup	flour	60 ml
	salt and freshly ground black pepper	
1 tsp	paprika	5 ml
2 tbsp	olive oil	30 ml
½ cup	red wine *or* chicken stock	125 ml
1 clove	garlic, *minced*	
2	fresh rosemary sprigs or	
1 tsp	dried rosemary	5 ml
1½ cups	good-quality tomato sauce *(see Tips, below)*	375 ml
¼ cup	35% cream *or* chicken stock	60 ml

TIPS:

• The Roasted Plum Tomato Sauce on p. 199 gives a wonderful taste to this dish.

• The recipe can be prepared through Step 5 a day or two ahead. Reheat gently, then stir in cream or stock.

This richly flavoured make-ahead dish is elegant enough to serve for a special dinner. Accompany with Saffron Rice Pilaf (p. 169), roasted potatoes, or egg noodles; and grilled mixed peppers, roasted fennel, or steamed fresh green beans.

1. Cut the pork tenderloins on the diagonal into ½" (1-cm) slices and pound to flatten.

2. Season flour with salt, pepper, and paprika, and dip each pork slice into the mixture, shaking off the excess.

3. In a large, heavy skillet, heat olive oil over medium-high heat. Add pork slices a few at a time and brown quickly on both sides. Remove and set aside.

4. Add wine or stock to the pan with garlic and rosemary and bring to a boil, scraping up the browned bits on the bottom of the pan.

5. Stir in the tomato sauce and simmer for 5 minutes, then return the pork slices to the pan and continue to simmer gently until they are cooked through, about 5 more minutes.

6. Stir in cream or stock. Taste and adjust seasoning.

Serves 4.

Lisa Olsson's Meatballs

2 slices	white bread	
1 cup	beef stock	250 ml
1 lb	ground beef	500 g
1 lb	ground pork	500 g
1	large boiled potato, *peeled and mashed*	
¼ cup	18% cream	60 ml
½ cup	Cheddar cheese, *grated*	125 ml
1½ tsp	baking powder	7 ml
1	large onion, *peeled and grated*	
2	egg yolks	
	salt and freshly ground black pepper	
1 tbsp	each butter and oil	15 ml

Sauce

1 cup	beef stock	250 ml
½ cup	18% cream	125 ml
2 tbsp	lingonberry sauce, grape jelly, *or* cranberry sauce	30 ml

*S*wedish meatballs are such a well-known buffet dish that they're almost a cliché. Don't let that reputation deter you from trying this recipe, which comes from a friend who grew up in Sweden. The sauce is sweetened with berries, the meatballs are light and tender, and the result is deliciously different. Serve over wide egg noodles as a main dish, or by themselves as a party appetizer.

1. Remove crusts from bread and soak slices in stock until soft. Squeeze dry.

2. Combine bread with all the other meatball ingredients except the butter and oil, blending well to form a smooth, light mixture. Form into small balls, about 1" (2.5 cm) in diameter.

3. Heat butter and oil in a large, heavy frying pan. Fry the meatballs, about a dozen at a time, over medium-high heat. Turn them frequently until well browned on all sides, about 7–8 minutes. Keep the cooked meatballs warm while you make the sauce.

4. Pour away the cooking fat from the pan. Add stock and cream, and set the pan over high heat, scraping up all the crispy brown bits stuck to the bottom. Reduce the sauce until slightly thickened, season to taste, and swirl in the lingonberry sauce, grape jelly, or cranberry sauce. Pour sauce over meatballs and serve immediately.

Makes about 60 meatballs.

TIP:
• The meatballs can be made ahead and gently reheated in the sauce.

Mushroom Ragout
over Pasta or Polenta

2–3 tbsp	olive oil	30–45 ml
½ lb	portobello mushroom caps, *thinly sliced*	250 g
1 lb	white mushrooms, *sliced*	500 g
	salt and freshly ground black pepper	
1	medium onion, *finely chopped*	
2 cloves	garlic, *finely chopped*	
1 tsp	fresh rosemary or **tarragon,** *chopped* or	5 ml
½ tsp	dried rosemary or **tarragon**	2 ml
pinch	hot red pepper flakes	
½ cup	vegetable stock	125 ml
1 tbsp	balsamic vinegar	15 ml
¼ cup	fresh parsley, *chopped*	60 ml
	Parmesan cheese, *grated*	

*P*ortobello mushrooms give this versatile (and quick-to-put-together) dish a rich, robust flavour and an almost meaty texture. (You will find it's a popular main course even among confirmed meat-eaters.)

1. Heat 1 tbsp (15 ml) oil in a large, heavy frying pan over medium-high heat. Add half the mushrooms and cook, tossing over the heat until lightly browned and almost tender. Season, scrape into a bowl, and set aside. Repeat with the remaining mushrooms, adding a little more oil to the pan if necessary.

2. Heat another 1 tbsp (15 ml) oil in the pan, add onion, and cook until soft and lightly browned, about 5 minutes. Add garlic, herbs, pepper flakes, and seasoning and cook for 2–3 minutes before stirring in the stock.

3. Return mushrooms and any collected juices to the pan. Stir all together, lower heat, and simmer for a couple of minutes to blend flavours. Taste, adjust seasoning, and add the vinegar. Serve hot over pasta or polenta (see Tip, below) with a garnish of fresh chopped parsley and grated Parmesan.

Serves 4.

TIPS:

• For polenta to serve with stews and sauces, follow the recipe on p. 50 through Step 2, but use 1 part cornmeal to 4 parts water or milk so the polenta is softer and creamier.

• Dried porcini mushrooms can be used in addition to, or instead of, the portobellos. Soak in warm water for 30 minutes to soften, then drain before using. Dried porcinis are a useful item to have in the pantry; look for them in the produce section of the supermarket.

V. SOUPS, SANDWICHES, & OTHER LIGHT BITES

Summer Minestrone

¼ cup	**olive oil**	60 ml
1	**onion,** *chopped*	
3 cloves	**garlic,** *chopped*	
2 stalks	**celery,** *thinly sliced*	
1	**red pepper,** *seeded and thinly sliced*	
1	**dried hot pepper**	
2	**medium zucchini,** *cut into chunks*	
1 can	**plum tomatoes** *(28 oz/796 ml)*	
1 can	**white beans** *rinsed and drained (19 oz/540 ml)*	
2 cups	**stock** *or* **water**	500 ml
1 tbsp	**each fresh basil and thyme,** *chopped* **or**	15 ml
1 tsp	**each dried basil and thyme**	5 ml
1	**bay leaf**	
	salt and freshly ground black pepper	
½ lb	**green beans,** *trimmed and cut in pieces*	250 g
	Parmesan cheese, *grated*	

A hearty combo of fresh summer vegetables topped with freshly grated Parmesan cheese. Accompany with crusty bread, Focaccia with Herbs (p. 241), or an Olive Baguette (p. 232) for lunch or a light dinner.

1. Heat oil in a large, heavy pot. Add onion and cook over medium heat until soft.

2. Add garlic, celery, red pepper, and hot pepper, and cook for 5 minutes. Add zucchini and stir and cook for 2 minutes to coat the chunks in flavoured oil.

3. Chop tomatoes and add, along with their juice. Stir in white beans, stock or water, and herbs. Season to taste. Simmer, partially covered, for 20 minutes. Add green beans during last 10 minutes of cooking.

4. Remove hot pepper and bay leaf before serving. Adjust seasoning. Serve the soup hot with grated Parmesan cheese sprinkled on top.

Serves 6.

TIPS:

• The minestrone has even richer flavour if left overnight, covered, in the refrigerator. It can also be frozen.

• For added flavour and slightly thickened texture, add a piece of Parmesan rind when you stir in the stock in Step 3. Remove the rind before serving.

• If you'd like the broth to have a thicker texture, remove 1 cup (250 ml) of the vegetables, mash with a potato masher, and stir back into the soup before serving.

• For a Provençal version (Soupe au Pistou), swirl 1 tbsp (15 ml) of Basil Pesto (p. 210) into each serving.

Carrot Ginger Soup

3 tbsp	butter	45 ml
1	large onion, *chopped*	
2 cloves	garlic, *minced*	
2 lbs	carrots *(about 8 large carrots), peeled and roughly chopped*	1 kg
2 tbsp	fresh ginger root, *peeled and grated*	30 ml
1 tsp	curry powder	5 ml
6 cups	chicken *or* vegetable stock	1.5 L
	salt and freshly ground black pepper	
	fresh lemon *or* lime juice *(to taste)*	

TIPS:

• If you're using a store-bought stock or stock cube, be sure to taste the soup before adding additional salt.

• The soup can be made ahead and stored in covered containers in the refrigerator for a day or two, or in the freezer for several weeks.

This simple puréed soup can be served hot or chilled. Garnish it with chopped coriander or parsley and a dollop of yogurt or a handful of garlic croutons.

1. Heat butter in a large, heavy-bottomed saucepan. Add onion and garlic and cook over moderate heat, stirring occasionally, until they are soft and lightly golden, about 8–10 minutes.

2. Add carrots, grated ginger, and curry powder. Toss over heat for a few minutes.

3. Add stock and seasoning and bring to a boil. Lower heat, cover, and simmer until carrots are very tender, about 20 minutes.

4. Purée soup in batches in a blender or food processor.

5. Add lemon or lime juice and adjust seasoning to taste.

Serves 6.

Spicy Black Bean Soup

½ lb	**black turtle beans**	250 g
6 cups	**water**	1.5 L
¼ lb	**pork rind** *or* **ham bone** *(optional)*	125 g
1–2	**onions,** *chopped*	
2–4 cloves	**garlic,** *chopped*	
1 tsp	**ground cumin**	5 ml
2 tbsp	**butter** *or* **vegetable oil**	30 ml
¼ lb	**lean bacon** *or* **ham,** *cubed (optional)*	125 g
2	**tomatoes** *(fresh or canned), peeled, seeded, and chopped*	
2–3	**serrano** *or* **jalapeño peppers,** *seeded and chopped (fresh or canned)*	
	salt and freshly ground black pepper	
2 tbsp	**fresh flat-leaf parsley,** *chopped*	30 ml
	sour cream, yogurt, *or* **crème fraîche** *(optional; for garnish)*	

Rich, spicy, and rib-sticking. Serve with crisp tortilla chips, spicy croutons (Quick Trick, p. 132), or corn bread (p. 335).

1. Rinse and pick over beans, removing any debris. Cover with water in a large pot. Bring to a fast boil for 2 minutes. Remove pot from heat, cover, and leave beans for an hour.

2. Drain beans and cover with 6 cups (1.5 L) fresh water. Add pork rind or ham bone if you like, onion, garlic, and cumin. Bring to a boil, lower heat, partially cover, and simmer until the beans are tender, about 1½ hours.

3. Discard pork rind or ham bone if using. Remove about 2–3 cups (500–750 ml) beans from the pot and either blend briefly in a food processor or mash. Return the puréed beans to the pot.

4. Brown bacon or ham in butter or oil, add tomatoes and peppers, and cook over moderate heat for 10 minutes. Stir mixture into beans and simmer all together for 15 minutes or so. Adjust seasoning. Serve hot, sprinkled with parsley and with a swirl of sour cream, yogurt, or crème fraîche.

Serves 6.

VARIATION:

• Vegetarian Black Bean Soup: Omit pork rind or ham bone when cooking beans. Omit bacon or ham, and simply soften peppers in hot butter or oil before adding tomatoes.

TIP:

• For heat with a hint of smokiness, add a spoonful of puréed chipotle chiles in adobo sauce (see p. 13) instead of the serranos or jalapeños.

This Spicy Black Bean Soup can be made with meat or without. Both ways, it's rich and satisfying.

Chicken Quesadillas

6	**large flour tortillas** *(10"/25 cm)*	
1 cup	**red** *or* **green salsa**	250 ml
½ lb	**Monterey Jack** *or* **mild Cheddar cheese,** *grated*	250 g
	jalapeño peppers, *chopped (optional)*	
	Spicy Shredded Chicken *(recipe on facing page)*	
	fresh coriander *or* **parsley,** *chopped*	

These tortillas, stacked with layers of tasty fillings, make great party food and are easy to serve since they can be assembled ahead of time and heated in the oven when needed.

1. Place 2 tortillas on a lightly oiled baking sheet. Spread each with a tablespoon or two of salsa and a layer of grated cheese, chopped jalapeños if desired, and shredded chicken.

2. Top with another tortilla and repeat the layers of salsa, cheese, jalapeños, and chicken. Add another tortilla, then spread more salsa and cheese on top.

3. Bake in 350°F (180°C) oven for about 15 minutes until the quesadillas are hot and the cheese is melted.

4. Serve hot, cut in wedges and sprinkled with coriander or parsley.

Serves 6.

TIPS:

• Steps 1 and 2 can be done a few hours ahead. Refrigerate until serving time.

• If you don't have time to make the Spicy Shredded Chicken, use shredded smoked chicken (sold in food shops and delicatessens).

Spicy Shredded Chicken

1 tsp	ground cumin	5 ml
¼ tsp	cayenne	1 ml
1 tsp	dried thyme	5 ml
2 cloves	garlic, *finely chopped*	
2 tbsp	onion, *chopped*	30 ml
4	boneless, skinless chicken breasts	
2 tbsp	vegetable oil	30 ml
½ cup	beer, white wine, *or* chicken stock	125 ml
	salt	

*U*se this recipe for the Chicken Quesadillas on the facing page, or roll the strips with avocado slices and salsa in a tortilla.

1. Combine cumin, cayenne, thyme, garlic, and onion, and mash together to make a paste.

2. Cut chicken breasts lengthwise into strips and coat with mixture. Leave to marinate at room temperature for 30 minutes (or longer in the refrigerator).

3. Heat oil in a large skillet. Add chicken and cook briefly over moderately high heat.

4. Add beer, wine, or stock, cover pan, and cook gently until chicken is cooked through and nicely glazed – about 5 minutes. Taste and season.

5. Shred chicken strips into convenient bite-sized lengths when ready to assemble the tortillas.

Makes enough for sandwiches or quesadillas to serve at least 6.

TIP:
• The chicken can be prepared the day before and refrigerated until needed.

Chilled Cantaloupe Soup

1	large, ripe cantaloupe
1 can	frozen orange juice concentrate, thawed (*12 oz/355 ml*)
	grated zest of 1 orange
pinch	salt
	fresh mint leaves

TIPS:

• This soup can also be made with honeydew melon, although the colour is not as vibrant.

• Top each serving with a spoonful of yogurt, sour cream, or crème fraîche if you wish.

𝓘t's hard to believe that a recipe with so few ingredients can taste so good. Serve this simple soup as part of a light lunch on a hot summer day, along with an antipasto platter or a chicken salad and homemade biscuits.

1. Remove rind and seeds from melon. Purée fruit in a food processor or blender or mash by hand until almost smooth.

2. Stir in juice concentrate (undiluted), orange zest, and salt. Mix well. Cover and chill until serving.

3. Serve cold, garnished with fresh mint.

Serves 6.

A few minutes and even fewer ingredients – all that Chilled Cantaloupe Soup requires.

Grilled Eggplant Soup
with Peppers & Tomatoes

3	red peppers	
1	large eggplant	
3 tbsp	olive oil	45 ml
6	plum tomatoes	
½	medium red onion, *chopped*	
3 cloves	garlic, *chopped*	
4 cups	chicken *or* vegetable stock	1 L
1 tsp	dried oregano	5 ml
	salt and freshly ground black pepper	
	sour cream, crème fraîche, *or* toasted croutons (*optional*)	

*W*hen dinner calls for veggies on the barbecue, grill extra eggplant, peppers, and tomatoes, and set them aside to make this soup the next day. Serve with corn bread (p. 335), Devilish Cheese Twists (p. 22), or Buttermilk Biscuits (p. 257).

1. Roast peppers on the barbecue over very high heat until skins are blistered and blackened on all sides, about 15 minutes. Set in a paper bag or in a bowl and cover with plastic wrap. Allow to steam for 10 minutes, then peel away charred skin, remove stem and seeds, and chop.

2. Cut eggplant in half and brush cut sides lightly with 1 tbsp (15 ml) of the oil. Lower heat to medium-high and grill, skin side down, until skin is blackened and flesh is soft (about a half-hour). Remove skin and chop flesh.

3. Cut tomatoes in half lengthwise, lightly brush with another 1 tbsp (15 ml) of oil, and set on grill, skin side down. Grill about 10 minutes. Remove skin and seeds and chop.

4. Heat remaining 1 tbsp (15 ml) oil in a large pot. Add onion, cook until lightly browned, then add garlic, eggplant, peppers, and tomatoes. Stir in stock, oregano, and seasoning, and simmer for about 30 minutes.

5. Purée soup in batches in a food processor or blender, or pass through a food mill until it is smooth. Taste and adjust seasoning. Top with sour cream, crème fraîche, or a few toasted croutons, and serve hot.

Serves 6.

Grilled Eggplant Soup with Peppers & Tomatoes: Make it during harvest season, when markets overflow with these vegetables.

Classic Gazpacho

1–2 cloves	garlic, *crushed*	
1 tsp	salt	5 ml
1 slice	white bread, *crusts removed*	
2 tbsp	olive oil	30 ml
2 cans	plum tomatoes, *drained and chopped; juice reserved (28 oz/796 ml cans)*	
½	onion, *chopped*	
2	English cucumbers, *peeled and chopped*	
2	sweet green peppers *(or mix green and red), seeded and chopped*	
¼ cup	red wine vinegar	60 ml
dash	hot sauce *(or to taste)*	
	additional salt and freshly ground black pepper	
	croutons, sour cream, green onions, *chopped (for garnish)*	

A refreshing summer soup that can easily be assembled ahead of time with a blender or food processor. Serve with toasted ham-and-cheese sandwiches for a quick lunch or evening snack.

1. Crush garlic with salt in a large bowl. Add bread and oil and leave for 30 minutes.

2. In batches, blend or finely chop vegetables in a blender or food processor. Mix with bread in bowl, adding vinegar and seasonings. Adjust consistency with the reserved juice from the tomatoes (or chilled stock or water). Refrigerate.

3. Serve gazpacho chilled with a topping of crisp croutons or sour cream and chopped green onions.

Serves 8.

TIPS:
• The gazpacho will keep 2–3 days in the fridge.

• It's a delicious addition to a picnic. Take it along in a Thermos, adding a couple of ice cubes to keep the soup nice and cold.

VARIATION:
• Grilled Gazpacho: Follow the recipe above, but grill some of the vegetables first to impart a slightly smoky flavour. Use 6–8 grilled fresh plum tomatoes (instead of canned), and grill the onion and peppers.

Mini-Meatball-Stuffed Pitas

½ cup	**fine bulgur**	125 ml
2 tbsp	**olive oil**	30 ml
1	**small onion,** *finely chopped*	
1 lb	**lean ground beef**	500 g
2 tbsp	**pine nuts,** *toasted and chopped (optional)*	30 ml
2 tbsp	**fresh parsley** *or* **coriander,** *chopped*	30 ml
2 tbsp	**fresh mint,** *chopped*	30 ml
	salt and freshly ground black pepper	
6	**pita breads**	
	Pico de Gallo *(p. 95)* *or* **Tuscan Pepper & Tomato Salad** *(p. 164)*	

These mini-meatballs were inspired by a picnic recipe from a Brazilian friend. Bake or grill them beforehand, then serve them cold, tucked into pitas and topped with Pico de Gallo (a Mexican uncooked tomato salsa; p. 95) or Tuscan Pepper & Tomato Salad (p.164). The meatballs are equally tasty served hot off the grill.

1. Cover bulgur with cold water and allow to stand for 30 minutes. Drain and squeeze dry.

2. Heat oil in a frying pan, add onion, and cook until soft.

3. Combine onion with soaked bulgur, ground beef, pine nuts, herbs, and salt and pepper. Add a few tablespoons of water, if necessary, to make a smooth, light mixture.

4. Form the mixture into small balls. (You should have about 24.) Place on a baking sheet and bake at 375°F (190°C) for about 20 minutes until browned and cooked through. Or thread on skewers and grill on barbecue for about 15 minutes, turning occasionally.

5. When ready to serve, tuck 4 meatballs into each pita and top with Pico de Gallo or Tuscan Pepper & Tomato Salad.

Makes 6 sandwiches.

TIP:
• If you're going on a picnic, transport the meatballs, salad, and pitas separately and assemble the sandwiches when it's time to eat.

Grilled Tomato-Basil Soup

2 lbs	ripe tomatoes, *halved*	1 kg
1	medium onion, *peeled and quartered*	
	olive oil	
	salt and freshly ground black pepper	
1	carrot, *chopped*	
1 clove	garlic, *minced*	
3–4 cups	chicken *or* vegetable stock	750 ml–1 L
	flavourings tied together: celery tops, thyme, parsley sprigs, and a bay leaf	
¼ cup	fresh basil, *chopped*	60 ml
1 tbsp	fresh lemon juice	15 ml
pinch	sugar	
	yogurt *(for garnish)*	
	basil sprigs *(for garnish)*	

TIP:

• 1 medium tomato weighs about 6 oz (170 g).

*G*rilling *the tomatoes and onion adds an interesting smoky flavour to the soup. Serve chilled or hot, topped with a swirl of yogurt and fresh herbs.*

1. Rub tomatoes and onion with oil, salt, and pepper. Set on the grill over low heat for about 10 minutes until flesh is lightly charred, turning once.

2. Combine tomatoes, onion, carrot, garlic, 3 cups (750 ml) of the stock, flavourings, and a little salt in a large pot. Bring to a boil, lower heat, and simmer for about 30 minutes until vegetables are soft.

3. Remove and discard flavouring bundle. Purée vegetables in a blender or food processor until smooth. Or press the soup through a food mill or sieve to remove seeds and skins, if you like. Stir in the chopped basil.

4. Adjust flavour with lemon juice and perhaps a pinch or two of sugar. Add more stock if necessary to achieve the desired consistency. Season to taste.

5. Serve chilled or hot with a spoonful of yogurt swirled in each bowl and a garnish of basil.

Serves 6.

TIPS:

• For a cream of tomato soup that's excellent both hot and chilled, heat 1 cup (250 ml) 18% cream for a few minutes and add to the puréed vegetables in place of the additional stock.

• The soup can also be made without grilling the vegetables first. Just chop roughly before adding to the pot.

Served chilled with yogurt, Grilled Tomato-Basil Soup is wonderful on a hot summer day.

Super Sandwich Combos

2 WAYS TO DRESS UP A BAGUETTE:

• **Olive Baguette:** Cut baguette on the diagonal into slices, not quite cutting all the way through. Brush each slice with a little garlic-flavoured olive oil, then spread with tapenade (black-olive purée; see p. 23). Re-form the baguette, lightly brush the outside with oil, and wrap in foil. Place in a 400°F (200°C) oven for 10 minutes, then open foil and heat a few more minutes until top is crispy. Serve hot.

• **Melted Brie & Roasted Pepper Baguette:** Slice baguette in half lengthwise and pull away some bread from the middle of each piece. Lightly brush each half with basil pesto (p. 210) or olive oil flavoured with fresh chopped basil. Place thinly sliced Brie and slices of roasted red pepper along the bottom. Cover with the top and press together firmly. Wrap tightly in foil. Bake in a 400°F (200°C) oven for 10 minutes, then open foil and heat a few more minutes to allow the bread to crisp. Cut sandwich into pieces and serve hot.

Let a main dish do double duty: Cook a little extra meat or veggies on the barbecue or stove the night before and use the leftovers for sandwiches the next day. Here are some tasty combos:

Pepper-Encrusted Loin of Pork Sandwich

Start with the Pepper-Encrusted Loin of Pork on p. 80. Stack thin slices on a crusty bun with sweet mustard; roasted red pepper slices or chili sauce; crisp greens such as arugula, romaine, or watercress; and mayo.

Cumin-Scented Lamb Wrap

Start with the grilled Cumin-Scented Leg of Lamb on p. 107. Spread tortillas with Red Pepper and Feta Spread (p. 28) or crumbled feta cheese. Add slices of cold grilled lamb and thin strips of grilled red and yellow peppers and zucchini, and roll up the tortillas.

Grilled Vegetables on Focaccia

Start with slices of grilled vegetables (pp. 124–127). Layer them with sliced bocconcini or provolone on homemade (p. 241) or storebought focaccia that has been sliced in half horizontally and spread with pesto (p. 210).

Lemon Chicken Sandwich

Start with slices of Very Lemon Chicken (p. 180). Spread Lemony Mayonnaise (Quick Trick, facing page) on a baguette. Add a layer of sliced chicken, crisp greens, and sliced roasted red and yellow peppers.

QUICK TRICKS:

Horseradish and Herb Mustards: Add a dab of horseradish or wasabi (green Japanese horseradish) to Dijon mustard to give it some zip. (Try it on a sliced steak or pork sandwich.) Or make your own herb mustard: Add about 1 tbsp (15 ml) of fresh chopped herbs to ½ cup (125 ml) Dijon mustard. Tarragon mustard goes particularly well with cold sliced steak.

• **Lemony Mayonnaise:** To ½ cup (125 ml) mayo, add 1 tsp (5 ml) grated lemon zest and 1 tbsp (15 ml) fresh lemon juice. Add a little fresh chopped dill if you like.

Island Chicken Wrap

Start with Island Beer Can Chicken (p. 117). (Barbecue two chickens at once to be sure you have leftovers.) Spread soft tortillas with Spicy Black Bean Dip (p. 46). Across the middle third of the tortilla arrange shredded chicken, slices of roasted peppers, and grated cheese. Add a spoonful of salsa if you like. Fold up the bottom, tuck in the ends, roll, and enjoy.

Steak Sandwich with Horseradish Cream

Start with leftover grilled steak (pp. 70, 73, 79), thinly sliced on the diagonal. Combine equal parts mayonnaise and sour cream with prepared horseradish (well drained) to taste. Spread the horseradish cream on lightly toasted slices of sourdough or French bread, add a layer of watercress or romaine lettuce, and the sliced steak. Top with grilled red onions (p. 126) or a sliced dill pickle, and season with salt and pepper. Serve open-faced.

Balsamic-Glazed Portobello Sandwich

Start with slices of Balsamic-Glazed Portobello Mushrooms (p. 111). Cut a focaccia or other soft flatbread or calabrese buns in half horizontally and toast lightly. Spread both halves with mayonnaise mixed with a few finely chopped fresh basil leaves and a squeeze of lemon. Arrange a layer of sliced mushrooms on the bottom half. Season lightly. Top with arugula leaves, leaf lettuce, or watercress, and thinly sliced Asiago cheese. Cover with the top half of the bread and press sandwich together gently.

Grilled Sausage with Roasted Peppers

Start with leftover grilled Italian sausage. Stuff the sausage into crusty kaisers and top with slices of roasted sweet and hot peppers and warm tomato sauce. Messy, but good.

Speedy Pizza Dough

2½–3 cups	all-purpose flour	625–750 ml
¾ tsp	salt	3 ml
1 tbsp	Fleischmann's Quick-Rise Instant Yeast *or* RapidRise Instant Yeast *(1 envelope)* *(see Tips, p. 337)*	15 ml
1 cup	water	250 ml
2 tbsp	olive oil	30 ml
	cornmeal *(for dusting pans)*	

TIPS:

• Vary the flavour of the crust by replacing ½ cup (125 ml) of the all-purpose flour with whole-wheat or buckwheat flour, or cornmeal.

• At the end of Step 4, the dough can be wrapped well and frozen or refrigerated for later use. Bring it back to room temperature before proceeding. (Frozen dough will take 2–3 hours to thaw at room temperature or overnight in the refrigerator.)

When there's no pizza delivery for miles, this quick-and-easy dough can be a lifesaver. If you like a thin, crisp crust, stretch the dough out and make two 12" (30-cm) thin-crust pizzas. If you like your crust soft and thick, shape the dough into a single 14" (35-cm) pizza and let it rise for half an hour before baking.

1. Toss 2 cups (500 ml) flour with salt and yeast in a large bowl.

2. Heat water and oil until hot (125°F/50°C). Briskly stir or beat the liquid into the flour mixture for about 2 minutes.

3. Stir in enough remaining flour to make a soft dough. Knead on lightly floured surface until smooth and elastic, about 4 minutes, adding more flour when the dough becomes sticky. (You may not need to use all the flour.)

4. Shape dough into a smooth ball, cover, and let rest 10 minutes. Divide dough in two if you want to make thin-crust pizzas.

5. Grease pizza pans or baking sheets well and dust with cornmeal. Stretch or roll dough to fit. Cover with your favourite toppings and bake in preheated 400°F (200°C) oven for 20–30 minutes until crust is nicely browned and topping is piping hot.

Makes one 14" (35-cm) thick-crust pizza or two 12" (30-cm) thin-crust pizzas.

Crispy Calzones

FOOD PROCESSOR METHOD:

• To make Speedy Pizza Dough in the food processor: Place 2¹/₂ cups (625 ml) flour in processor with yeast and salt, and pulse to combine. Heat liquid ingredients (as in Step 2) and add through feed tube with motor running. If dough is too sticky, add 1–2 tbsp (15–30 ml) more flour. Dough should pull away from sides of bowl. Process for 30 seconds to knead, remove from bowl, knead briefly on floured surface, form into a ball, and proceed as with basic dough.

TO COOK PIZZA OR CALZONES ON THE BBQ:

• Assemble pizza or calzones on a wooden board. Preheat barbecue to medium. Gently slide pizza or calzones onto grill rack, close lid, and bake over direct heat for 10–15 minutes. Lift pizza crust and take a look every 5 minutes; if the bottom is browning too quickly, move to a cooler spot on the grill or turn off one of the burners and move the pizza to that side, baking with indirect heat for the remainder of the time. Turn calzones after 5 minutes and continue to bake, checking as above and moving to a cooler spot if underside browns too quickly.

Stuff these turnovers with the same ingredients you'd put on top of a pizza. Bite-sized ones make a popular party snack – try them filled with the toppings for Let's Go Greek Pizza (p. 238).

1. Divide the Speedy Pizza Dough (facing page) in half, then roll or stretch out each half as you would if you were making pizza. From each half, cut either two 8" (20-cm) circles, for calzones that each serve 1 as a substantial snack; or eight 4" (10-cm) circles, for mini party-size calzones.

2. On half of each circle, arrange layers of your favourite pizza toppings. Leave a ¹/₂" (1-cm) border around the edge of each circle.

3. Moisten the edge with water and fold the uncovered half of the dough over the filling. Pinch the edges securely closed. Prick the tops a couple of times with a fork to allow steam to escape. Brush the tops lightly with a mixture of egg yolk beaten with milk.

4. Place on lightly oiled baking sheets dusted with cornmeal and bake in a preheated 400°F (200°C) oven for 20 minutes until lightly golden.

Makes 4 large calzones or 16 bite-sized ones.

Leek & Potato Soup with Stilton

4	**leeks,** *thinly sliced (white and tender green parts only)*	
3	**medium potatoes,** *peeled and diced*	
5 cups	**vegetable** *or* **chicken stock**	**1.25 L**
	salt and freshly ground black pepper	
¼ cup	**35% cream**	**60 ml**
½ cup	**Stilton cheese,** *crumbled*	**125 ml**
	fresh chives *or* **parsley,** *chopped*	

*P*otatoes and leeks make a tasty combination that's open to all manner of variations. Just remember to add approximately equal amounts of liquid and chopped vegetables.

1. Combine leeks, potatoes, stock, and about ¼ tsp (1 ml) salt in a large pot. Bring to a boil, reduce heat, and simmer, partially covered, until vegetables are tender – about 20–30 minutes.

2. Purée mixture until smooth. Just before serving, stir in cream and Stilton, and heat through. Season to taste.

3. Garnish with fresh chives or parsley and a little extra crumbled cheese on top of each bowl if desired.

Serves 4–6.

TIPS:

• For a different taste, omit the cheese but include another ¼ cup (60 ml) cream or a tablespoon or two (15–30 ml) of butter.

• Instead of puréeing the soup, serve it chunky-style. Thicken it by puréeing just a cup or so of cooked vegetables and stock, then stir the purée back into the pot.

• Add 1 cup (250 ml) broccoli or watercress, or 2 packed cups (500 ml) fresh spinach, to the cooked potato/leek mixture. Simmer all together gently for 5 minutes. Purée if desired, then add a dash of grated nutmeg and the cream.

• To make a classic vichyssoise to serve cold, purée the cooked potato/leek mixture and press through a sieve to make a smooth cream. Stir in ½ cup (125 ml) 35% cream and chill. Season to taste. Serve garnished with chopped fresh chives.

Sweet Potato & Chile Soup

2 tbsp	**unsalted butter**	30 ml
2	**medium onions,** *finely chopped*	
2	**cloves garlic,** *finely chopped*	
3	**medium sweet potatoes,** *peeled and sliced*	
1	**jalapeño pepper** *(or more to taste), seeded and chopped*	
1 tsp	**chipotle chiles in adobo sauce,** *puréed (optional; see p. 13)*	5 ml
4–5 cups	**chicken** *or* **vegetable stock**	1–1.25 L
	salt	
¼ cup	**fresh lime juice,** *or to taste*	60 ml
	sour cream *or* **yogurt**	

The sweetness of the potatoes, the heat of the chiles, and the tartness of the lime create a wonderfully complex flavour. For an informal south-of-the-border dinner that can be completely made ahead, serve the soup with Chicken Quesadillas (p. 222) and Corn & Black Bean Salad (p. 156).

1. Heat butter in a large pot. Add onions and soften over medium heat. Add garlic, sweet potatoes, jalapeño pepper, and chile purée (optional), and stir to coat with the buttery onions.

2. Add 4 cups (1 L) chicken or vegetable stock and a dash of salt. Bring to a boil, reduce heat, and simmer, partially covered, until the vegetables are tender – about 20 minutes. Purée the mixture.

3. Reheat gently, add lime juice, and season to taste. The soup will thicken as it rests, so adjust consistency with additional stock as needed.

4. Serve hot with a swirl of sour cream or yogurt in each bowl.

Serves 4–6.

TIP:
• This soup is even better when made a day or two ahead, so the flavours have a chance to blend. It also freezes well.

½	**recipe Speedy Pizza Dough** (p. 234)	
1 tbsp	**olive oil**	**15 ml**
½	**medium red onion,** *finely chopped*	
1 clove	**garlic,** *finely chopped*	
½ cup	**spinach,** *cooked, squeezed dry, and chopped*	**125 ml**
	salt and freshly ground black pepper	
½ cup	**mozzarella cheese,** *grated*	**125 ml**
¼ cup	**pitted black olives,** *sliced*	**60 ml**
½ cup	**feta cheese,** *crumbled*	**125 ml**
¼ cup	**flavoured olive oil** (see Tip, below)	**60 ml**
1 tbsp	**fresh parsley,** *chopped (optional)*	**15 ml**

TIP:

• To make a flavoured olive oil for this pizza, put a sliced clove of garlic, a twist of lemon peel, and some chopped fresh or dried rosemary into ¼ cup (60 ml) extra-virgin olive oil. Allow to stand at least 15 minutes before using.

Let's Go Greek Pizza

A delicious change from the familiar pizza with tomato sauce. If you prepare the dough and the spinach mixture ahead – see Tips, p. 234 and below – you can have hot, crispy pizza on the table in 30 minutes or less.

1. Heat olive oil in a heavy frying pan, add onion, and cook over medium heat until soft. Add garlic and cooked spinach, season lightly, and continue to cook over medium heat for 3–4 minutes.

2. On a lightly floured surface, stretch or roll the dough to form a 12" (30-cm) circle, or cut into ten 3" (8-cm) rounds. Place on oiled baking sheets that have been dusted with cornmeal.

3. Cover dough with half the mozzarella. Sprinkle on the spinach mixture, the remaining mozzarella, the olives, and the crumbled feta. Drizzle half the flavoured olive oil on top.

4. Bake in a preheated 400°F (200°C) oven for about 20 minutes, until the crust is lightly golden on the bottom and the topping is very hot. Sprinkle with chopped parsley and remaining oil if desired and serve immediately.

Serves 2 as a main course, 4–6 for snacks.

TIP:

• You can make the spinach topping (Step 1) a day or two ahead; keep refrigerated until needed.

Eggplant & Basil Pesto Pizza

½ recipe	**Speedy Pizza Dough** (p. 234)	
2 tbsp	**basil pesto** (p. 210)	30 ml
1	**medium eggplant,** *thinly sliced and grilled or roasted*	
½	**roasted red pepper,** *chopped (optional)*	
	salt and freshly ground black pepper	
drizzle	**garlic-flavoured olive oil** (optional)	
¼ cup	**goat cheese** *or* **feta cheese**	60 ml
	fresh parsley, *chopped (optional)*	

This pizza is a real crowd pleaser – particularly when made in 3" (8-cm) rounds for bite-sized versions.

1. On a lightly floured surface, stretch or roll the dough to form two 8" (20-cm) circles, or cut into ten 3" (8-cm) rounds. Place on oiled baking sheets that have been dusted with cornmeal.

2. Spread a light, even layer of basil pesto on the dough, and top with a layer of eggplant and red pepper, if using. (Chop the eggplant into smaller pieces if you are making 3"/8-cm pizzas.) Season with salt and pepper and a little garlic-flavoured olive oil if you like.

3. Bake in a preheated 400°F (200°C) oven for 15 minutes. Remove from oven and add a topping of crumbled goat cheese or feta cheese. Return to oven to bake for about 5 minutes longer, until the crust is lightly golden on the bottom. Sprinkle with chopped parsley if desired and serve immediately.

Serves 2 as a main course, or 4–6 for snacks.

Red Lentil Soup
with Cumin & Lemon

2 cups	**split red lentils**	500 ml
8 cups	**chicken** *or* **vegetable stock**	2 L
1	**large tomato,** *peeled, seeded, and chopped*	
1	**onion,** *chopped*	
2 cloves	**garlic,** *chopped*	
1 tbsp	**butter**	15 ml
2 tsp	**ground cumin**	10 ml
	salt and freshly ground black pepper	
	lemon slices	
	fresh parsley, *chopped*	
	sour cream, crème fraîche, *or* **yogurt** *(optional)*	

TIP:

• Take care to read the cooking directions on the packages of lentils and beans you buy. Some brands have been processed to cook quickly; adjust the cooking time accordingly.

Lentils, peas, and dried beans are useful basics to have on hand in the cupboard. This wonderfully fragrant soup uses red lentils – and is very easy to make. Crisped pita bread is a tasty accompaniment.

1. Rinse lentils and discard any debris.

2. Bring stock to a boil in a large pot. Add lentils, tomato, onion, and garlic. Simmer, partially covered, until lentils are tender – about 45 minutes.

3. Purée soup in a food processor or food mill and press through a sieve if you prefer a very smooth texture. Return soup to the pot.

4. Melt butter in a small pan, add ground cumin, and stir over low heat for a couple of minutes. Stir the spice into the soup, heat through, and season with salt and lots of freshly ground pepper.

5. Top each serving with a lemon slice, chopped parsley, and a spoonful of sour cream, crème fraîche, or yogurt if you wish.

Serves 6.

Focaccia with Herbs

1 recipe	**Speedy Pizza Dough** *(p. 234)*	
2 tbsp	**fresh herbs** *(rosemary, oregano, thyme, or basil), chopped* **or**	**30 ml**
2 tsp	**dried herbs**	**10 ml**
¼ cup	**extra-virgin olive oil**	**60 ml**
1 clove	**garlic**	
	cornmeal *(for dusting baking sheet)*	
	coarse salt	
	toppings *(optional; see Tips, below)*	

TIPS:

• Before the focaccia goes in the oven, add toppings such as goat cheese, ricotta, grated Parmesan, slivers of fresh garlic, sliced grilled onions, chopped sun-dried tomatoes, olives, or roasted peppers if desired.

• The wonderful crisp crusts typical of good country breads result from baking in brick and stone ovens with a high degree of natural humidity. Commercial ovens create this effect with a burst of steam; to get it at home, use a fine spritz of water from a spray bottle on the interior of your hot oven.

Focaccia is a crusty Italian flatbread, about an inch or two high, baked with a variety of savoury toppings. It makes a great snack on its own, can be served with salads, soups, and eggs, or split in half for sandwiches. You can prepare dozens of variations, using different combinations of herbs and toppings.

1. Prepare Speedy Pizza Dough through Step 4 as described on p. 234, adding half the fresh or dried herbs to the dry ingredients.

2. Slice garlic into olive oil and set aside.

3. Press dough into an 8" (20-cm) square or oval, about ¾" (2 cm) thick. Place on a well-greased baking sheet sprinkled with cornmeal. Cover with a damp tea towel and leave in a warm, draft-free spot until doubled in size, about 30–40 minutes.

4. Using your fingertips, press "dimples" in the surface to about ¾ of the depth. Brush surface with some of the garlic-flavoured olive oil. Sprinkle surface of dough with the remaining herbs and coarse salt, and add toppings of your choice if desired, pressing them into the dough. Mist lightly with water using a spray bottle.

5. Mist interior of a preheated 400°F (200°C) oven with a quick spritz from a spray bottle. Slip bread into the hot oven. After 5 minutes, mist oven again, then continue baking for 20–30 minutes until bread has a golden crust. Remove from oven and brush top with more of the olive oil.

Makes 1 loaf.

Vegetable Enchiladas

2 tbsp	**vegetable oil**	30 ml
1	**medium onion,** *chopped*	
1	**red pepper,** *seeded and chopped*	
2	**zucchini,** *halved lengthwise and sliced*	
1½ cups	**corn kernels** *(fresh or frozen)*	375 ml
dash	**salt**	
2 tbsp	**jalapeño peppers** *(fresh or canned), diced*	30 ml
2 tbsp	**fresh coriander** *or* **parsley,** *chopped*	30 ml
½ cup	**Monterey Jack** *or* **mild Cheddar cheese,** *grated*	125 ml
8	**medium corn** *or* **flour tortillas** *(8"/20 cm)*	
2 cups	**mild tomato salsa** *or* **tomato sauce**	500 ml
½ cup	**sour cream**	125 ml

A spicy vegetable filling is wrapped in either corn (yellow) or flour (white) tortillas and baked with tomato sauce or salsa. Serve with sour cream on top and diced fresh tomato, finely shredded lettuce, and red onion alongside.

1. Heat oil in a large frying pan over moderate heat. Add onion and cook until soft and lightly browned, about 10 minutes. Add red pepper, zucchini, corn, and salt and cook for about 5 minutes longer.

2. Remove pan from heat and stir in jalapeño peppers, coriander or parsley, and cheese.

3. If you're using corn tortillas, soften them by frying in hot oil for a few seconds on each side (you'll need about ½ cup/125 ml of oil in a large frying pan), then drain on paper towels. Flour tortillas don't require softening.

4. Place about ⅓ cup (75 ml) of the vegetable filling along the bottom third of each tortilla and roll up neatly.

5. Spread a thin layer of tomato salsa or sauce in the bottom of a 9" x 13" (23 cm x 33 cm) baking dish and arrange the filled tortillas on top, side by side. Drizzle the remaining sauce over the top.

6. Bake in a 375°F (190°C) oven for about 20 minutes or until heated through. Serve hot, topped with sour cream.

Serves 4.

VI. BREAKFAST & BRUNCH

Banana Buttermilk Pancakes

1 cup	very ripe bananas *(about 2 large bananas), mashed*	250 ml
2 tsp	fresh lemon juice	10 ml
1 cup	buttermilk	250 ml
1	egg	
1 tsp	vanilla	5 ml
1 tsp	lemon zest, *grated*	5 ml
3 tbsp	butter, *melted and cooled*	45 ml
1 cup	all-purpose flour *or* part all-purpose and part buckwheat *or* whole wheat	250 ml
2 tbsp	sugar	30 ml
2 tsp	baking powder	10 ml
½ tsp	baking soda	2 ml
½ tsp	salt	2 ml

A delicious way to use up those overripe bananas in the fruit bowl. Serve these light, fluffy cakes with Blueberry Maple Syrup (Quick Trick, facing page) or plain maple syrup poured over top and sliced bananas or strawberries alongside.

1. Blend mashed bananas and lemon juice.

2. Combine banana mixture with buttermilk, egg, vanilla, lemon zest, and melted butter in a large bowl.

3. In a separate bowl, combine dry ingredients. Stir dry ingredients into banana-buttermilk mixture, taking care not to overmix.

4. Brush surface of a large non-stick frying pan with butter. When the pan is hot, spoon in the batter using a small ladle or ¼ cup (60-ml) measure. Cook for 2–3 minutes over medium-high heat. When the surface of the pancake is smooth and small bubbles appear, turn it over once only and cook briefly to brown the other side.

Makes a dozen 4" (10-cm) pancakes.

MAKING BREAKFAST FOR A BUNCH:

• When cooking a lot of pancakes, French toast, or omelettes, keep a small pot of melted butter and a pastry brush nearby so you can quickly grease the pan between batches.

TIPS:

• You can substitute sour milk for the buttermilk: Put 1 tbsp (15 ml) lemon juice or vinegar in a measuring cup. Add milk to make 1 cup (250 ml). Let stand 5 minutes; stir well.

• The batter can be prepared the night before and kept, covered, in the refrigerator.

Blueberry Corn Griddle Cakes

½ cup	cornmeal	125 ml
½ tsp	salt	2 ml
1 tbsp	maple syrup	15 ml
½ cup	boiling water	125 ml
½ cup	all-purpose flour	125 ml
2 tsp	baking powder	10 ml
1	egg	
3 tbsp	butter, *melted and cooled*	45 ml
½ cup	milk	125 ml
1 cup	blueberries	250 ml
1 tsp	lemon zest, *grated*	5 ml

*E*very cook should have a pancake recipe in his or her repertoire for those times when there's no boxed mix on hand. Besides, from-scratch batter gives you a chance to make pancakes that are a little out of the ordinary. The cornmeal gives these a pleasing crunch, and the blueberries make them taste like summer. Serve a sky-high pile in a pool of Blueberry Maple Syrup (Quick Trick, below).

1. In a large bowl, combine cornmeal with salt, maple syrup, and boiling water. Stir and set aside.

2. Combine flour and baking powder. In a small bowl, combine egg, melted butter, and milk.

3. Mix dry ingredients alternately with liquid ingredients into cornmeal mixture, stirring lightly until smooth. Fold in blueberries and lemon zest. Don't overmix.

4. Spoon the batter onto a hot, lightly buttered griddle or frying pan, using a small ladle or ¼ cup (60-ml) measure. Cook until small bubbles appear on the top of each pancake, then turn to brown the other side.

5. Serve hot on warm plates with warm Blueberry Maple Syrup.

Makes a dozen 4" (10-cm) griddle cakes.

QUICK TRICK:

Maple Butter: Cream ¼ cup (60 ml) butter until fluffy, then slowly beat in 2 tbsp (30 ml) maple syrup and ¼ tsp (1 ml) cinnamon. A delicious spread for toast or scones.

QUICK TRICK:

Blueberry Maple Syrup: In a small saucepan, combine ¼ cup (60 ml) water, 2 strips lemon zest, 1 cup (250 ml) blueberries, and ½ cup (125 ml) maple syrup. Bring gently to a simmer, cover, and cook 5 minutes. Serve warm or at room temperature. The syrup will keep 3–5 days in the refrigerator.

Poached Eggs with Spinach
& Quick Hollandaise Sauce

1 tbsp	**butter**	15 ml
1	**small onion,** *finely chopped*	
½ cup	**35% cream**	125 ml
	salt and freshly ground black pepper	
2 cups	**fresh** *or* **frozen spinach,** *cooked and drained*	500 ml
pinch	**nutmeg,** *freshly grated*	
pinch	**cayenne**	
¼ cup	**Parmesan cheese,** *freshly grated*	60 ml
4	**English muffins,** *toasted*	
4–8	**poached eggs** *(see Quick Trick)*	
1–2 cups	**Quick Hollandaise** *or* **Virtuous Hollandaise** *(p. 248)*	250–500 ml

TIPS:

• Prepare the spinach mixture the night before, cover and refrigerate; warm before serving.

• The spinach mixture also makes a delicious omelette filling.

A sublime combination when you're in the mood for something special. This is an easy dish to make – although an extra pair of hands helps ensure everything is ready at the right moment when you're serving a number of people.

1. Heat butter in a medium-sized frying pan, add onion, and cook until soft. Add cream and a dash of salt and pepper, and simmer until cream is reduced by half, 3–5 minutes. Stir in cooked spinach, nutmeg, cayenne, and Parmesan cheese, and adjust seasoning.

2. Divide the spinach mixture between the toasted English muffins; top with a poached egg and Quick Hollandaise or Virtuous Hollandaise Sauce.

Serves 4.

QUICK TRICK:

Perfect Poached Eggs: Fill a frying pan, preferably non-stick, with water to a depth of about 2" (5 cm). Add 1 tsp (5 ml) white vinegar and ¼ tsp (1 ml) salt. (This helps to keep the eggs together.) Bring water to a boil, then lower heat to a gentle simmer. One at a time, crack each egg into a small bowl and slide the egg into the simmering water. Simmer about 2 minutes for a soft egg. Remove with a slotted spoon and drain.

If you are poaching eggs for a crowd, slide the cooked eggs into a bowl of ice water. Slip them back into simmering water for a minute to reheat at serving time.

Poached Eggs with Spinach and Hollandaise, with bacon on the side. If you're worried about being too decadent, you can opt for the Virtuous Hollandaise (p. 248.)

Two Hollandaise Sauces

Quick Hollandaise

4	large egg yolks	
3 tbsp	fresh lemon juice	45 ml
1 tbsp	water	15 ml
pinch	salt	
pinch	cayenne	
1 cup	unsalted butter, *melted*	250 ml

Virtuous Hollandaise

1½ cups	light mayonnaise	375 ml
½ cup	sour cream	125 ml
2 tsp	fresh lemon juice	10 ml
1 tsp	Dijon mustard	5 ml
pinch	cayenne	
	salt and freshly ground black pepper	

Quick Hollandaise

A classic Hollandaise sauce uses raw eggs. The method here, put forward by the American Egg Board, heats the egg yolks to kill any lurking salmonella bacteria, first diluting the yolks with a healthy amount of lemon juice and a dash of water to prevent hardening.

1. Combine the egg yolks, lemon juice, and water in a small, preferably non-stick, frying pan and stir constantly over very low heat just until the mixture bubbles at the edge and becomes creamy, about 1 minute. Immediately lift from the heat, stir constantly while mixture cools, then scrape into a blender or food processor. Blend briefly and season with salt and cayenne.

2. With motor running, pour in warm melted butter in a slow steady stream. The sauce will thicken as the butter is added. Taste and adjust seasoning. If necessary, keep the sauce warm for a short period in a bowl over hot water.

Makes about 1½ cups (375 ml).

Virtuous Hollandaise

If the butter- and egg-yolk-laden Hollandaise is too rich for your blood, try this one. If you want a really virtuous version, use light sour cream too.

1. Combine ingredients thoroughly. Taste and adjust seasoning.

Makes 2 cups (500 ml).

Baked Eggs in Tomatoes

4	**just-ripe firm tomatoes**	
	salt and freshly ground black pepper	
1 clove	**garlic,** *minced*	
4	**eggs**	
3 tbsp	**35% cream**	**45 ml**
1 tbsp	**tomato paste**	**15 ml**
½ tsp	**dried oregano**	**2 ml**
½ tsp	**dried basil**	**2 ml**
2 tbsp	**Parmesan cheese,** *grated*	**30 ml**

QUICK TRICK:

Breakfast Trifle: A delicious breakfast starter, and a feast for the eyes, too. For 6–8 people, you'll need 3 cups (750 ml) granola, 4 cups (1 L) 1% French vanilla yogurt, 2 sliced bananas, 3 oranges cut into sections, and 1 pint (500 ml) sliced strawberries. Starting at the bottom of a large glass bowl, layer half the granola, half the yogurt, the bananas, oranges, and strawberries, and the remainder of the yogurt. Top with remaining granola. Garnish with whole berries if desired.

Eggs and sun-ripened field tomatoes are just made for each other. This is a perfect dish for August mornings, when flavourful tomatoes are easy to come by. Serve with peameal bacon and hot buttered corn bread (p. 335) or Buttermilk Biscuits (p. 257).

1. Slice stem ends from tomatoes, scoop out seeds and pulp, sprinkle with salt and pepper, and set upside down for a few minutes to drain juices.

2. Place tomatoes in a buttered ovenproof dish; make it a tight fit so they don't tip over. Sprinkle a little garlic in each tomato shell and break an egg on top.

3. Combine cream, tomato paste, and herbs and spoon a little over each egg. Sprinkle with Parmesan cheese.

4. Bake in a 350°F (180°C) oven for about 20 minutes or until eggs are set. Serve immediately.

Serves 4.

Refrigerator-Rise
Caramel Pecan Sticky Buns

½ recipe	**Refrigerator-Rise Potato Bread dough** *(p. 336)*	
2 tbsp	**butter,** *melted and cooled*	30 ml

Nut Filling

¼ cup	**brown sugar**	60 ml
½ tsp	**cinnamon**	2 ml
¼ tsp	**nutmeg**	1 ml
¼ cup	**raisins** *or* **sultanas**	60 ml
3 tbsp	**pecans,** *toasted and finely chopped*	45 ml
	zest of ½ orange, *chopped*	
	zest of ½ lemon, *chopped*	

Caramel Topping

¼ cup	**butter**	60 ml
¼ cup	**corn syrup**	60 ml
½ cup	**brown sugar,** *packed*	125 ml
¼ cup	**pecan halves,** *toasted*	60 ml
¼ cup	**dried cherries** *(optional)*	60 ml

*S*erved warm from the oven, these sticky buns will become a favourite morning treat. Double the recipe if you like – the baked buns can be frozen and reheated.

1. Prepare dough through Step 5 (p. 336). When ready to make buns, remove a scant half of the dough from the refrigerator. (Freeze the rest for another time, use it for bread or burger buns, or make 2 pans of sticky buns.)

2. Punch dough down and knead briefly. On a lightly floured surface, roll out into a rectangle approximately 10" x 16" (25 cm x 40 cm) and about ¼" (6 mm) thick. Brush with melted butter.

3. Combine all ingredients for nut filling and sprinkle evenly on top of dough. Starting from the shorter side, roll up dough jelly-roll fashion. Pinch seam to seal. Cut into 8 slices.

4. To make the caramel topping, place butter, corn syrup, and brown sugar in a small saucepan. Set over medium heat and stir while sugar melts. Raise heat and allow mixture to bubble for 4–5 minutes. Pour into a buttered 9" (23-cm) round cake pan and sprinkle with nuts and cherries (if using).

5. Lay the slices of dough in the prepared pan cut side down. Let stand, covered with a damp tea towel, in a warm, draft-free spot for about 25 minutes, or overnight in the refrigerator.

6. Preheat oven to 375°F (190°C). If dough has been refrigerated, return to room temperature. Bake 25–30 minutes until golden on top and springy to the touch. Immediately turn out onto a serving platter. Serve warm.

Makes 8 buns.

Make the dough ahead of time, then bake the buns in the morning.

Huevos Rancheros

2 cups	red or green salsa	500 ml
6	medium corn or wheat tortillas (8"/20 cm)	
3 tbsp	butter	45 ml
6	eggs	
handful	fresh coriander, *chopped, for garnish (optional)*	

In this traditional Mexican dish, fried eggs are topped with salsa. You can make your own (p. 40) or substitute a good store-bought one. This simple dish has become a staple for leisurely summer breakfasts.

1. Place salsa in a small saucepan to warm.

2. In a small frying pan, heat tortillas one at a time for about 30 seconds per side to warm and soften. Stack and wrap in a towel to keep warm.

3. Heat butter in a large frying pan over medium heat. Break eggs one at a time into a saucer and slip them into the hot butter. Tip and shake the pan a little – just like at the diner – to keep the eggs from sticking and to flip a little hot butter over them to cook the tops.

4. Place a tortilla on a warm plate. Top with a fried egg, spoon salsa on egg, and sprinkle with chopped coriander if desired.

Makes 6.

QUICK TRICK:

Continental-Style Cold Breakfast: For a nice alternative to a cooked breakfast on a warm summer morning, bagels with deli-style cream cheese, slices of smoked salmon, capers, raw onion rings, and lemon slices are always popular. Or put out slices of mild, nutty cheeses (Emmenthal, Gruyère, Fontina, Jarlsberg, and Gouda) and sliced ham, or perhaps some smoked trout. Add a basket of rye, pumpernickel, and walnut breads, and a platter of fresh fruit or a Breakfast Trifle (p. 249).

Special Scrambled Eggs

¼ cup	butter	60 ml
8	eggs	
¼ cup	milk *or* cream	60 ml
	salt and freshly ground black pepper	
2 tbsp	deli-style cream cheese	30 ml

Additions

	smoked salmon, *slivered*
	fresh dill or chives, *chopped*

	mushrooms, *sliced and sautéed in butter,*
	green onions, *chopped*
	squeeze of lemon juice

QUICK TRICK:

Fried Tomatoes: Heat equal amounts of butter and oil until very hot in a large frying pan. Sprinkle firm tomato wedges with a little salt and cook until nicely browned on both sides (about 2–3 minutes per side); remove with a slotted spoon. Add a couple splashes of balsamic vinegar to juices in pan and stir. Pour over tomatoes and sprinkle with freshly ground pepper and some chopped herbs. A great accompaniment to eggs.

The secret to creamy scrambled eggs is diligent stirring over gentle heat. If you try to hurry them up, they turn instantly dry and lumpy.

1. Melt butter in a non-stick frying pan. Beat eggs with milk or cream and a dash of salt and pour into pan.

2. Stir constantly over moderate-to-low heat until eggs thicken to creamy consistency. Lift pan from heat and stir in cream cheese and whatever additions you like.

3. Season with salt and pepper and serve at once.

Serves 4.

MAKING BREAKFAST FOR A BUNCH:

• The most convenient way to cook bacon for a crowd is to broil it instead of frying. Preheat broiler, spread bacon on the rack of the broiler pan, and put a cup of water in the pan to catch the fat and prevent flare-ups. Place the pan about 5" (13 cm) from the heat. Keep watch. When one side is lightly browned (about 3 minutes), turn the strips over and brown the other side. Remove to a tray lined with paper towel to drain off excess fat, and keep warm in the oven.

• Delegate the tasks of broiling the bacon, making coffee and toast, and setting the table to helpers. A designated toast butterer is also helpful.

Overnight French Toast
with Blueberries

1 cup	brown sugar, *packed*	250 ml
1¼ tsp	cinnamon	6 ml
¼ cup	butter, *melted*	60 ml
12 slices	bread	
1½ cups	fresh blueberries	375 ml
5	eggs	
1½ cups	milk	375 ml
1 tsp	vanilla	5 ml
½ tsp	salt	2 ml

TIPS:

• You can substitute raspberries, peaches, or nectarines for the blueberries.

• Try raisin or egg bread, brioche, or even stale croissants instead of plain white bread.

This blueberry-filled breakfast and brunch dish is a lazy cook's dream: You can prepare it entirely ahead the night before and then just bake it in the morning. Serve warm with maple syrup and grilled bacon or sausage alongside.

1. Combine brown sugar, cinnamon, and melted butter. Mix well. Sprinkle ⅓ of mixture evenly in bottom of a 9" x 13" (23 cm x 33 cm) pan.

2. Cover with 6 slices of bread. Sprinkle another ⅓ of sugar mixture over bread and scatter berries on top.

3. Place remaining bread on fruit. Sprinkle with remaining sugar mixture.

4. Beat eggs, milk, vanilla, and salt together. Pour evenly over bread. Press down lightly. Cover with plastic wrap and refrigerate overnight, or let stand at room temperature for 2 hours.

5. Bake, uncovered, at 350°F (180°C) for 40–45 minutes, or until puffed and golden.

Serves 6.

QUICK TRICK:

Start-the-Day Fruit Smoothie: Combine ¾ cup (175 ml) orange juice, 1 cup (250 ml) sliced strawberries, and 2 sliced bananas and whirl in a blender with 2 crushed ice cubes until smooth. (If you prepare the fruit ahead and freeze it, you can eliminate the ice.) For a different taste, substitute ½ cup (125 ml) cranberry juice and ½ cup (125 ml) plain yogurt for the orange juice. Serves 2.

Assemble the Overnight French Toast the night before you want to serve it. Then just slip it in the oven in the morning.

Stuffed French Toast

Mascarpone Apricot Filling

1 cup	**mascarpone** (see Tips, below)	250 ml
1 tbsp	**maple syrup**	15 ml
½ cup	**dried apricots,** thinly sliced	125 ml

French Toast

1 loaf	**egg bread**	
4	**eggs**	
1 tbsp	**brown sugar**	15 ml
½ tsp	**vanilla**	2 ml
¼ tsp	**orange zest,** grated	1 ml
pinch	**cinnamon**	
¾ cup	**milk** or **10% cream**	175 ml
¼ cup	**unsalted butter** (approx.)	60 ml
2 tbsp	**vegetable oil** (approx.)	30 ml
	maple syrup	

Imagine a French toast sandwich with a decadent filling.

1. To make the filling, combine mascarpone, maple syrup, and apricots. Set aside.

2. Cut egg bread to make 12 even slices, about ⅜" (1 cm) thick.

3. Spread the filling on 6 slices of the egg bread and top each with another slice. Gently press bread slices together to make 6 neat sandwiches.

4. Whisk together eggs, sugar, vanilla, zest, and cinnamon. Add milk or cream. Pour mixture into a shallow dish.

5. Dip each sandwich into the egg mixture, about 2–3 seconds for each side. Let excess egg mixture drip off.

6. Heat about 2 tbsp (30 ml) butter and 1 tbsp (15 ml) oil in a large, preferably non-stick, frying pan over medium heat. Add 1 or 2 sandwiches and cook for about 2 minutes on each side until nicely golden. Repeat with other sandwiches, adding more butter and oil to the pan as needed. Serve sandwiches hot with maple syrup.

Serves 6.

TIPS:

• Mascarpone is a very rich cream cheese available in 500-ml containers in the dairy section of supermarkets and in specialty food stores. If you can't find it, substitute a rich deli cream cheese.

• Experiment with different filling combinations to come up with your favourite. Try sliced fresh mango or peaches, or cranberry conserve.

Buttermilk Biscuits
with Herbs and Ham

3 cups	all-purpose flour	750 ml
½ tsp	salt	2 ml
½ tsp	baking soda	2 ml
4 tsp	baking powder	20 ml
pinch	cayenne	
⅔ cup	vegetable shortening *or* part butter, part shortening	150 ml
2 tbsp	each fresh parsley and chives, *or* a combination of fresh herbs *(parsley, chives, thyme, oregano), finely chopped* or	30 ml
1 tsp	each dried oregano and thyme	5 ml
1 cup	ham, *finely diced (optional)*	250 ml
1¼ cups	buttermilk	300 ml
1	egg, *mixed with* 1 tbsp (15 ml) milk *or* cream *(for egg wash; optional)*	

ℒ ight and tender, these are a treat to serve with eggs. The dry mix can be made quickly ahead of time in the food processor and kept in a plastic bag in the refrigerator until needed.

1. Preheat oven to 425°F (220°C). Grease and flour 2 baking sheets.

2. Combine dry ingredients in a large bowl and cut in shortening until mixture resembles coarse crumbs. (Use a knife and your fingertips, or pulse briefly in a food processor.) Store the mix in a plastic bag in the refrigerator until needed.

3. Place mix in a large bowl with herbs and ham (if using), sprinkle with the buttermilk, and lightly toss all together with a fork just to combine.

4. Drop spoonfuls of dough onto baking sheets. Brush with egg wash if desired and bake in a preheated oven until biscuits are lightly browned, about 12–15 minutes. Serve immediately.

Makes 18–20 biscuits.

TIPS:

• Omit ham and herbs; add either 1 cup (250 ml) grated Cheddar cheese or ¼ cup (60 ml) grated Parmesan cheese with 1 tsp (5 ml) each dried thyme and oregano.

• You can also cut these biscuits into rounds: Knead the dough briefly, pat into a sheet about ½" (1 cm) thick, and cut with a 2" (5-cm) cutter. Bake as above.

• You can substitute sour milk for the buttermilk; for how to sour milk, see p. 244.

(The Buttermilk Biscuits are shown as drop biscuits with Cheddar cheese in the photo following p. 329.)

Crab Strata

1 loaf	**French bread,** *cut in ¹/₂" (1-cm) slices on the diagonal*	
1 cup	**milk**	250 ml
2 tbsp	**butter**	30 ml
2 tbsp	**green onions,** *chopped*	30 ml
1 can	**crab meat,** *drained and chopped (4.2 oz/120 g)*	
¹/₂ tsp	**dried thyme**	2 ml
	salt and freshly ground black pepper	
1 pkg	**frozen leaf spinach,** *cooked, drained, and chopped*	
1 cup	**Swiss** *or* **mild Cheddar cheese,** *grated*	250 ml
4	**eggs**	
¹/₂ cup	**35% cream**	125 ml

*P*uffed and golden – like a soufflé without the finickiness – a strata is a baked savoury egg dish that is elegant enough to serve guests for breakfast or brunch. Do the work the night before and pop the strata in the oven the next morning.

1. The night before serving, dip bread slices in milk and gently press out as much liquid as possible. Arrange a layer of bread slices in the bottom of a buttered ovenproof dish approximately 8" x 8" (20 cm x 20 cm).

2. Melt butter in a skillet and cook onions until soft over moderate heat. Add the crab and thyme, and heat for a few minutes. Season with salt and pepper.

3. Layer ¹/₂ the spinach on top of the bread slices, then ¹/₂ the crab mixture and ¹/₃ of the cheese. Repeat layers with remaining ingredients, ending with a layer of bread and cheese.

4. Beat eggs with a little salt and pepper and pour over layers. Cover with plastic wrap and leave overnight in the refrigerator.

5. The following day, bring to room temperature. Pour a layer of cream over the top. Bake at 350°F (180°C) until puffed and lightly browned, about 40–50 minutes. Serve hot.

Serves 6.

QUICK TRICK:
Mimosas – half fresh orange juice, half sparkling white wine or champagne – are the perfect addition to a summer weekend brunch.

Asparagus Prosciutto Strata

1 loaf	**French bread,** *cut in* 1/2" *(1-cm) slices on the diagonal*	
1 cup	**milk**	250 ml
1 lb	**asparagus,** *trimmed*	500 g
1/4 lb	**prosciutto,** *chopped*	125 g
1 cup	**Swiss** *or* **provolone cheese,** *grated*	250 ml
1/4 cup	**Parmesan cheese,** *grated*	60 ml
4	**eggs**	
1/4 tsp	**nutmeg,** *freshly grated*	1 ml
	salt and freshly ground black pepper	
1/4 cup	**35% cream**	60 ml

VARIATION:

• For a vegetarian option, replace the prosciutto with 1 roasted red pepper, peeled, seeded, and cut in slivers.

A variation on the strata theme. Accompany with a roasted pepper salad or a simple tossed green one.

1. The night before serving, dip bread slices in milk and gently press out as much liquid as possible. Arrange a layer of bread slices in the bottom of a buttered ovenproof dish approximately 8" x 8" (20 cm x 20 cm).

2. Blanch the asparagus in boiling water for 5 minutes. Cut in 1" (2.5-cm) pieces.

3. Spread 1/2 the asparagus pieces evenly over the bread slices and sprinkle with 1/2 the prosciutto and 1/3 of the Swiss (or provolone) and Parmesan cheeses. Repeat layers with remaining ingredients, ending with a layer of bread and cheese.

4. Beat eggs together with nutmeg and a little salt and pepper, and pour over the strata. Cover with plastic wrap and leave overnight in the refrigerator.

5. The following day, bring strata to room temperature. Pour the cream over top. Bake at 350°F (180°C) until puffed and lightly browned, about 40–50 minutes. Serve hot.

Serves 6.

Ricotta Dill Bread

2 cups	all-purpose flour	500 ml
2 tbsp	sugar	30 ml
2 tsp	baking powder	10 ml
½ tsp	baking soda	2 ml
½ tsp	salt	2 ml
½ cup	smooth ricotta cheese *(10% MF)*	125 ml
2 tbsp	fresh dill, *chopped*	30 ml
½ tsp	freshly ground black pepper	2 ml
2	large eggs, *beaten*	
2 tsp	lemon zest, *grated*	10 ml
½ cup	butter, *melted and cooled*	125 ml
1 cup	buttermilk *or* sour milk *(see Tip, p. 244)*	250 ml

𝒯his savoury quick bread is wonderful with cream cheese for breakfast or brunch. Try it with smoked salmon or glazed ham.

1. Preheat oven to 350°F (180°C). Grease and lightly flour a 9" x 5" (2 L) loaf pan.

2. In a large bowl, combine flour, sugar, baking powder, baking soda, and salt.

3. In another bowl, combine ricotta, dill, pepper, eggs, lemon zest, butter, and buttermilk or sour milk.

4. Stir liquid mixture into dry ingredients with quick, light strokes, just until combined. Do not overmix.

5. Spoon batter evenly into prepared loaf pan. Bake in preheated oven 40–50 minutes, or until a wooden skewer inserted in centre comes out clean.

6. Let loaf stand in pan for 10 minutes, then turn out onto a rack to cool.

Makes 1 loaf.

TIPS:

• If you are baking a quick bread ahead, cool completely, wrap well in foil, and store at room temperature overnight. To keep for 2–4 days, store the bread in the refrigerator. Warm before serving – about 10 minutes in a 325°F (170°C) oven.

• For longer storage (4 days–1 month), wrap the bread well in foil and place in a freezer-proof plastic bag; store in the freezer. Transfer to the refrigerator the day before using and warm before serving.

Ricotta Dill Bread pairs well with a smear of cream cheese and a slice of smoked salmon.

The Ultimate Bran Muffin

1²/₃ cups	natural bran	400 ml
¾ cup	all-purpose flour	175 ml
1 tsp	baking soda	5 ml
½ tsp	salt	2 ml
¼ tsp	baking powder	1 ml
1	egg	
¾ cup	brown sugar, *packed*	175 ml
¼ cup	oil *or* melted butter	60 ml
1 cup	buttermilk	250 ml
2 tbsp	molasses	30 ml
¾ cup	raisins	175 ml

This recipe, the creation of professional baker Jill Snider, produces the best bran muffins I know. They're full of bran flavour – but, unlike some bran muffins, are very moist and light. And the batter will keep for up to a week in the fridge.

1. Preheat oven to 375°F (190°C). Grease muffin cups or line them with muffin papers.

2. Combine bran, flour, baking soda, salt, and baking powder. Set aside.

3. In a large bowl, combine egg, brown sugar, oil or butter, buttermilk, molasses, and raisins. Mix well.

4. Add dry ingredients, stirring until moistened.

5. Fill muffin cups ¾ full. Bake for 20–25 minutes, or until top springs back when lightly touched.

Makes 12 muffins.

TIP:

• Replace raisins with your favourite dried or fresh fruit. Try chopped dried apricots or dates, dried cranberries, fresh blueberries, grated apple, or chunks of nectarine.

Carrot Apple Muffins

3 cups	all-purpose white flour *or* half each whole wheat and white	750 ml
1 tsp	baking soda	5 ml
2 tsp	baking powder	10 ml
1 tsp	cinnamon	5 ml
½ tsp	salt	2 ml
1½ cups	sugar	375 ml
1¼ cups	vegetable oil	300 ml
4	large eggs	
2½ cups	carrots *(about 5–6 carrots), grated*	625 ml
2 cups	apples *(about 2 apples), peeled and chopped*	500 ml
1 tsp	fresh orange zest, *grated*	5 ml

TIP:

• Golden Delicious apples are indeed delicious in this recipe.

Even when the pantry is just about empty, you're likely to find a few carrots and apples around for these moist muffins. They can be made ahead – the recipe makes a big batch – stored in the freezer, and warmed for a quick breakfast.

1. Preheat oven to 375°F (190°C). Grease muffin cups or line them with muffin papers.

2. Combine flour, baking soda, baking powder, cinnamon, and salt. Set aside.

3. In a separate bowl, beat sugar, oil, and eggs until light and fluffy.

4. Blend dry mixture into beaten egg mixture. Fold in carrots, apples, and orange zest.

5. Spoon batter into muffin cups, filling about ¾ full. Bake for 25–35 minutes, or until a toothpick inserted in the centre comes out clean.

Makes about 2 dozen medium-sized muffins.

QUICK TRICK:

Melon Medley: To serve 4, slice half a honeydew and half a cantaloupe into thin wedges and remove skin. Arrange melon slices on a platter. In the middle, pile fresh strawberries that have been tossed with a little sugar (if desired) and fresh chopped mint. Accompany with a basket of fresh-from-the-oven muffins.

TIP:

Select melons that feel heavy for their size and have a pronounced aroma.

Diner-Style Sausage Hash

³/₄–1 lb	sausages	375–500 g
3 cups	cooked potatoes (baked or boiled), peeled and cut into small cubes	750 ml
1	medium onion, finely chopped	
1 tbsp	fresh parsley, chopped	15 ml
	salt and freshly ground black pepper	
1 tbsp	vegetable oil	15 ml
2 tbsp	butter	30 ml

TIPS:

• Bake or boil a few extra potatoes when you're making supper to get a quick start on next morning's breakfast or brunch.

• The hash mixture can be prepared the night before (through Step 2) and stored, covered, in the refrigerator.

• Add a chopped stalk of celery, half a chopped pepper (red or green), or a few lightly browned, sliced mushrooms to the hash if you like.

*C*rispy browned potatoes, just like the diner makes, are essential with eggs. This twist on classic hash uses your favourite sausage instead of corned beef. Serve hot with fried or poached eggs on top (for perfect poached eggs, see Quick Trick, p. 246), or scrambled eggs on the side, and brown toast.

1. Prick sausages and simmer in enough water to cover for 5 minutes. Remove from water and allow to cool, then pull away the casing and roughly chop the filling.

2. Toss crumbled sausage with potatoes, onion, parsley, and salt and pepper to taste.

3. Heat oil and butter in a non-stick frying pan. Add sausage mixture and press down with a spatula to make an even layer. Cook, covered, over moderate heat for about 10 minutes to heat through.

4. Remove lid, raise heat, and cook 5 minutes longer until nicely browned on the bottom. Flip the hash out onto a plate.

5. Add a little more butter to the pan. When it's hot, slide the hash back in, unbrowned side down. Cook for a few more minutes until the underside is golden. Serve in hot wedges straight from the pan with eggs alongside or on top.

Serves 4.

Zucchini Frittata

2 tbsp	olive oil	30 ml
1 clove	garlic, *sliced*	
2	zucchini, *trimmed and thinly sliced*	
	salt and freshly ground black pepper	
2	green onions, *finely chopped*	
1/2 cup	parsley, *finely chopped*	125 ml
10	eggs, *lightly beaten*	
3 tbsp	butter	45 ml
1/2 cup	Swiss cheese, *grated*	125 ml
3 tbsp	Parmesan cheese, *grated*	45 ml

TIP:

• To save time in the morning, Step 1 can be done the night before and the zucchini mixture refrigerated.

VARIATIONS:

• Add half a sliced or chopped roasted red pepper.

• Replace the zucchini with a 14-oz (398-ml) can of artichoke hearts, rinsed, well drained, and sliced, or 1 1/2 cups cooked asparagus cut into 2" (5-cm) pieces.

This Italian-style omelette is quickly prepared, hearty enough to feed a group, and very flexible, since you can combine odds and ends of cheese (try fontina, Gruyère, or Cheddar) and vegetables that have been languishing in the fridge.

1. Heat oil in a small frying pan and toss in garlic. When garlic has coloured, scoop it out and discard. Add zucchini and toss over medium heat until browned. Season lightly and sprinkle with green onions and half the parsley.

2. Combine eggs and zucchini mixture, and season with salt and pepper.

3. Preheat broiler. Over medium-high heat, melt 2 tbsp (30 ml) butter in a large (about 10"/25-cm) well-seasoned or non-stick pan that can go into the oven. Pour in egg mixture. Leave for a couple of minutes to set the bottom, then shake pan gently over the heat.

4. When underside is lightly browned and top is still runny (another minute or two), sprinkle cheeses on top and dot with remaining butter. Slide frittata under the broiler until cheese melts and the top starts to brown. Cut in wedges, sprinkle with the rest of the parsley, and serve at once.

Serves 4–5.

Pear Crumble Coffee Cake

Cake

	batter for Save-the-Day Pound Cake (p. 281)	
3	ripe pears, *peeled, cored, and cut into thick slices*	

Ginger Crumble Topping

½ cup	brown sugar	125 ml
⅓ cup	flour	75 ml
1 tsp	ground ginger	5 ml
1 tbsp	crystallized ginger, *diced (optional)*	15 ml
¼ cup	cold butter, *cut in small chunks*	60 ml

TIPS:

• The cake can be baked ahead and frozen. (It's best when used within a couple of weeks.) Warm briefly before serving.

• Substitute sliced apples or plums for the pears.

Delicious warm for breakfast or as a mid-morning snack.

1. Make the crumble topping: In a large bowl, combine brown sugar, flour, and ginger(s). Cut in cold butter until mixture resembles coarse crumbs. (Or combine in a food processor using on/off pulses.) Set aside.

2. Preheat oven to 350°F (180°C). Lightly grease, or line with parchment, a 9" (23 cm) springform pan or a 9" x 9" (23 cm x 23 cm) baking pan.

3. Spoon pound cake batter into prepared pan. Arrange sliced pears on top and cover evenly with topping.

4. Bake on the middle rack of the preheated oven for about an hour, or until a wooden skewer inserted in the centre of the cake comes out clean. (Test after 45 minutes.) Cool in pan on a wire rack for 10 minutes, then remove from pan and cool completely, right side up. Serve warm or at room temperature.

Makes 12–16 slices.

VARIATION:

• **Blueberry Streusel Coffee Cake:** Mix 2 cups (500 ml) blueberries into the batter instead of putting sliced pears on top. Replace the crystallized and ground ginger in the topping with ½ tsp (2 ml) cinnamon. Cover batter with crumble topping and bake as above.

Lazy-Day Sticky Buns

2 cups	**pecan halves** *or* **pieces**	500 ml
	frozen white dinner-roll dough *(enough for 24 rolls)* *(see Tips, below)*	
1 pkg	**butterscotch pudding and pie filling** *(not instant)* *(6 oz/170 g)*	
½ cup	**butter,** *cut in small pieces*	125 ml
½ cup	**brown sugar,** *lightly packed*	125 ml

TIPS:

• Be sure to buy frozen roll dough, not prebaked frozen rolls. Rhodes is one brand to look for.

• Save the leftover pudding mix. When you've made 3 batches of sticky buns, you'll have enough mix for 1 more batch.

This prize-winning recipe from one of Cottage Life magazine's readers has earned countless fans. It requires little preparation since the buns start with storebought frozen dinner-roll dough and use pudding mix to create their caramel sauce. Assemble them the night before and leave them to rise overnight.

1. Spray a 9" (3-L) bundt or tube pan with non-stick cooking spray or grease lightly with shortening. Spread pecans in bottom of pan.

2. Arrange frozen rolls closely together in single layer over pecans. (You'll need about 24 rolls.)

3. Measure out ¾ of pudding mix – about ⅔ cup (150 ml). Sprinkle mix evenly over rolls. Scatter butter pieces on top; sprinkle with brown sugar.

4. Cover loosely with plastic wrap or greased foil. Let stand at room temperature for 6–9 hours, or until buns are just below top of pan. Rising time will vary depending on how warm or cool your "room temperature" is.

5. Place pan on a piece of aluminum foil or a baking sheet to catch any drips that run over. Bake at 350°F (180°C) for 30–35 minutes, or until golden brown and firm, and buns sound hollow when lightly tapped.

6. Immediately after removing from oven, loosen buns from sides of pan and invert onto serving plate. Enjoy warm, cool, or reheated, if there are any left.

Makes about 8 servings.

Lemon Blueberry Scones

2 cups	all-purpose flour	500 ml
½ cup	sugar	125 ml
1 tbsp	baking powder	15 ml
½ tsp	salt	2 ml
¼ cup	cold butter, *cut in pieces*	60 ml
1 cup	fresh blueberries	250 ml
1 tbsp	lemon zest, *grated*	15 ml
1	large egg	
1	large egg, *separated*	
½ –¾ cup	10% cream	125–175 ml
	Lemon Sugar *(2 tbsp/30 ml sugar mixed with 1 tbsp/15 ml grated lemon zest)*	

TIPS:

• The dough can also be baked as 2 large rounds. Score the top into 8 equal wedges before baking for easy cutting afterwards. (Baking time will be longer; check after 15 minutes.)

VARIATION:

• Cranberry Orange Scones: In fall and winter, substitute cranberries for the blueberries and orange zest for the lemon zest in both the scones and the sugar topping. Bake as above.

Serve these irresistible scones warm with butter or Maple Butter (Quick Trick, p. 245) for breakfast, with cream or crème fraîche for tea.

1. Preheat oven to 400°F (200°C). Grease and lightly flour a large baking sheet.

2. Place flour, sugar, baking powder, salt, and cold butter in the bowl of a food processor. Pulse until mixture resembles coarse crumbs, then turn into a large bowl. (Or combine dry ingredients in a bowl and cut in butter using a pastry blender, 2 knives, or your fingers to make coarse crumbs.)

3. Stir blueberries and lemon zest into flour mixture.

4. In a bowl, whisk egg, egg yolk, and ½ cup (125 ml) cream. (Reserve egg white.) Stir egg-cream mixture into the other ingredients with quick, light strokes, just until combined, adding more cream if necessary to make a soft dough. Do not overmix.

5. Turn dough out onto a floured surface and knead briefly with a light hand until smooth. Pat into a disc about 1" (2.5 cm) thick and cut into rounds with a 2" (5-cm) cookie cutter or glass. Place on prepared baking sheet.

6. Whisk reserved egg white, then brush on surface of each scone and sprinkle with Lemon Sugar.

7. Bake on the middle rack of a preheated oven 10–15 minutes, until tops are nicely browned and a wooden skewer or cake tester inserted close to the centre of a scone comes out clean. Cool on a rack. Serve warm.

Makes at least 12 scones.

Depending on the season, make either Cranberry Orange Scones (shown here) or Lemon Blueberry ones.

Sausage & Vegetable Strata

1 loaf	**French bread,** *cut in ¹/₂" (1-cm) slices on the diagonal*	
1 cup	**milk**	**250 ml**
2–3	**Italian sausages**	
1 tbsp	**olive oil**	**15 ml**
	Piperade, *made without ham (recipe on facing page)*	
1 cup	**Cheddar cheese,** *grated*	**250 ml**
4	**eggs,** *beaten*	
	salt and freshly ground black pepper	
1 tbsp	**butter**	**15 ml**

TIPS:

• Make up a double batch of piperade and serve some alongside the strata. Add a romaine salad, and you've got an easy Sunday supper.

• If you have any mushrooms in the fridge, you can sauté them and add them to the strata as well.

When surprise guests show up and you have to make something out of nothing, a hunt in the refrigerator may reveal a couple of sausages, a few eggs, and a vegetable or two that can be turned into a special breakfast dish. Assemble it the night before and bake it in the morning.

1. The night before serving, dip bread slices in milk and gently press out excess liquid. Arrange a layer of slices in the bottom of a buttered ovenproof dish approximately 8" x 8" (20 cm x 20 cm).

2. Remove sausage meat from casings. Heat oil in a large frying pan. Add sausage meat, breaking it up with a fork, and cook until lightly browned. Remove meat with a slotted spoon and pour away excess fat.

3. Prepare the piperade in the same pan, omitting the ham.

4. Layer half the sausage on top of the bread slices, then add half the piperade and a third of the cheese. Repeat the layers with remaining ingredients, ending with a layer of bread and cheese.

5. Beat eggs with salt and pepper and pour over the layers. Cover with plastic wrap and refrigerate.

6. The next day, bring the strata to room temperature and dot the top with butter. Bake at 350°F (180°C) until puffed and lightly browned, about 40–45 minutes. Serve hot.

Serves 6.

Piperade with Eggs

½–¾ cup	**butter**	125–175 ml
16–20	**eggs**	
	fresh parsley, *chopped*	

Piperade

2 tbsp	**olive oil**	30 ml
½ lb	**cooked smoked ham,** *thinly sliced and cut in strips*	250 g
1	**onion,** *finely chopped*	
2 cloves	**garlic,** *minced*	
2	**green peppers,** *seeded and sliced*	
2	**red peppers,** *seeded and sliced*	
2 lbs	**firm ripe tomatoes,** *seeded and chopped* **or**	1 kg
1 can	**plum tomatoes,** *drained and chopped (28 oz/796 ml)*	
1 tbsp	**fresh basil,** *chopped* **or**	15 ml
1 tsp	**each dried basil and oregano**	5 ml
2 dashes	**hot sauce**	
	salt and freshly ground black pepper	

*P*iperade, from the Basque region of France, is a savoury mixture of peppers and tomatoes that is particularly good with eggs. Tuck spoonfuls of it into omelettes, or pile it in the centre of a platter of scrambled eggs for an easy breakfast dish for a crowd. Serve with brioche or whole-grain toast.

1. Make the piperade: Heat oil in a large frying pan. Add ham strips, brown lightly, then lift out and reserve.

2. Add onion and garlic to the pan and cook until soft. Toss in pepper strips and cook until lightly browned and beginning to soften.

3. Add tomatoes, herbs, and seasonings, and stir over moderately high heat for a few minutes until most of the liquid has evaporated. Return ham to pan, partially cover, and set aside until needed.

4. Whisk the eggs with a little salt in two batches of 8–10. Melt half the butter in a non-stick frying pan, pour in one batch of eggs, and stir constantly over medium heat until eggs are set and creamy. Turn out onto a large platter and keep warm. Cook the second batch in the remaining butter; add to platter.

5. Reheat the piperade and pile in the middle of the platter. Sprinkle with pepper and parsley, and serve at once.

Serves 8.

TIP:
• The piperade (Steps 1–3) can be made up to 2 days ahead and kept refrigerated.

Pan-Fried Fresh Fish

1½ lbs	fish fillets	750 g
	salt and freshly ground black pepper	
6 tbsp	unsalted butter	90 ml
	juice of 1 lemon	
	fresh parsley, *chopped*	

Cornmeal-Crusted Fish

1 cup	fine cornmeal	250 ml
1 cup	buttermilk	250 ml

Egg-Battered Fish

1 cup	flour	250 ml
2	eggs	
¼ cup	milk	60 ml

*T*wo great ways to showcase the catch at breakfast. Accompany the fish with browned onions, home fries, and warm cornmeal muffins (Tip, p. 335).

1. Season cornmeal or flour with a dash of salt and pepper.

2. For Cornmeal-Crusted Fish: Dip fillets first in buttermilk, then in the seasoned cornmeal to coat evenly.

3. For Egg-Battered Fish: Beat eggs and milk together lightly. Dip fish fillets one at a time into the seasoned flour, then into the egg mixture, and then again into the flour, dusting off excess.

4. Heat 3 tbsp (45 ml) of the butter in a large, heavy skillet over moderate heat. Sauté fish until lightly browned on one side, about 5 minutes; turn and cook other side a minute or two more. The fish is done when the flesh becomes opaque and separates into moist flakes.

5. Remove fish from pan and pour away cooking fat. Add lemon juice and remaining butter to the pan, and cook until butter melts. Pour sauce over fish, season to taste, and sprinkle with parsley. Enjoy at once.

Serves 4.

TIPS:
• If you're also preparing bacon, fry the fillets in the bacon fat instead of butter.

• Instead of the lemon-butter sauce, serve the fish with your favourite salsa on the side. (The Roasted Tomato Corn Salsa on p. 54 goes well.)

The classic cottage breakfast – pan-fried fish with fried onions and potatoes.

1	**sausage** *(sweet or hot Italian)*
4 slices	**lean side bacon,** **peameal bacon,** *or* **ham**
½ recipe	**Speedy Pizza Dough** *(p. 234)*
	cornmeal *(for dusting pan)*
2 tbsp	**tomato sauce** **30 ml**
½ cup	**mozzarella** **125 ml** **cheese,** *grated*
1	**egg**
	fresh parsley, *chopped* *(optional)*

TIP:

• The sausage and bacon can be cooked
a day ahead and refrigerated.

Breakfast Pizza

*𝒯ry this twist on the bacon-and-eggs theme for a hearty breakfast or brunch.
Serve it with a Melon Medley (Quick Trick, p. 263) to start, a romaine salad on
the side, and perhaps a morsel of Pear Crumble Coffee Cake (p. 266) to finish.*

1. Remove casing from sausage. Break up sausage meat in a frying pan set
over moderate heat, and cook until no longer pink, about 5 minutes.
Remove and set aside.

2. Cut ham or bacon slices in half. Grill or lightly fry until half cooked.
Drain on paper towel and set aside.

3. On a lightly floured surface, stretch or roll the dough to form one 10"–12"
(25–30-cm) circle. Place on an oiled baking sheet or pizza pan that has been
dusted with cornmeal.

4. Spread a light, even layer of tomato sauce over the dough, add about half
the mozzarella, then the crumbled sausage, ham or bacon slices, and the rest
of the cheese. Make a small hollow in the cheese in the centre of the pizza
and break an egg into it.

5. Bake in a preheated 400°F (200°C) oven for 15 minutes. Remove from
oven and carefully break the egg yolk with a fork, pulling the yolk gently
through the cheese topping towards the edge of the pizza. Continue baking
for about 5 minutes longer until the crust is lightly golden on the bottom
and the topping is piping hot. Serve hot, sprinkled with parsley if you like.

Serves 2–4.

VII. BAKING & DESSERTS

Mix-in-the-Pan Cake

Cake

1½ cups	all-purpose flour	375 ml
1 cup	sugar	250 ml
¼ cup	cocoa	60 ml
1 tsp	baking powder	5 ml
1 tsp	baking soda	5 ml
¼ tsp	salt	1 ml
⅓ cup	butter, *melted*	75 ml
1 tbsp	lemon juice *or* vinegar	15 ml
1 cup	warm water	250 ml

Brown-Sugar Frosting

1 cup	brown sugar, *packed*	250 ml
¼ cup	milk	60 ml
2 tbsp	butter	30 ml
3 tbsp	icing sugar	45 ml

A chocolate cake that you mix and bake all in one pan – what could be easier? There's no egg in this cake, so it's ideal for the days you forget to pack the eggs or someone eats the last few for breakfast. The brown-sugar frosting is different and delicious – or, for a double hit of chocolate, try the Chocolate Ganache Frosting on the facing page.

1. Preheat oven to 350°F (180°C). Combine first 6 dry ingredients in an ungreased 8" (20-cm) square cake pan. Mix well.

2. Add butter, lemon juice, and water. Mix well with fork until smoothly blended.

3. Bake in preheated oven for 35–40 minutes, or until cake springs back when lightly touched. Cool slightly.

4. Combine first 3 frosting ingredients in a medium saucepan. Boil 2 minutes. Cool slightly.

5. Beat in icing sugar until smooth and starting to thicken (about 5 minutes). Spread right away on warm cake. (Icing hardens quickly.)

Makes about 9 servings.

TIP:
• The cake is also delicious without frosting, perhaps topped with a dollop of whipped cream.

(Mix-in-the-Pan Cake with Brown-Sugar Frosting is included in the photo following p. 329.)

Couldn't-Be-Easier
Chocolate Banana Cake

2 cups	sugar	500 ml
1¾ cups	all-purpose flour	425 ml
¾ cup	cocoa	175 ml
1½ tsp	baking powder	7 ml
1½ tsp	baking soda	7 ml
1 tsp	salt	5 ml
2	eggs	
1 cup	ripe banana (2 large bananas), mashed	250 ml
1 cup	warm water	250 ml
½ cup	milk	125 ml
½ cup	oil	125 ml
1 tsp	vanilla	5 ml

QUICK TRICK:
Chocolate Ganache Frosting: Bring 1 cup (250 ml) 35% cream to a boil, then pour it on top of 8 oz (250 g) chopped semi-sweet chocolate. Stir while chocolate melts, then beat until smooth. Cover and refrigerate until frosting is cool and slightly set, about 45 minutes. (If the frosting becomes too firm, soften at room temperature to spreading consistency.) Makes enough to frost one 9" x 13" (23 cm x 33 cm) cake or 24 cupcakes.

This cake is a great way to use up a couple of overripe bananas. It can be whipped up in minutes, and is so dark and moist it doesn't really require any frosting – though you certainly can't go wrong with a swirl of Chocolate Ganache Frosting on top. (See Quick Trick, below.) Or serve it with vanilla ice cream, crème fraîche, or custard instead.

1. Preheat oven to 350°F (180°C). Grease a 9" x 13" (23 cm x 33 cm) pan.

2. Combine sugar, flour, cocoa, baking powder, baking soda, and salt. Mix well.

3. In a large bowl, whisk together eggs, banana, warm water, milk, oil, and vanilla until blended.

4. Add dry ingredients, whisking until smooth and thoroughly blended. Batter will be thin.

5. Pour into prepared pan. Bake for 35–40 minutes, or until toothpick inserted in centre comes out clean.

6. Cool cake in pan on wire rack.

Makes about 16 servings.

VARIATION:
Couldn't-Be-Easier Chocolate Banana Cupcakes: Preheat oven to 400°F (200°C). Scoop batter into regular-sized muffin cups lined with muffin papers, filling them about ⅔ full. Bake approximately 20 minutes, or until toothpick inserted in centre comes out clean. Makes 24 cupcakes.

Strawberry Meringue Cake

¾ cup	all-purpose flour	175 ml
¼ cup	cornstarch	60 ml
1½ tsp	baking powder	7 ml
½ cup	soft butter	125 ml
1½ cups	sugar	375 ml
4	eggs, *separated*	
2 tsp	vanilla	10 ml
2 tbsp	milk	30 ml
½ cup	sliced almonds, *toasted*	125 ml

Filling and decoration

1 cup	35% cream	250 ml
½ tsp	vanilla	2 ml
1 tbsp	icing sugar	15 ml
1 qt	fresh strawberries	1 L

This take on the classic strawberry shortcake features crunchy meringue layers with lashings of whipped cream and juicy berries in between. It looks impressive, but is easy to make. You can bake the meringue layers a couple of days ahead, then assemble the cake shortly before serving.

1. Preheat oven to 350°F (180°C). Lightly butter and flour two 9" (23-cm) round cake pans.

2. Sift together flour, cornstarch, and baking powder, and set aside.

3. Beat butter until light. Add ½ cup (125 ml) sugar and continue beating until mixture is light and fluffy. Beat in egg yolks, one at a time. Add 1 tsp (5 ml) vanilla.

4. Blend in dry ingredients and milk. Spread batter in prepared cake pans.

5. Let egg whites reach room temperature, then beat until soft peaks form. Gradually beat in the remaining sugar and vanilla. Spread a layer of meringue on top of each layer of batter and sprinkle with almonds.

6. Bake in preheated oven about 25 minutes, or until a toothpick inserted in the centre of the cake comes out clean and the top is an even light brown. Set aside to cool in the pans.

Please turn to next page

The almond-covered meringue on each layer gives a delectable crunch to this take on traditional strawberry shortcake.

Strawberry Meringue Cake, *continued*

To assemble the cake:

1. Whip cream, vanilla, and icing sugar together until soft peaks hold their shape.

2. Trim and halve the berries, saving the nicest ones to decorate the top of the cake.

3. Remove cake layers from pans and place one on a platter meringue side down. Spread with a layer of whipped cream and a layer of berries.

4. Top with the other cake layer meringue side up. Decorate top with berries and swirls of whipped cream. Serve any remaining berries alongside.

Makes 8 slices.

QUICK TRICK:

Strawberry Yogurt Popsicles (shown in photo following p. 305): Crush 2 cups (500 ml) hulled strawberries in a food processor or with a potato masher. Stir in 1½ cups (375 ml) plain yogurt and 2 tbsp (30 ml) icing sugar. Process or mix until smoothly blended. Divide the mixture evenly into 10 small paper drink cups (the 3-oz/ 100-ml size). Cover each with foil. Make a small slit in centre of foil and insert a wooden stick or plastic spoon handle through the foil and into each cup. (Or use plastic Popsicle-style moulds.) Freeze until firm, at least 3 hours. To serve, tear away the foil and paper cup. Makes 10.

Save-the-Day Pound Cake

2 cups	all-purpose flour	500 ml
2 tsp	baking powder	10 ml
¼ tsp	salt	1 ml
½ cup	butter, *softened*	125 ml
1 cup	sugar	250 ml
3	eggs, *lightly beaten*	
1 tsp	vanilla	5 ml
2 tsp	lemon or orange zest, *grated*	10 ml
1 cup	sour cream	250 ml

QUICK TRICK:
Citrus Glaze: For a light, citrusy icing for pound cake, combine ¼ cup (60 ml) fresh lemon or orange juice with ½ cup (125 ml) sugar. Simmer for 3 minutes. Pour over warm pound cake in pan. Let stand 10 minutes, then remove from pan and cool completely.

This recipe is a lifesaver, as it can help you create a number of quick desserts. Top it with fresh berries or Mixed Berry Sauce (p. 295) – and a dollop of whipped cream or ice cream. Layer it with custard and fruit to make a summer trifle. Turn it into a Pear (or Apple or Plum) Crumble Coffee Cake (p. 266). Dip it in egg and grill it for a French-toast-like dessert (p. 282). Or drizzle it with a lemon or orange glaze (Quick Trick, below) and serve it on its own for tea time or dessert.

1. Preheat oven to 350°F (180°C). Lightly grease (or line with parchment) an 8" x 8" (2-L) square pan or a 9" x 5" (2-L) loaf pan.

2. Combine flour, baking powder, and salt. Set aside.

3. Cream butter and sugar until light and fluffy. Add eggs, one at a time. Stir in vanilla and lemon or orange zest.

4. Fold in flour mixture alternately with sour cream.

5. Spoon batter into prepared pan. Bake on the middle rack of the oven for about an hour, or until a wooden skewer poked into the centre of the cake comes out clean. (Test cake after 45 minutes.) Cool in pan on a wire rack for 10 minutes, then remove from pan and cool completely.

Makes 12–16 slices.

Grilled Pound Cake
with Warmed Strawberries

2 cups	**strawberries,** *halved or quartered*	500 ml
¼ cup	**sugar**	60 ml
1	**egg,** *lightly beaten*	
2 tbsp	**milk**	30 ml
2 tbsp	**orange liqueur** *(such as Cointreau or Grand Marnier)*	30 ml
4 slices	**pound cake** *(¾"/2 cm thick)*	
	whipped cream *(optional)*	

When you're eating outdoors on a warm summer night, it's appealing to serve a dessert prepared on the barbecue. Use the pound cake on the previous page to make this exotic version of French toast, or take a shortcut and start with a store-bought cake.

1. Combine berries and sugar in an aluminum pie plate. Let stand at room temperature to allow juices to form. Stir occasionally.

2. Preheat grill on high for a few minutes.

3. Place pie plate with strawberry mixture on one side of grill to warm. Stir occasionally.

4. Beat egg, milk, and liqueur in a small shallow dish. Dip each slice of cake into egg mixture, turning to coat both sides thoroughly. Using egg lifter, place each slice on grill. Turn after 3 or 4 minutes, or when nicely browned, and brown second side.

5. Place each slice of cake on a dessert plate and spoon berries on top. Garnish, if desired, with whipped cream. Serve immediately.

Serves 4.

TIPS:
• Add in other berries, such as raspberries or blueberries.
• Replace the orange liqueur with orange juice plus ¼ tsp (1 ml) vanilla extract.

Strawberries and cream on top of pound cake treated like French toast – who could resist?

Easy Apple Cake

Topping

⅓ cup	sugar	75 ml
1½ tsp	cinnamon	7 ml

Cake

2 cups	sugar	500 ml
1 cup	vegetable oil	250 ml
4	eggs	
½ cup	orange *or* apple juice	125 ml
1 tbsp	vanilla	15 ml
3 cups	all-purpose flour	750 ml
1 tbsp	baking powder	15 ml
½ tsp	salt	2 ml
5	medium apples, *peeled, cored, and chopped*	

TIP:

• **Use tart apples such as Granny Smiths for the best flavour.**

*M*oist and delicious, with a hint of spice. This is an ideal cottage cake – it makes a large pan, needs no icing, and keeps well. It's versatile, too: Serve it for dessert, with tea, or as a coffee cake for breakfast.

1. Preheat oven to 350°F (180°C). Grease a 9" x 13" (23 cm x 33 cm) cake pan.

2. Combine sugar and cinnamon for topping; set aside.

3. Beat first 5 cake ingredients in a large bowl.

4. Combine flour, baking powder, and salt. Stir into egg mixture, mixing until smooth. Spread half of batter in prepared pan. Arrange apples over top. Sprinkle half of topping mixture over apples. Spread remaining batter over top. Sprinkle with remaining topping.

5. Bake in preheated oven for 50–60 minutes, or until cake springs back when lightly touched. Serve warm or cool.

Makes about 16 servings.

(The Easy Apple Cake is included in the photo following p. 329.)

Apricot Upside-Down Cake

¼ cup + 6 tbsp	butter	150 ml
¼ cup	brown sugar	60 ml
¼ cup	maple syrup	60 ml
1 can	apricot halves, *well drained* *(14 oz/398 ml)*	
1½ cups	all-purpose flour	375 ml
1 tsp	baking powder	5 ml
¼ tsp	baking soda	1 ml
pinch	salt	
¾ cup	white sugar	175 ml
	zest of 1 lemon, *grated*	
2	eggs	
¾ cup	sour cream	175 ml

TIP:

• Substitute thinly sliced apples, pears, peaches, or nectarines for the apricots.

*O*ne of the big pluses of this yummy fruit-topped cake is that you can make it even when you don't have any fresh fruit around. Just make sure you keep a can of apricots in the cupboard.

1. Thoroughly butter a 9" (23-cm) round cake pan. Preheat oven to 350°F (180°C).

2. In a small saucepan combine ¼ cup (60 ml) of the butter with the brown sugar and maple syrup. Stir over moderate heat until sugar is dissolved. Pour into the cake pan and arrange apricot halves on top, cut side up.

3. Combine flour, baking powder, baking soda, and salt. Set aside. In a mixing bowl, cream the remaining 6 tbsp (90 ml) butter with white sugar and grated lemon zest until light. Beat in eggs one at a time. Fold in flour mixture alternately with sour cream.

4. Spoon batter evenly over apricots. Bake for about 40 minutes, until the top is golden and a toothpick inserted in the centre comes out clean.

5. Set cake pan on a rack for 5 minutes, then loosen the edges of the cake and turn out onto a serving plate. Serve warm with whipped cream or Maple Cream (see below).

Makes about 8 servings.

QUICK TRICK:

Maple Cream: Beat ¾ cup (175 ml) whipping cream until soft peaks form. Gradually add ¼ cup (60 ml) maple syrup and a drop of vanilla. Continue beating until firm. Serve Maple Cream on Apricot Upside-Down Cake or a fruit pie or crisp.

Chocolate Toffee Crunch

1 cup	**butter,** *softened*	250 ml
1 cup	**brown sugar,** *packed*	250 ml
1	**egg yolk**	
2 cups	**all-purpose flour**	500 ml
1½ cups	**crunchy toffee bits** *(see Tips), divided*	375 ml
2 cups	**semi-sweet chocolate chips**	500 ml
1 cup	**white chocolate chips**	250 ml

QUICK TRICK:

Coffee Ice Cream Float: Fill a large mug or heatproof glass ⅔ full of black coffee and sweeten to taste. Add a scoop of vanilla ice cream, and stir slightly. Add another scoop of ice cream, sprinkle with grated chocolate or cinnamon, and you have dessert and coffee in the same cup. Serve at once – with a spoon and a straw.

The flavour combination of butter, caramel, and chocolate with a crunchy texture is sure to be a winner. Luckily, this recipe makes a big pan because these bars will disappear in a flash.

1. Preheat oven to 350°F (180°C).

2. In a large bowl, beat butter with an electric mixer or by hand until creamy. Add brown sugar and egg yolk, beating until smooth. Stir in flour and half the toffee bits, mixing until well blended.

3. Press mixture firmly into ungreased 15" x 10" x 1" (2-L) jelly-roll pan or cookie sheet with sides. Bake in preheated oven until golden, about 15–18 minutes.

4. Remove from oven. Immediately sprinkle semi-sweet chocolate chips on top. Let stand 5 minutes, or until chips are softened. Smooth evenly over top with a knife. Sprinkle white chocolate chips and remaining toffee bits over chocolate. Cool completely, then cut into bars.

Makes about 5 dozen bars.

TIPS:

• Look for toffee bits in bags in your supermarket – they're usually shelved with the chocolate chips. (Hershey's Skor Toffee Bits is the common brand.) One 225-g package is enough for this recipe.

• Try replacing the white chocolate chips with ⅔ cup (150 ml) sliced almonds.

Chocolate Toffee Crunch: two types of chocolate and crunchy toffee bits. Lemon Squares (p. 288): lots of lemon on a shortbread crust.

Lemon Squares

Crust

1 cup	all-purpose flour	250 ml
¼ cup	sugar	60 ml
½ cup	butter	125 ml

Topping

1 cup + 2 tbsp	sugar	280 ml
3 tbsp	all-purpose flour	45 ml
3	eggs	
1 tsp	lemon zest, *grated*	5 ml
½ cup	fresh lemon juice	125 ml

*T*his recipe comes from my friend and colleague Jill Snider, a master baker. The squares combine an intensely lemony topping with a rich, shortbread-like crust.

1. Preheat oven to 350°F (180°C) and grease an 8" (20-cm) square cake pan.

2. Combine all ingredients for crust, mixing until crumbly. Press firmly into pan. Bake in preheated oven for 15–20 minutes, or until light golden.

3. In a small bowl, whisk topping ingredients together until smooth. Pour over crust. Bake 30–35 minutes longer, or until set. Cool in pan on rack, then cut into squares.

Makes about 25 squares.

(The Lemon Squares are shown in the photo on the previous page.)

Double-Chocolate Peanut Bars

½ cup	peanut butter	125 ml
⅓ cup	corn syrup	75 ml
⅓ cup	honey	75 ml
½ cup	cocoa	125 ml
¼ cup	brown sugar, *lightly packed*	60 ml
3 cups	miniature marshmallows	750 ml
1 tsp	vanilla	5 ml
3 cups	crisp rice cereal	750 ml
1 cup	peanuts	250 ml
1–1½ cups	semi-sweet chocolate chips	250–375 ml

A no-bake goodie that takes only minutes to make. The combination of chocolate and peanut butter is irresistible to kids of all ages.

1. Combine the first 5 ingredients in a large saucepan. Heat, stirring constantly, until smooth and almost boiling. Reduce heat to low, add marshmallows, and stir constantly until mixture is melted and smooth.

2. Remove from heat. Stir in vanilla, cereal, and peanuts, and mix well. Press firmly into a greased 8" (20-cm) or 9" (23-cm) square pan.

3. Melt chocolate chips and spread evenly over bars. Cool until chocolate is set. Cut into squares.

Makes about 25 bars.

TIPS:

• Replace peanuts with another cup (250 ml) of cereal.

• Chocolate chips can also be sprinkled over squares and melted in the oven at 350°F (180°C) for 2–3 minutes until soft, then spread evenly over top.

One-Pot Brownies
with Chocolate Marshmallow Topping

Brownies

2 oz	unsweetened chocolate (2 squares)	56 g
1/3 cup	butter	75 ml
1 cup	sugar	250 ml
2	eggs	
1/2 tsp	vanilla	2 ml
3/4 cup	flour	175 ml
1/2 tsp	baking powder	2 ml
1/2 tsp	salt	2 ml
1/2 cup	nuts, chopped	125 ml

Topping

5	large marshmallows, sliced in half	
2 tbsp	butter	30 ml
1 oz	unsweetened chocolate (1 square)	28 g
1/4 cup	water or milk	60 ml
1 1/4 cups	icing sugar	300 ml
1/2 tsp	vanilla	2 ml

One of the best cottage cooks I know has a talent for effortlessly bringing out one yummy treat after another. This version of the all-time favourite fudgy square comes from her collection. It can be stirred up in just one pot.

1. Preheat oven to 350°F (180°C). Grease a 9" x 9" (23 cm x 23 cm) pan.

2. In a medium saucepan melt chocolate and butter. Add sugar, eggs, and vanilla, and stir until smooth.

3. Stir in flour, baking powder, salt, and nuts.

4. Spread mixture in prepared pan. Bake for about 20 minutes, or until the brownies dimple slightly when you press the centre of the pan.

5. Remove from the oven and place marshmallows on top, cut side down.

6. In the brownie-making saucepan (wash first), melt chocolate for topping with butter over low heat. Add water or milk, then stir in icing sugar until mixture is smooth. Stir in vanilla.

7. Drizzle topping over and around the marshmallows. Leave to cool before cutting into squares.

Makes 36.

TIP:
• If you're going to have a campfire, leave the topping off the brownies. Then hand out roasting sticks and marshmallows around the fire and let people top their brownies with warm, gooey toasted marshmallows.

Caramel Almond Squares

40	**soda crackers**	
	(plain or five-grain, salted or unsalted)	
	or	
30	**graham cracker squares**	
1 cup	**butter**	**250 ml**
1 cup	**brown sugar,** *packed*	**250 ml**
1 cup	**sliced almonds**	**250 ml**

TIPS:

• Sandwich 2 squares with a generous helping of ice cream in the middle, about 1" (2.5 cm) thick. Press firmly together. Slip each sandwich into a plastic bag or wrap tightly in plastic wrap. Freeze.

• For a more elegant presentation, cut the squares into triangles or fingers and serve them alongside a dish of ice cream.

A quick crispy sweet that's wonderful served with ice cream. No one will guess how simple these cookies are.

1. Preheat oven to 375°F (190°C). Generously grease a 10" x 15" (25 cm x 38 cm) jelly-roll pan or baking sheet with sides.

2. Line the pan with a single layer of crackers, trimming to fit if necessary.

3. Melt butter in a medium-sized saucepan. Add sugar. Cook over medium heat, stirring constantly until mixture is thoroughly blended, 3–4 minutes. (Do not allow it to boil.)

4. Stir in almonds. Carefully spread mixture over crackers.

5. Bake in preheated oven for 7–8 minutes, or until golden. Cool about 30 minutes. Cut into squares while still warm.

Makes about 30 squares.

(Ice cream sandwiches made with Caramel Almond Squares are shown in the photo following p. 305.)

Plum Crumble Squares

Crust & Topping

1 cup	slivered almonds	250 ml
2 cups	flour	500 ml
1 cup	icing sugar	250 ml
2 tsp	baking powder	10 ml
½ tsp	ground ginger	2 ml
1 cup	cold unsalted butter	250 ml
2 tbsp	crystallized ginger, *chopped*	30 ml
1	egg	
1	egg yolk	
1 tsp	vanilla	5 ml

Plum Filling

6	large plums, *sliced* (*a generous 4 cups/1 L*)	
½ cup	sugar	125 ml
¼ cup	cornstarch	60 ml
pinch	salt	

*S*harp, juicy plums combine with a crisp, sweet shortbread crust to make a tempting bite – no forks or plates required. For a real dessert, serve warm with whipped cream, ginger ice cream, or yogurt.

1. Preheat oven to 350°F (180°C). Lightly butter a 9" x 13" (23 cm x 33 cm) baking pan.

2. To make the crust and topping: Place ½ cup (125 ml) of the almonds in the bowl of a food processor and process until finely ground. Add flour, icing sugar, baking powder, and ground ginger, and combine briefly. Add cold butter and pulse to make coarse crumbs. Turn dry mix into a large bowl and add chopped crystallized ginger.

3. Combine egg, egg yolk, and vanilla. Gradually add to dry mix, tossing with a fork and your fingers until mixture begins to come together. Set ⅓ of mixture aside and press remainder into the prepared pan. Prick all over with a fork, then refrigerate 15–20 minutes. Bake in preheated oven for 18–20 minutes until lightly golden. Set aside to cool.

4. Meanwhile, combine the filling ingredients. Spread on baked crust and sprinkle reserved crumbs and remaining almonds on top. Bake 45–50 minutes until plums are bubbling around a golden topping.

Makes 36 squares.

TIP:

• If you don't have a food processor at hand, use store-bought ground almonds; combine the ingredients in a large bowl, cutting in the butter with 2 knives, a pastry blender, or your fingers.

Ginger Shortbread

2 cups	all-purpose flour	500 ml
1 cup	dark brown sugar	250 ml
2 tbsp	ground ginger	30 ml
1 tsp	baking soda	5 ml
pinch	salt	
1 cup	butter, *softened*	250 ml
2 tbsp	crystallized ginger, *finely chopped (optional)*	30 ml

VARIATION:

• Add 1 oz (28 g) finely grated unsweetened dark chocolate to half the mixture. Bake as above.

TIP:

Low-fat yogurt – 1% M.F. or 2% M.F. – can be turned into a wonderful substitute for high-fat whipped cream: Set the yogurt, with a pinch of salt added, to drain in a sieve lined with a double layer of cheesecloth or a paper coffee filter. Refrigerate. After about 30 minutes, the yogurt will have the consistency of lightly whipped cream. Stir in a little honey and serve as a dessert topping.

A crisp, spicy, buttery cookie that's fabulous with fruit, especially summer berries, rhubarb, peaches, and pears. (Try the shortbread with one of the fruit toppings on the next page or the Mixed Berry Sauce on p. 295.) Pile the fruit on the cookie and add a dollop of lightly sweetened whipped cream or yogurt. (See Tip, below.)

1. Preheat oven to 325°F (170°C). Lightly butter and flour two 9" (23-cm) round cake pans.

2. In a large bowl toss together the flour, sugar, ginger, soda, and salt. Blend in butter with your fingers or a pastry blender until mixture forms fine crumbs. Add crystallized ginger (if using).

3. Press mixture into the two prepared pans to form a smooth, even layer. Prick surface all over lightly with a fork.

4. Bake in preheated oven for 40–45 minutes until edges are lightly browned. Let cool in the pan for 5 minutes, then cut into narrow wedges and cool on racks. Store in an airtight container.

Make 32 wedges.

Mix & Match Fruit Toppings

Strawberry Rhubarb Compote

½ cup	sugar	125 ml
¼ cup	orange juice	60 ml
1 strip	orange zest, *(orange part only, no pith)*	
2 cups	rhubarb, *chopped*	500 ml
2 cups	strawberries, *sliced*	500 ml

Ginger Spiced Pears

½ cup	sugar	125 ml
1 cup	water	250 ml
1	cinnamon stick *(3"/8 cm)*	
2 strips	lemon zest	
3 slices	fresh ginger root, *(¼"/6 mm thick)*	
6	almost-ripe pears, *peeled, cored, and quartered*	

TIP:

• You can use the same method with plums, peaches, or apples.

Strawberry Rhubarb Compote

Serve over Ginger Shortbread (previous page) or pound cake (p. 281) and top with whipped cream or yogurt. Also try the compote on pancakes at breakfast.

1. Combine sugar, orange juice, and orange zest in a saucepan over moderate heat. Stir until sugar dissolves, then add rhubarb and simmer, covered, until tender (about 20 minutes).

2. Fold in strawberries and simmer for about 5 minutes. Set aside to cool, remove zest, and then refrigerate until serving. *Makes 4 servings.*

Ginger Spiced Pears

Serve on top of Ginger Shortbread (previous page) or alongside Pear Crumble Coffee Cake (p. 266) to dress it up for dessert. The pears are also wonderful with a scoop of vanilla ice cream on top drizzled with hot fudge sauce.

1. Combine sugar, water, cinnamon, lemon zest, and ginger in a medium-sized saucepan over moderate heat. Stir while sugar dissolves, then simmer the syrup for 5 minutes.

2. Add pears to the syrup, cover the pot, and simmer for about 5 minutes more, or until pears are just tender. (Cooking time will vary depending on the variety of pear and the ripeness of the fruit.)

3. Set aside and chill. Remove whole spices before serving. *Makes 6 servings.*

(The Strawberry Rhubarb Compote is shown in the photo on the previous page.)

Cheesecake Squares
with Mixed Berry Sauce

Crumb Crust

2 cups	graham cracker crumbs	500 ml
6 tbsp	butter, *melted*	90 ml
¼ cup	sugar	60 ml

Filling

1½ lbs	cream cheese	750 g
1 cup	sugar	250 ml
3 tbsp	flour	45 ml
1 tbsp	lemon zest, *grated*	15 ml
1 tsp	vanilla	5 ml
3	eggs	

Mixed Berry Sauce

2 cups	each raspberries and blueberries, *fresh or frozen*	500 ml
1 tbsp	lemon juice	15 ml
¾ cup	sugar *(or to taste)*	175 ml
¼ cup	orange liqueur *or* brandy *(optional)*	60 ml

A treat to take to a party or potluck. Carry the berry sauce along in a separate container and spoon a little on each square right before serving.

1. Line a 10" x 15" (25 cm x 38 cm) jelly-roll pan or baking sheet with sides with parchment paper or foil. Preheat oven to 325°F (170°C).

2. Combine crust ingredients and spread in the pan, patting down to make an even layer. Bake in preheated oven for 10 minutes. Set aside to cool.

3. In a large bowl, using a hand mixer, combine cream cheese and sugar. Mix in flour, lemon zest, vanilla, and eggs.

4. Pour mixture over prepared crust and bake in a 325°F (170°C) oven for 20–30 minutes or until filling in the centre of the pan is almost firm to the touch. Set aside to cool, then refrigerate before cutting into squares.

5. To make sauce, combine berries, lemon juice, and sugar in a blender or food processor and whirl until smooth. (If using frozen berries, thaw partially before using.) Add liqueur or brandy to taste, if you wish.

6. Press berry mixture through a sieve and store in a covered container in the refrigerator. Spoon over squares before serving.

Makes 24 squares.

TIP:
• The Mixed Berry Sauce will keep in the refrigerator for about 2 weeks. Keep it on hand to use with pancakes, waffles, ice cream, frozen yogurt, and pound cake.

Giant Oatmeal Cookies
with *Cranberries & Pecans*

¾ cup	butter	175 ml
1 cup	brown sugar, *packed*	250 ml
¼ cup	honey	60 ml
1	egg	
1 tsp	vanilla	5 ml
	zest of 1 orange, *finely grated*	
¾ cup	all-purpose flour	175 ml
½ tsp	salt	2 ml
½ tsp	baking soda	2 ml
3 cups	old-fashioned oats	750 ml
1½ cups	dried cranberries	375 ml
1 cup	pecans, *chopped*	250 ml

TIP:

• Use a heaped tablespoon of batter to make medium-sized cookies. Reduce baking time to 10–12 minutes.

*M*ake the batter ahead and store it in covered containers – it will keep in the refrigerator for a few days – then have fresh-baked cookies when the urge strikes.

1. Preheat oven to 350°F (180°C). Lightly grease 2 baking sheets or line them with parchment.

2. Cream butter, sugar, and honey together in a large bowl at medium speed with an electric mixer. Add egg, vanilla, and orange zest, and continue to beat until light and creamy.

3. In a separate bowl, combine flour, salt, and baking soda, and stir into the creamed mixture.

4. Add oats, cranberries, and pecans, and stir until well mixed.

5. Drop batter by ¼ cup (60-ml) measures onto prepared baking sheets. Wet your hands with water and use your palms to flatten the cookies, so they are about ⅜" (1 cm) thick. Bake for 14–16 minutes until lightly browned at the edges but still soft in the centres. Remove with a lifter to wire racks to cool.

Makes 2 dozen large cookies.

VARIATION:

• For Chocolate Chip Oatmeal Cookies, omit the orange zest and cranberries. Add 1 tsp (5 ml) cinnamon and 1½ cups (375 ml) chocolate chips. Bake as above.

Giant Oatmeal Cookies with Cranberries & Pecans and Decadent Fudge Cookies (next page): guaranteed not to make it to the cookie jar.

Decadent Fudge Cookies

14 oz	**semi-sweet chocolate,** *cut in chunks (about 2 full cups/500 ml)*	**400 g**
2 oz	**unsweetened chocolate,** *cut in chunks (about 1/3 cup/75 ml)*	**56 g**
1/4 cup	**unsalted butter**	**60 ml**
3	**large eggs,** *lightly beaten*	
1/2 cup	**white sugar**	**125 ml**
1 1/2 cups	**brown sugar**	**375 ml**
1 tsp	**vanilla**	**5 ml**
1/2 cup	**all-purpose flour**	**125 ml**
1/2 tsp	**baking soda**	**2 ml**
pinch	**salt**	
1/2 cup	**pecans,** *toasted and chopped*	**125 ml**
1 cup	**semi-sweet chocolate chips**	**250 ml**
1/2 cup	**dried cherries,** *softened in water and patted dry (optional)*	**125 ml**

If you want to keep these triple-chocolate cookies from disappearing in the blink of an eye, you'll need to store them in a locked tin under your bed! They're great for making ice cream sandwiches, by the way.

1. Preheat oven to 375°F (190°C). Grease and flour baking sheets or line them with parchment.

2. Melt semi-sweet chocolate, unsweetened chocolate, and butter in a bowl set over simmering water.

3. Beat eggs, white and brown sugar, and vanilla until light and fluffy.

4. In a separate bowl, toss together the flour, baking soda, salt, pecans, chocolate chips, and dried cherries (if using); set aside.

5. Pour egg/sugar mixture into melted chocolate and combine thoroughly. Stir in dry ingredients. Set aside for a few minutes until mixture cools and batter is firm enough to scoop.

6. Drop by teaspoonfuls onto prepared baking sheets. Bake for about 6 minutes – just until the tops begin to crack and the insides are still fudgy.

7. Cool on the baking sheets for 10 minutes, then transfer to racks. When completely cool, store in an airtight tin.

Makes 3 dozen cookies.

(The triple-chocolate Decadent Fudge Cookies are shown in the photo on the previous page.)

Chocolate Chunk Shortbreads

1 cup	unsalted butter	250 ml
1/2 cup	sugar	125 ml
1 tsp	vanilla	5 ml
1 3/4 cups	all-purpose flour	425 ml
1/4 cup	rice flour *or* cornstarch	60 ml
1 cup	semi-sweet chocolate chunks *(plus additional for decorating; optional)*	250 ml

A sophisticated variation of the chocolate chip cookie. These shortbreads keep well and have a pleasing crunch.

1. Preheat oven to 325°F (170°C). Lightly butter and flour a baking sheet.

2. Cream butter, sugar, and vanilla until light.

3. Combine flours (or flour and cornstarch) and blend into creamed mixture. Do not overmix. Add chocolate chunks.

4. Pinch off a tablespoon or so of mixture and place on prepared baking sheet. Press roughly into shape with two fingers and top with an extra chocolate chunk if you like.

5. Bake in preheated oven until firm but not brown, about 15–20 minutes.

Makes 16 cookies.

QUICK TRICK:

Fudge Cookie Ice Cream Pie: Bake a giant Decadent Fudge Cookie (facing page) in a pie plate at 375°F (190°C) for 15 minutes. (Use about 2 cups/500 ml of dough.) Allow to cool, top with softened ice cream, and refreeze until serving time. Decorate the top with melted chocolate and toasted pecans if you wish.

Chocolate Raspberry Terrine

6 oz	**bittersweet chocolate**	170 g
1 cup	**cream cheese,** *at room temperature*	250 ml
½ cup	**icing sugar**	125 ml
2 cups	**fresh raspberries**	500 ml
	Raspberry Syrup *(p. 305)*	

TIPS:

• If you see raspberries in the market with the hull and stem still attached, steer clear: It's a sign they were picked when they were underripe and they will likely be tart.

• Ripe, flavourful berries always have that wonderful berry aroma – I take a surreptitious sniff to make sure!

• For the smoothest, most sensuous desserts, use fine-quality dark, semi-sweet, or bittersweet chocolate such as Callebaut, Valrhona, or Lindt.

*E*ach bite of this frozen dessert combines rich, creamy chocolate flavour and the intense fruity taste of ripe raspberries.

1. Roughly chop or shave the chocolate. Place in a bowl set over a pot of simmering water until chocolate is just melted, stirring occasionally.

2. Soften the cream cheese with a rubber spatula. Add sugar and melted chocolate. Stir until well combined and smooth. Gently fold in 1 cup (250 ml) raspberries.

3. Spoon mixture into an 8½" x 4½" (1.5-L) loaf pan lined with plastic wrap or, for individual servings, scoop by ¼-cup (60-ml) measures into medium-sized muffin tins lined with paper cups. Cover with plastic wrap and freeze for at least 3 hours.

4. Unmould from loaf pan and slice, or remove individual servings from muffin papers. Drizzle each serving with Raspberry Syrup and garnish with remaining raspberries.

Makes 10–12 servings.

QUICK TRICK:

Brownies with Raspberry Coulis: Chocolate and raspberries go together like lakes and loons. For another easy-but-elegant dessert, serve a fudgy brownie in a pool of Raspberry Syrup (p. 305). Scatter some fresh raspberries over top.

Freeze the Chocolate Raspberry Terrine in a loaf pan and serve in slices. Or freeze it in muffin tins lined with paper cups for attractive individual servings.

Blueberry Coconut Cream

1 block	**pure creamed coconut** *(see Tip, below)*	
1 cup	**cream cheese,** *at room temperature*	250 ml
1 cup	**icing sugar**	250 ml
1 tsp	**coconut** *or* **rum extract**	5 ml
2 cups	**blueberries**	500 ml
	Blueberry Syrup *(p. 305)*	

TIP:

• Pure creamed coconut, which comes packaged in blocks, adds intense tropical flavour to desserts, muffins, and cakes. It is also a handy product to use in curries, coconut rice, and other Asian or African dishes. Look for it in your supermarket near the canned coconut milk.

A frozen dessert that combines a northern fruit with a taste of the tropics.

1. Soften creamed coconut by squishing it with your hands in its plastic package. Measure out $^1/_2$ cup (125 ml).

2. Soften cream cheese with a rubber spatula. Add sugar, the $^1/_2$ cup (125 ml) creamed coconut, and the extract, and stir until well combined. Gently fold in 1 cup (250 ml) blueberries.

3. Spoon mixture into an $8^1/_2$" x $4^1/_2$" (1.5-L) loaf pan lined with plastic wrap or, for individual servings, scoop by $^1/_4$-cup (60-ml) measures into medium-sized muffin tins lined with paper cups. Cover with plastic wrap and freeze for at least 3 hours.

4. Unmould from loaf pan and slice, or remove individual servings from muffin papers. Drizzle each serving with Blueberry Syrup and garnish with remaining blueberries.

Makes 10–12 servings.

Lemon Mousse

4	eggs, *separated*	
½ cup	sugar	125 ml
¼ cup	fresh lemon juice	60 ml
¼ cup	butter	60 ml
1 tsp	lemon zest, *grated*	5 ml
1 cup	35% cream	250 ml

QUICK TRICK:
Rum-Glazed Pineapple: Remove skin and eyes from a ripe pineapple. Cut into ½" (1-cm) slices and remove core. Combine ¼ cup (60 ml) each of dark rum, unsalted butter, and brown sugar in a small saucepan and stir over low heat until butter is melted and sugar dissolved. Add 2 tbsp (30 ml) fresh orange or lime juice. Brush mixture on pineapple and grill over medium heat about 5 minutes a side. Serve hot with ice cream.

*S*erve this simple, light dessert with a crispy cookie such as brandy snaps, gingersnaps, or the Maple Lace Cookies on p. 312. The mousse starts with a fresh lemon curd. You can also use the curd as a filling for little tarts, between sponge cake layers, or on toast or scones.

1. To make the lemon curd, combine egg yolks, sugar, lemon juice, and butter in a small pot over medium-low heat. Stir constantly until mixture coats the back of a spoon (5–7 minutes). Be careful mixture doesn't get too hot.

2. Remove from heat and stir in zest. Refrigerate until needed.

3. To finish the mousse, beat the egg whites until stiff. Fold into cool curd.

4. Whip cream until stiff and gently fold into mixture until thoroughly combined. Pile into a pretty serving bowl or individual wineglasses.

Makes 8 servings.

Berry Syrup

½ cup	sugar	125 ml
½ cup	water	125 ml
2 strips	lemon zest *(approx. ½" x 3"/1 cm x 8 cm)*	
2 cups	fresh berries *(strawberries, raspberries, blueberries, blackberries, or a mixture)*	500 ml

TIP:

• The syrup will keep in the refrigerator for a long time, but the flavour will be best if it's used within 2 weeks. It can also be frozen.

QUICK TRICK:

Berry Pops: Combine 2 cups (500 ml) of the Berry Syrup with 1 cup (250 ml) apple juice. Pour mixture into Popsicle-style moulds and freeze overnight, or for about 12 hours. Makes 6 pops.

You can use both red and blue summer berries for this intensely flavoured fruit syrup. Make separate batches for each berry variety – Raspberry Syrup or Blueberry Syrup, for instance – or mix them up. Every batch will be different, and each one will taste amazing. Serve the syrup pooled around slices of lemon tart, chocolate cake, or a fudgy brownie. Drizzle it over ice cream, sorbets, or waffles. Make fruity pops for the kids (Quick Trick, below) and use the syrup to flavour sodas, shakes, and smoothies. For the grown-ups, splash it into a glass of bubbly or make an awesome summer Berry Margarita (p. 19).

1. Combine sugar, water, and lemon zest in a small saucepan, and bring to a boil for 1 minute, or until sugar dissolves. Remove from heat and cool. Remove zest.

2. Rinse berries. Sort through them to remove any stems or leaves, and hull strawberries (if using). Place the berries in a small saucepan, crush gently, and bring to a boil over medium heat. If you're making the syrup with blueberries or blackberries alone, add ¼ cup (60 ml) water to the pot; no water is necessary if you're using strawberries, raspberries, or a mixture of red and blue berries. Reduce heat to low and simmer, uncovered, for 5–7 minutes.

3. Push the cooked berries through a fine mesh sieve (to purée them, leaving the seeds and skins behind), then add the cooled sugar syrup. Or purée the berries in a blender or food processor with the sugar syrup, then strain through a fine mesh sieve. Store covered in the refrigerator.

Makes 1⅔–2 cups (400–500 ml).

Mix the syrup with apple juice and freeze it for colourful, flavourful Berry Pops.

Espresso Ice Cream Loaf

2 cups	**chocolate ice cream,** *slightly softened*	500 ml
3 cups	**vanilla ice cream,** *slightly softened*	750 ml
1½ tsp	**instant espresso powder**	7 ml
2–3	**Skor chocolate bars,** *crushed (39 g each)*	
¼ cup	**toasted almonds,** *chopped (optional)*	60 ml
	chocolate sauce *(optional)*	

A layer of dark chocolate and a layer of mocha toffee crunch combine to make an irresistible grown-up frozen dessert. You don't have to tell anyone how easy it is to make.

1. Line an 8½" x 4½" (1.5-L) loaf pan with plastic wrap, leaving the ends hanging over the sides of the pan. Spread chocolate ice cream evenly in pan. Place in freezer while making the top layer.

2. Mix vanilla ice cream and espresso powder until blended. Stir in 2 crushed chocolate bars and nuts (if using). Spread over chocolate ice cream. Bring edges of plastic wrap over the top to seal tightly and freeze in the loaf pan until firm, at least 8 hours.

3. To serve, unmould onto cutting board, Remove plastic wrap. Cut into slices. If desired, drizzle slices with chocolate sauce or an additional crushed Skor bar.

Makes about 12 servings.

QUICK TRICKS:

Chocolate Crackle Sundae Sauce: Just like the soda-fountain favourite, this warm sauce hardens on cold ice cream. Chop 4 squares (4 oz/112 g) of semi-sweet or white chocolate and melt with ¼ cup (60 ml) butter on low heat or in a microwave until smooth. Spoon warm sauce on ice cream and leave for a few minutes to harden.

Design-Your-Own-Flavour Ice Cream: Slightly soften regular vanilla ice cream. Stir in your favourite goodies and refreeze until serving time. Try crushed peanut brittle, chopped almond bark, crushed striped mint candies, chopped fudge cookies, crushed candy bars, or other treats.

Previous page, clockwise from left: Espresso Ice Cream Loaf, Peachy Thick Shake (Quick Trick, facing page), ice cream sandwiches made with Caramel Almond Squares (p.291), Strawberry Yogurt Popsicles (p.280), and ice cream in Chocolate Nests and Crunchy Peanut Butter Shells (facing page).

Chocolate Nests
& Crunchy Peanut Butter Shells

Chocolate Nests

1 cup	chocolate chips	250 ml
½ cup	corn syrup	125 ml
½ cup	peanut butter	125 ml
4 cups	crisp rice cereal	1 L

Crunchy Peanut Butter Shells

1 cup	brown sugar, *packed*	250 ml
1 cup	corn syrup	250 ml
1 cup	peanut butter	250 ml
7 cups	corn flake cereal, *slightly crushed*	1.75 L
1¼ cups	peanuts, *chopped*	300 ml

QUICK TRICK:

Peachy Thick Shake: Combine about 1½ cups (375 ml) fresh peeled and sliced peaches with ¾ cup (175 ml) cold milk, ¼ cup (60 ml) orange, peach, or pineapple juice, and 1 tbsp (15 ml) honey in a blender. Process until smooth, then add 6 scoops vanilla ice cream and blend just until thick and smooth. Pour into glasses and garnish each with a peach slice. Serves 4.

These crispy shells make edible bowls for your favourite ice cream – a change from plain old cones that will delight kids and adults alike.

Chocolate Nests

1. Heat chips and syrup in a large saucepan until chips are melted. Add peanut butter and stir over heat until smooth. Add cereal. Mix well.

2. Scoop mixture into greased, large muffin cups until they're about ¾ full. Press a large indentation in the centre of each to form a shell. Chill in refrigerator until firm.

Makes about 15 shells.

Crunchy Peanut Butter Shells

1. Heat sugar and syrup in a large saucepan to dissolve. Add peanut butter and stir over heat until smooth.

2. Combine cereal and nuts in a large bowl. Add syrup mixture. Mix well. Cool slightly.

3. Scoop mixture into greased, large muffin cups until they're about ¾ full. Press a large indentation into the centre of each to form a shell. Chill in refrigerator until firm.

Makes about 18 shells.

Barbecued Peaches, Two Ways

4–6	**peaches,** *peeled, halved, and pitted*	

Caramelized Peaches

3 tbsp	**butter**	**45 ml**
½ cup	**brown sugar,** *lightly packed*	**125 ml**
2 tbsp	**brandy, orange liqueur,** *or* **maple syrup**	**30 ml**
2 tsp	**fresh lemon juice**	**10 ml**

Mint Julep Peaches

½ cup	**butter**	**125 ml**
½ cup	**bourbon**	**125 ml**
2 tbsp	**brown sugar**	**30 ml**
2 tbsp	**fresh mint,** *chopped* (plus extra for garnish)	**30 ml**

QUICK TRICK:
Peach Melba: Place a scoop of vanilla ice cream in an individual dessert dish, top with slices of Caramelized or Mint Julep Peaches, drizzle with Raspberry Syrup (p. 305), add a generous swirl of whipped cream, and sprinkle with toasted slivered almonds.

The flavour of peaches intensifies after a short time over the fire. Here are two ways to barbecue them. Either way, they're fabulous served over ice cream.

Caramelized Peaches

1. Spread 1 tbsp (15 ml) of the butter in an aluminum pie plate or on a large piece of foil.

2. Slice peaches and toss with sugar, flavouring, and lemon juice. Spoon onto pie plate or foil. Dot with remaining butter. Cover pie plate with foil and seal tightly, or fold foil around fruit, seal, and wrap with a second layer of foil.

3. Cook on barbecue, over low heat, for 20–30 minutes, or until fruit is tender. Spoon fruit with juices over ice cream or cake. *Serves 4.*

Mint Julep Peaches

1. Soak bamboo skewers or long, skinny cinnamon sticks in water for about an hour. Combine butter, bourbon, and sugar in a small saucepan, stirring over low heat for a couple of minutes until sugar and butter melt.

2. Thread peach halves horizontally onto skewers or cinnamon sticks, so that the cut sides will be exposed to the fire. (Depending on the size of the fruit, you may need to use 2 parallel skewers for each peach.)

3. Place on lightly oiled barbecue over medium heat. Turn and baste with glaze until peaches are tender, about 10–12 minutes. Serve warm over ice cream with any remaining glaze poured over top and a sprinkling of chopped fresh mint. *Serves 4.*

The Barbecued Peaches go particularly well with vanilla ice cream.

Maple Lace Cookies

¼ cup	butter	60 ml
¼ cup	pure maple syrup	60 ml
⅓ cup	brown sugar, *packed*	75 ml
½ cup	flour	125 ml
½ cup	nuts, *toasted and finely chopped*	125 ml
pinch	cinnamon	

TIPS:

• Be sure to preheat the oven and prepare your cookie sheets ahead so you can work quickly once the batter is made. It will harden if left in the pot very long.

• Try making curled cookies: Leave the baked cookies on the parchment paper for a minute or two to set. While they are still warm and pliable, curl them individually over the handle of a wooden spoon or a rolling pin and allow to cool. (Quick work and a light hand are required.)

*M*ake these lacy cookies with toasted walnuts, pecans, pine nuts, or pistachios. They go wonderfully with Lemon Mousse (p. 303), Ginger Spiced Pears (p. 294) – or a bowl of chocolate ice cream topped with fudge sauce.

1. Preheat oven to 375°F (190°C). Line 3 cookie sheets with cooking parchment.

2. In a small saucepan set over medium heat, combine butter, syrup, and sugar; stir until butter melts. Remove from heat and stir in flour, nuts, and cinnamon.

3. Drop batter by the tablespoon onto prepared baking sheets, leaving 3" (8 cm) between cookies.

4. Bake 5–6 minutes, or until edges are slightly brown. Remove cookie-covered parchment to a rack to cool. Store cooled cookies in tightly covered containers.

Makes approx. 12 cookies.

Maple Caramel Corn

1½ cups	sugar	375 ml
½ cup	water	125 ml
½ cup	maple syrup	125 ml
3 tbsp	butter	45 ml
2 tbsp	vinegar	30 ml
½ tsp	salt	2 ml
½ tsp	baking soda	2 ml
8 cups	popped corn, *no salt, no butter*	2 L
1 cup	pecans, *roughly chopped*	250 ml

TIP:
• For over-the-top delicious, melt semi-sweet chocolate and pour over the cooled caramel corn. Allow chocolate to harden, then break into clusters.

Fun to make, these caramel popcorn-and-nut clusters are even better than the store-bought kind.

1. Combine sugar, water, maple syrup, butter, vinegar, and salt in a small heavy saucepan. Cook over high heat for about 10 minutes until a spoonful of the mixture forms a hard ball when dropped into ice water or the mixture registers 260°F (125°C) on a candy thermometer.

2. Remove pan from heat and stir in baking soda. The mixture will foam up and become creamy.

3. Place the popped corn and pecans in a large bowl. Pour the caramel syrup over top and stir to coat evenly. Spread on a large cookie sheet to cool, then break into clusters.

Makes about 8 cups (2 L).

QUICK TRICK:
S'mores: To make this summer classic, you need lots of large marshmallows, graham crackers – or, if you want to get fancy, thin gingersnaps – and squares of dark chocolate. Toast a marshmallow over the fire until it's golden outside and molten inside, then plop it onto a graham cracker. Top with a piece of chocolate and another graham cracker. Eat instantly.

VARIATION: **Skip the graham cracker and the square of chocolate and squish the toasted marshmallow between two Decadent Fudge Cookies (p. 298).**

Peach & Blueberry Shortcakes

Filling

6	**large, ripe peaches** *peeled*	
1 cup	**blueberries**	250 ml
	sugar *or* **maple syrup,** *to taste*	

Shortcakes

2 cups	**all-purpose flour**	500 ml
1 tbsp	**baking powder**	15 ml
½ tsp	**salt**	2 ml
2 tbsp	**sugar,** *plus additional for sprinkling on top*	30 ml
¼ cup	**butter**	60 ml
⅔ cup	**milk**	150 ml
1 cup	**35% cream**	250 ml

TIP:

• Substitute raspberries for the blueberries, or use a combination of raspberries and blueberries.

*S*hortcakes are not just for strawberries. This recipe combines peaches and blueberries – which look and taste wonderful together – in individual little cakes.

1. Preheat oven to 425°F (220°C) and lightly grease a baking sheet. Cut peaches in half, remove pits, and slice. Toss them with blueberries and a little sugar or maple syrup, and let stand for a while at room temperature.

2. In a mixing bowl stir together flour, baking powder, salt, and 2 tbsp (30 ml) sugar. Cut in butter until mixture resembles coarse crumbs. Add milk gradually, tossing mixture gently with a fork to form a soft dough.

3. Turn dough out onto a lightly floured surface and pat into an even layer about ½" (1 cm) thick. Cut into 8 rounds. Brush tops with a little of the cream and sprinkle with sugar.

4. Place rounds on prepared baking sheet. Bake for 15 minutes, or until nicely browned and cooked through.

5. Whip the cream until soft peaks form. Split the shortcakes while they're still warm. Pile fruit on the bottom half of each shortcake, replace other half, and top with the lightly whipped cream and more fruit. Enjoy immediately.

Serves 8.

TIPS:

• The shortcakes can be made the day before serving. Cool, then wrap well in foil. Warm briefly before serving.

• The best way to remove the skins from peaches is to drop them, one at a time, into boiling water for 30 seconds. Remove and immediately plunge into ice water for a few seconds. The skins should slip off easily.

These individual Peach & Blueberry Shortcakes capture the look and taste of summer.

Bumbleberry Crisp

Fruit

6 cups	mixed berries	1.5 L
1/3 cup	sugar (or to taste)	75 ml
1 tsp	lemon zest, grated	5 ml
1 tbsp	fresh lemon juice	15 ml

Topping

1/4 cup	flour	60 ml
1/2 cup	old-fashioned oats	125 ml
2/3 cup	brown sugar	150 ml
pinch	salt	
1 tsp	cinnamon	5 ml
1/3 cup	cold butter	75 ml
1/2 cup	almonds, slivered	125 ml

TIP:

• Include tart sliced apples with the berries, using a total of 6 cups (1.5 L) fruit.

You won't find bumbleberries growing in the woods. This is the name that has taken root to describe a concoction of mixed berries – blackberries, raspberries, blueberries, strawberries – and sometimes even including rhubarb and apples. Whatever's handy at baking time goes into the mix. Serve the crisp warm with lightly sweetened, vanilla-flavoured whipped cream, custard, crème fraîche, sweetened yogurt, or vanilla ice cream.

1. Thoroughly butter a 9" x 13" (23 cm x 33 cm) baking dish. Preheat oven to 375°F (190°C).

2. Toss the berries, sugar, and lemon zest and juice together and place in the prepared baking dish.

3. In a large bowl combine flour, oats, brown sugar, salt, and cinnamon. Cut in cold butter until mixture resembles coarse crumbs. (Or combine in a food processor using on/off pulses.) Stir in nuts. Spread evenly over fruit.

4. Bake in preheated oven for 30–40 minutes, until the juices are bubbling and the topping is lightly browned. Serve warm.

Serves 8.

TIPS:

• Prepare several batches of the topping and store in plastic bags in your freezer, ready to make this favourite dessert in a hurry.

• Add a pinch of an additional spice to the topping to suit the fruit: a pinch of nutmeg, for instance, with peaches and blueberries; a pinch of cloves with apples and blackberries; a pinch of ginger with pears.

Caramel Peach Cobbler

8	ripe peaches (about 2 lbs/1 kg)	
¼ cup	butter	60 ml
½ cup	dark brown sugar	125 ml
¼ tsp	cinnamon	1 ml
pinch	freshly grated nutmeg	
½ cup	fresh blueberries or	125 ml
⅓ cup	dried blueberries	75 ml
½ cup	sour cream or yogurt	125 ml
½ cup	almonds, roughly chopped	60 ml

Biscuit Topping

1½ cups	flour	375 ml
1 tbsp	baking powder	15 ml
1 tsp	salt	5 ml
⅓ cup	cold unsalted butter	75 ml
2 tbsp	maple syrup	30 ml
1	egg, lightly beaten	
¼ cup	milk	60 ml

In this cobbler, the peaches are sautéed first, creating a rich caramel syrup that combines with the crunchy biscuit topping to make an utterly delicious mouthful. Serve warm with whipped cream, vanilla ice cream, or yogurt.

1. Preheat oven to 400°F (200°C).

2. Peel peaches and cut into fat wedges.

3. Heat butter and ¼ cup (60 ml) of the brown sugar together in a heavy saucepan until melted. Add peaches and toss over medium heat for 5 minutes. Add cinnamon and nutmeg.

4. Spoon peaches in an even layer in a 9" x 13" (23 cm x 33 cm) shallow baking dish. Sprinkle blueberries over top and dot with sour cream or yogurt.

5. To make the biscuit topping, combine dry ingredients in a bowl. Cut in butter to form coarse crumbs. Lightly mix maple syrup, egg, and milk. Add to dry ingredients, tossing all together until just combined.

6. Drop spoonfuls of biscuit topping over fruit. Sprinkle with remaining brown sugar and almonds. Bake 15–20 minutes until top is lightly browned.

Serves 8.

TIPS:

• The cobbler can be made up to a day ahead. Warm in a 350°F (180°C) oven before serving.

• You can also use Buttermilk Biscuit dough (p. 257) for the topping: Make the dough omitting the ham, herbs, and cayenne, and adding ¼ cup (60 ml) sugar to the dry ingredients. Proceed with Step 6 above.

Grilled Mango Slices
with Ginger Coconut Cream

Grilled Mangoes

2	**mangoes,** *peeled and sliced*	
2 tbsp	**fresh lime juice**	30 ml
1 tbsp	**brown sugar**	15 ml
2 tbsp	**dark rum** *(optional)*	30 ml

Ginger Coconut Cream

1 cup	**35% cream,** *chilled*	250 ml
1 can	**coconut milk,** *chilled (14 oz/400 ml)*	
1 tbsp	**fresh ginger root,** *grated*	15 ml
1 tsp	**sugar** *(or to taste)*	5 ml
2 tbsp	**desiccated coconut,** *lightly toasted* *(for garnish)*	30 ml

A special ending for an Asian or Caribbean meal. Serve the mango slices and cream on their own, or spoon over meringues or slices of grilled pound cake.

1. Toss mango slices with lime juice, brown sugar, and rum (if using). Mound fruit in the centre of a square of heavy-duty foil and fold to make a secure package.

2. Place the foil package on the grill over moderately high heat for about 15 minutes.

3. Whip cream until soft peaks form.

4. Carefully remove the top of the chilled can of coconut milk without shaking it and scoop out about $\frac{1}{4}$ cup (60 ml) of the thick coconut cream on the top. Add to the softly whipped cream.

5. Stir in grated ginger root and sugar to taste. Whip again to reach desired consistency.

6. Serve the warm glazed mangoes topped with the cream and garnished with a sprinkling of toasted coconut.

Serves 4.

TIPS:

• Freeze the remainder of the can of coconut milk, or use it to make Fragrant Coconut Rice (p. 172).

• See p. 94 for a diagram of how to cut the fruit off a mango easily and efficiently.

Grilled Mango Slices with Ginger Coconut Cream brings a taste of the tropics to dessert.

Summer Fruit Tart

2 lbs	plums	1 kg
1 cup	all-purpose flour	250 ml
1 cup	sugar	250 ml
1 tsp	baking powder	5 ml
pinch	salt	
¼ cup	butter	60 ml
1	egg, *beaten*	
1 tsp	vanilla	5 ml

Topping

3 tbsp	sugar	45 ml
3 tbsp	butter, *melted*	45 ml
1 tsp	cinnamon	5 ml
1	egg, *beaten*	

My favourite version of this tart is made with plums, but you can substitute any fresh fruit you have on hand. It's also good, for instance, with sliced apples, peaches, nectarines, or cherries.

1. Preheat oven to 350°F (180°C). Halve plums, remove stones, and cut each half into equal wedges.

2. Combine flour, sugar, baking powder, and salt in a mixing bowl. Cut in butter until mixture resembles small crumbs; add egg and vanilla and toss together.

3. Press mixture evenly into the bottom and sides of a 9" (23-cm) pie plate. Arrange fruit in circles to cover top, and bake in preheated oven for 40 minutes.

4. Combine topping ingredients and spoon over hot tart. Continue baking 10–15 minutes longer until topping is set and lightly browned.

5. Serve warm or cool with lightly sweetened whipped cream, crème fraîche, or plum sauce. (See below.)

Serves 6–8.

QUICK TRICK:

Fresh Plum Sauce: Simmer about 2 cups (500 ml) sliced plums with a little water and sugar until tender. Force the mixture through a sieve, or whirl in a food processor and then sieve to make a purée. Great with this fruit tart or over ice cream or sorbet.

Raspberry Cream Crunch Pie

1	unbaked 9" (23-cm) Sweet Crust pie shell *(p. 325)*	
4 cups	fresh raspberries	1 L
¼ cup	all-purpose flour	60 ml
1 cup	vanilla yogurt	250 ml
	crème fraîche *or* additional vanilla yogurt	

Almond Crunch Topping

¼ cup	all-purpose flour	60 ml
½ cup	brown sugar	125 ml
1 tsp	cinnamon	5 ml
¼ cup	butter	60 ml
½ cup	whole almonds, *roughly chopped, or* **slivered** *or* **sliced** almonds	125 ml

If you make only one pie a summer, this should be it. Sweet crisp crust, tart raspberries mellowed by a creamy yogurt filling, and an almond crunch topping – utterly decadent.

1. Preheat oven to 400°F (200°C). Prick unbaked pie shell with a fork. Line with foil and fill with pastry weights or dried beans. Bake for 12 minutes. Remove foil and weights and set aside.

2. To make the Almond Crunch Topping: Combine flour, sugar, and cinnamon. Cut in butter and add almonds. Set aside.

3. Toss raspberries with flour and gently fold in the yogurt. Pile filling in prepared crust and cover with the topping.

4. Bake in a 350°F (180°C) oven for 45 minutes, or until raspberries are bubbling and topping is golden. (If crust begins to get too brown while baking, cover pie loosely with aluminum foil.)

5. Cool to room temperature. Serve with crème fraîche or additional vanilla yogurt.

Serves 6–8.

TIP:
• You can't beat a homemade sweet crust (p. 325) for this pie; its sweetness is the perfect counterpoint to the slightly tart and tangy filling. However, an unbaked store-bought pie shell can be used as a shortcut in a pinch.

Muskoka Blueberry Pie

¾ cup	sugar	175 ml
2½ tbsp	cornstarch	35 ml
⅔ cup	water	150 ml
4 cups	fresh blueberries	1 L
2 tbsp	butter	30 ml
1	**lemon,** *grated zest and juice*	
2 tbsp	orange liqueur	30 ml
1	**unbaked 9"(23-cm) pie shell** (*Basic Pastry, p. 325*)	
	whipped cream	

TIP:

• Replace blueberries with raspberries, or combine a mixture of summer berries for another great taste.

*T*his version of the summer classic gets its wonderful flavour from a combination of cooked and raw berries and its name from the lakes region north of Toronto.

1. Combine sugar, cornstarch, water, and 1 cup (250 ml) blueberries in a small saucepan. Bring to a boil, then simmer, stirring constantly until thickened, about 10–15 minutes. (Time will vary with moisture in berries.)

2. Remove from heat and add butter, lemon zest and juice, and liqueur. Mix well. Chill at least 1 hour.

3. Preheat oven to 425°F (220°C). Prick pie shell and bake 12–15 minutes. Allow to cool before filling.

4. Remove sauce from refrigerator about 1 hour before serving. Fold in remaining berries. Spoon into pie shell. Chill 1 hour.

5. To serve, top with whipped cream, or serve each piece with a dollop of whipped cream or a scoop of vanilla or maple walnut ice cream.

Makes 6–8 servings.

The pies have it: Muskoka Blueberry Pie and Double-Crust Mixed-Fruit Pie (p. 324).

Double-Crust Mixed-Fruit Pie

Basic Pastry for a 2-crust pie *(facing page)*		
2 cups	**apples,** *peeled and sliced*	500 ml
1 cup	**rhubarb,** *sliced*	250 ml
¾ cup	**raspberries**	175 ml
1 cup	**sugar**	250 ml
¼–⅓ cup	**all-purpose flour**	60–75 ml
1	**egg,** *beaten*	

Topping

2 tsp	**milk**	10 ml
2 tsp	**sugar**	10 ml

A lovely combination of fresh fruits baked to perfection in a glistening, tender, golden-brown crust.

1. Preheat oven to 400°F (200°C).

2. Combine all filling ingredients. (Use the extra flour if fruit is quite juicy.)

3. On a floured board, roll out half the pastry. Fit into a 9" (23-cm) pie plate. Fill with fruit mixture.

4. Roll out remaining pastry and place over fruit. Trim extra pastry off bottom and top crusts, leaving about ½" (1 cm) beyond the outer edge of the pie plate. Fold top edge under bottom, seal, and flute around rim. Cut vents in top crust.

5. Brush top crust lightly with milk and sprinkle with sugar. Bake on bottom shelf of preheated oven for 10 minutes, then reduce heat to 350°F (180°C) and bake 30–35 minutes longer, or until fruit is tender. Cool on wire rack.

Makes 6–8 servings.

(Double-Crust Mixed-Fruit Pie is shown in the photo opposite p. 323.)

Basic Pastry & Sweet Crust

Basic Pastry

2 cups	all-purpose flour	500 ml
¾ tsp	salt	4 ml
1 cup	shortening	250 ml
1	egg	
2 tbsp	ice water	30 ml
1 tbsp	white vinegar	15 ml

Sweet Crust

1½ cups	all-purpose flour	375 ml
pinch	salt	
¼ cup	icing sugar	60 ml
½ cup	unsalted butter, *at room temperature*	125 ml
1	large egg, *beaten*	

TIP:

• Roll pastry and shape in pie plates. Stack, wrap well, and store in freezer. A pie, tart, or quiche can then be ready for the oven in minutes.

Use the basic pastry with both sweet and savoury pies. The sweet crust complements pies with a slightly tart fruit filling. Both are easy to work with.

Basic Pastry

1. Combine flour and salt in a bowl. Cut in shortening until mixture resembles coarse crumbs.

2. Combine egg, water, and vinegar. Add to flour mixture and toss with a fork until mixture is moistened. Gather into a ball, then divide in two.

3. On a floured surface, flatten 1 ball into a circle and turn it over to flour both sides. Roll dough to a uniform thickness, flouring the rolling pin and surface as necessary to prevent sticking. Transfer dough to a 9" (23-cm) pie plate. Trim and flute. Repeat with other ball. *Makes enough pastry for 2 9" (23-cm) single pie shells or 1 double-crust pie.*

Sweet Crust

1. Combine flour, salt, and sugar in a bowl. Cut in butter until mixture resembles coarse crumbs. Add egg and quickly toss the mixture with a fork until pastry comes together.

2. Turn out mixture onto a floured work surface. Using the heel of your hand, push the pastry away from you 2 or 3 times, then form it into a round disk, wrap in plastic, and refrigerate for an hour.

3. Roll out pastry as above. Set in refrigerator for 10 minutes before baking. (See p. 321 for baking instructions.) *Makes one 9" (23-cm) single pie shell.*

Decadent Dipping Sauces

**selection of fruit
and other sweets,**
*cut into bite-size pieces
(see Tip, below)*

Caramel Rum Sauce

1 cup	sugar	250 ml
¼ cup	fresh orange *or* apple juice *or* water	60 ml
¼ cup	35% cream	60 ml
1 tbsp	butter	15 ml
2–4 tbsp	spiced rum	30–60 ml

Chocolate Orange Sauce

1 lb	chocolate, *grated or chopped into small pieces*	500 g
¼–½ cup	35% cream	60–125 ml
1 tbsp	orange liqueur	15 ml

TIP:

• Some ideas for dipping: cubes of pound cake and gingerbread; whole strawberries, grapes, and dates; wedges of peeled apple, pear, and fresh fig; chunks of papaya, mango, pineapple, and fresh coconut; melon balls; dried apricots; mandarin orange segments; marshmallows; crystallized ginger.

*E*quip each guest with a long-handled fondue fork or skewer, put out a selection of treats for dipping, and have everyone gather round a fondue pot or flame-proof ceramic bowl filled with one of these sensuous sauces.

Caramel Rum Sauce

Combine sugar and juice or water in a small heavy saucepan. Over moderately high heat, melt the sugar until it becomes an amber colour – about 10 minutes. Swirl the pan gently as it darkens. Remove pan from heat and watch the bubbling sugar for a minute. It will mellow and you will be able to see and smell the caramel. Quickly add cream and whisk carefully. Add butter and rum, and pour into a fondue pot or flame-proof bowl.

Chocolate Orange Sauce

Place the grated or chopped chocolate and ¼ cup (60 ml) of the cream in a small fondue pot or flame-proof bowl and set over very low heat. Stir constantly while the chocolate melts and the sauce becomes smooth. Add additional cream as necessary to achieve dipping consistency. Stir in liqueur.

Keep the sauces warm over a very low flame at the table (a tea light works well). Serve with fruit and other sweets for dipping.

Each sauce serves 4–6.

TIP:

• The sauces can be made well ahead and refrigerated in covered containers. Reheat in a small saucepan over very low heat or warm in the microwave, then transfer to a small fondue pot or flame-proof ceramic bowl.

Dip fruit, cake, and other treats into Chocolate Orange Sauce (shown here) or Caramel Rum Sauce. The sauces are also excellent served warm over ice cream.

Old-Fashioned Rice Pudding

½ cup	white rice *(preferably jasmine)*	125 ml
2 cups	whole milk	500 ml
1 cup	10% cream	250 ml
1	cinnamon stick *(3"/8 cm)*	
2	egg yolks	
½ cup	35% cream	125 ml
¼ cup	sugar	60 ml
pinch	salt	
pinch	freshly grated nutmeg	

VARIATION:

• For a fragrant, East Indian-style pudding, use rinsed and soaked basmati rice. Lightly crush the grains first to release the starch. (This creates a creamier consistency.) Flavour the milk with green cardamom pods and cinnamon.

*R*ich, *creamy, and thick. Serve with Strawberry Rhubarb Compote (p. 294) or Ginger Spiced Pears or Plums (p. 294) on top.*

1. Rinse rice and drain well. Combine in the top of a double boiler with the milk, 10% cream, and cinnamon stick. Set over simmering water and cook, uncovered, stirring occasionally, for 30–40 minutes, until rice is just tender and creamy.

2. In a small bowl, whisk egg yolks with 35% cream and ladle in a few spoonfuls of hot, creamy rice. Stir the mixture back into the pot of rice, adding the sugar, salt, and nutmeg. Continue to cook gently in the double boiler for 5 minutes or so. Remove the cinnamon stick.

3. Set aside, covered, for 15 minutes. Serve warm or at room temperature.

Serves 4–6.

TIPS:

• For a lighter pudding, replace the whole milk and creams with 2 cups whole milk mixed with 1 cup of water.

• When refrigerated overnight, the pudding becomes very thick; thin out with additional milk or cream.

• Instead of topping the pudding with fruit, add ¼ cup (60 ml) raisins, dried cranberries, or dried cherries during the last 5 minutes of cooking.

Blueberry Bread Pudding
with Blueberry Sauce

1 loaf	**day-old challah** *or* **other sweet eggbread** *or* **white French country bread,** *cut in 1"(2.5-cm) cubes*	
3 cups	**milk**	**750 ml**
1 cup	**sugar**	**250 ml**
good pinch	**cinnamon**	
1 tsp	**vanilla**	**5 ml**
2 cups	**fresh blueberries**	**500 ml**
6	**eggs**	

Blueberry Sauce

2 cups	**blueberries**	**500 ml**
½ cup	**orange juice**	**125 ml**
1 tsp	**orange zest,** *grated*	**5 ml**
2 tbsp	**sugar**	**30 ml**
1 tsp	**cornstarch** *dissolved in ¼ cup (60 ml) cold water*	**5 ml**

TIP:

• Raisins, chopped dried apricots, or other berries can be substituted for the blueberries.

*B*read pudding is an old-fashioned dessert that has come back into vogue, and this version is wonderful to make during blueberry season. Any day-old bread can form the base as long as it has good taste and texture and is not so assertive that it dominates the flavour of the eggs and berries.

1. Soak bread in milk for 1 hour. Mix in sugar, cinnamon, vanilla, and blueberries.

2. Whisk eggs and fold into mixture. Pour into a 10" (25-cm) lightly buttered springform pan, or equivalent large baking dish, and bake at 350°F (180°C) for about 1 hour or until a toothpick inserted in the centre comes out clean.

3. Cool slightly before removing from the springform pan, or serve directly from the baking dish. Serve warm, with Blueberry Sauce on top and cream or custard alongside.

Serves 6–8.

Blueberry Sauce

1. Combine all ingredients in a small, heavy saucepan. Set over medium heat and stir while sauce comes to a boil. Set aside to cool.

Makes about 2 cups (500 ml).

Chocolate Chip Crisps

1 cup	butter	250 ml
1 cup	sugar	250 ml
¾ cup	brown sugar, *packed*	175 ml
2	eggs	
1 tsp	vanilla	5 ml
2 cups	all-purpose flour	500 ml
1½ cups	old-fashioned oats	375 ml
1 tsp	baking soda	5 ml
¼ tsp	salt	1 ml
2 cups	crisp rice cereal	500 ml
1½ cups	chocolate chips	375 ml

TIP:

• Try butterscotch chips, raisins, or nuts instead of the chocolate chips.

The addition of rice cereal gives these oatmeal chocolate chip cookies pleasing crunch. And the kids in the family will be happy that this recipe makes a nice, big batch.

1. Preheat oven to 375°F (190°C). Grease baking sheets.

2. Beat butter, sugars, eggs, and vanilla in a large bowl on medium speed of an electric mixer until light and creamy.

3. Combine flour, oats, soda, and salt. Add to creamed mixture, stirring until blended.

4. Gently mix in cereal and chips. Drop by spoonfuls onto baking sheets. Bake for 8–12 minutes, or until lightly browned. Underbake for chewy cookies; bake longer for crisp ones. Cool on wire rack.

Makes about 5 dozen cookies.

QUICK TRICK:

Banana Boats: Peel down one or two flaps of peel and hollow out a little trench along the length of the banana. Stuff with mini-marshmallows and chocolate chips. Replace the flaps of peel, fastening them in place with toothpicks. Place the "boat" on the grill for a couple of minutes until chocolate and marshmallows melt. Eat with a spoon. Great fun for the kids (and the kids at heart).

Previous page, clockwise from top left: Chocolate Chip Crisps, Mix-in-the-Pan Cake (p. 276), Easy Apple Cake (p. 284), Buttermilk Biscuits with cheese (p. 257), and Raisin Soda Bread (facing page).

Raisin Soda Bread

2 cups	all-purpose flour	500 ml
2 tbsp	sugar	30 ml
1 tbsp	baking powder	15 ml
½ tsp	baking soda	2 ml
½ tsp	salt	2 ml
½ cup	butter	125 ml
½ cup	raisins *(optional)*	125 ml
¾ cup	buttermilk *or* sour milk *(see Tips, p. 244)*	175 ml

A quick and easy alternative when you run out of bread. Great toasted.

1. Preheat oven to 425°F (220°C). Lightly grease a baking sheet.

2. Combine first 5 ingredients in a large bowl. Cut in butter with pastry blender or 2 knives to make small crumbs. Stir in raisins.

3. Add buttermilk to flour mixture, stirring just until moistened. Dough will be crumbly. Turn out onto lightly floured surface. Knead lightly 12–15 times or until a smooth ball forms. Place on prepared baking sheet. Pat dough out to a circle about 7" (18 cm) in diameter. With a sharp knife, score top of dough with a large X.

4. Bake in preheated oven for 20–25 minutes, or until golden. Serve warm.

Makes 1 loaf.

Chewy Butterscotch Bars

¼ cup	butter	60 ml
1 cup	brown sugar, *packed*	250 ml
1	egg	
1½ tsp	vanilla	7 ml
¾ cup	all-purpose flour	175 ml
1 tsp	baking powder	5 ml
¼ tsp	salt	1 ml
⅔ cup	nuts, *chopped*	150 ml

TIP:

• For a tropical taste, replace nuts with ½ cup (125 ml) shredded coconut and 1 tsp (5 ml) grated lime zest.

This recipe takes only a few minutes to put together, and all the ingredients are mixed in one saucepan.

1. Preheat oven to 325°F (170°C). Grease an 8" (20-cm) square cake pan.

2. Melt butter in medium saucepan. Stir in brown sugar, egg, and vanilla. Mix well.

3. Add remaining ingredients, stirring until smooth. Spread evenly in prepared pan.

4. Bake in preheated oven for 25–30 minutes. Cool, then cut into squares.

Makes about 25 bars.

QUICK TRICK:

Cheater's Poppy Seed Lemon Cake: Always have at least one lemon cake mix on hand in the cupboard. For a delicious cake to serve with berries or tropical fruits, mix up the "richer" version using extra oil and eggs, following the instructions on the box. Reduce the water required by ¼ cup (60 ml) and soak ¼ cup (60 ml) poppy seeds in ¼ cup (60 ml) milk for a few minutes. Stir mixture into the batter. Combine 1 tbsp (15 ml) each of cinnamon, cocoa, and sugar. Spoon half the batter into a greased bundt or angel food cake pan and sprinkle half the spice mixture over the batter. Spoon in the remaining batter and sprinkle with the rest of the spice mixture. Bake according to box directions.

World's Best Corn Bread

1½ cups	cornmeal	375 ml
1 cup	flour	250 ml
⅓ cup	sugar	75 ml
1 tbsp	baking powder	15 ml
1 tsp	salt	5 ml
1½ cups	buttermilk	375 ml
2	**eggs,** *lightly beaten*	
¾ cup	**butter,** *melted and cooled*	175 ml

TIPS:

• Add half a roasted red pepper, chopped, and/or 2 tbsp (30 ml) of chopped jalapeño pepper to the batter.

• Other good additions: ½ cup (125 ml) grated Cheddar or Monterey Jack cheese and ½ cup (125 ml) cooked corn kernels. (Corn roasted on the barbecue adds a wonderful smoky flavour.)

The perfect quick bread to serve with eggs, chili, or southern-style barbecues. The butter in the batter is what makes this version so good.

1. Preheat oven to 400°F (200°C). Grease a 9" square (23-cm) baking pan.

2. Combine dry ingredients in a large bowl.

3. Lightly beat together buttermilk, eggs, and melted butter. Stir quickly into cornmeal mixture; don't overmix.

4. Pour batter into prepared pan. Bake until golden and a toothpick inserted in the centre comes out clean, about 20–25 minutes. Serve hot.

Serves 8.

TIPS:

• To make this quick bread even quicker, combine the dry ingredients ahead of time and store in a plastic bag.

• The corn bread can be wrapped well and frozen.

• The batter also makes good muffins: Pour into greased muffin tins and bake at 400°F (200°C) for 15–20 minutes. Makes 12 large muffins.

Refrigerator-Rise Potato Bread

2	**medium potatoes** *(see Tip, below)*	
6–7 cups	**all-purpose flour**	1.5–1.75 L
2 tbsp	**Fleischmann's Quick-Rise Instant Yeast** *or* **RapidRise Instant Yeast** *(2 envelopes) (see Tips, facing page)*	30 ml
½ cup	**sugar**	125 ml
¼ cup	**skim-milk powder**	60 ml
1½ tsp	**salt**	7 ml
½ cup	**butter**	125 ml
2	**eggs** *(at room temperature)*	
	milk *or* **egg white** *(for brushing tops of bread and buns)*	

TIP:

• Use Idaho or russet potatoes; they make fluffier mashed potatoes and will give the bread better texture.

This is a handy recipe if you have a summer place located far from a source of good fresh baking. Make the multi-purpose dough at leisure on a cool evening, then use as needed for bread or hamburger buns (facing page), or fabulous pecan sticky buns (p. 251). Although the dough has to rise for at least 3 hours, it does so in the refrigerator, and it can stay there for up to 36 hours before being used.

1. Cook potatoes in at least 3 cups (750 ml) water. Drain, saving the potato-cooking water, and mash until smooth. You should have about 1 cup (250 ml) of mashed potatoes. Set aside.

2. Combine 2 cups (500 ml) flour, yeast, sugar, milk powder, and salt in a large bowl. Heat 1½ cups (375 ml) of the reserved potato-cooking water, butter, and the mashed potatoes to 125°F (50°C). With electric mixer at low speed or a large spoon, mix the hot liquid into dry ingredients until blended, then beat vigorously for 2 minutes. Add eggs and beat 2 minutes more.

3. Using a large spoon, add 3–3½ cups (750–875 ml) more flour and combine to make a soft, moist dough. Turn out on a lightly floured surface, and knead for 4 or 5 minutes until dough is smooth and elastic, adding more flour as necessary to keep the dough workable. (You may not use all of it.)

4. Shape dough into a ball and put in a large, lightly greased bowl. (Turn the dough so the surface is greased.) Cover bowl with a slightly damp tea towel, or plastic wrap, and set aside in a warm spot for 20 minutes.

5. Punch dough down and knead briefly in bowl. Shape into a ball, turn to grease top, cover bowl tightly with plastic wrap, and put in the refrigerator for at least 3 hours or up to 36 hours.

TIPS:

• **The dough rises up to 50% faster when you use Quick-Rise Instant Yeast (the name given to the Fleischmann's brand of fast-acting yeast in Canada, and the one most available in Canadian supermarkets; in the U.S., substitute the same amount of Fleischmann's RapidRise Instant Yeast). These instant yeasts do not have to be dissolved in water, but rather can be mixed in directly with the other dry ingredients.**

• **A traditional method of forming bread dough into loaves is to pat or roll the dough into a rectangle whose short side is slightly shorter than the pan; then, starting from the short side, roll up the dough jelly-roll fashion. Pinch the seam and ends. Place in well-greased pan seam side down.**

Bread

1. When ready to bake, remove dough from refrigerator, punch down, and knead briefly in the bowl.

2. Divide dough in half and, with well-greased hands, form into 2 loaves. (See Tips, at left.) Place in well-greased loaf pans, cover with a damp tea towel, and set in a warm spot for about 30 minutes.

3. For a soft surface, brush tops with milk; for a crisper, glazed top, brush with beaten egg white. Bake in preheated 375°F (190°C) oven for about 30 minutes. Turn out on racks to cool. Tops should be nicely browned and bottoms should sound hollow when tapped.

Makes 2 loaves.

Hamburger Buns

1. When ready to bake, remove dough from refrigerator, punch down, knead briefly in the bowl, and divide in half. Cut each half into 8 or 9 equal pieces.

2. With greased hands, form each piece into a smooth ball, set on a well-greased baking sheet, and press to flatten slightly. Cover with a slightly damp tea towel and leave in a warm spot for about 25 minutes.

3. For a soft surface, brush buns with milk; for a crisper, glazed top, brush with beaten egg white. Bake in preheated 375°F (190°C) oven for about 15 minutes until tops are nicely browned and rolls sound hollow when tapped.

Makes about 1½ dozen buns.

Aunt Mabel's
Date & Nut Bread

8 oz	dates, *roughly chopped* *(about 2 cups/500 ml)*	250 g
1 tsp	baking soda	5 ml
1 cup	boiling water	250 ml
2 cups	all-purpose flour	500 ml
½ cup	sugar	125 ml
1 tsp	baking powder	5 ml
½ tsp	salt	2 ml
2 tsp	lemon zest, *grated*	10 ml
1	large egg, *beaten*	
1 cup	walnuts, *chopped*	250 ml

This dense sweet loaf is an updated version of a '50s family favourite, with the advantage that it tastes smooth and rich without any added fat. You can still feel virtuous when you slather on the cream cheese!

1. Preheat oven to 350°F (180°C). Grease and lightly flour a 9" x 5" (2-L) loaf pan.

2. Place dates and baking soda in a bowl and cover with boiling water. Set aside to cool.

3. In a large bowl, combine flour, sugar, baking powder, and salt.

4. Add lemon zest and beaten egg to the date mixture, then stir into dry ingredients with quick, light strokes, just until combined. Stir in nuts. Do not overmix.

5. Spoon batter into prepared loaf pan in an even layer. Bake in preheated oven 50–55 minutes, or until a wooden skewer or cake tester inserted close to the centre comes out clean.

6. Let loaf stand in pan for 10 minutes, then turn out onto a rack to cool.

Makes 1 loaf.

TIPS:

• When making any quick bread, lightly mix the liquid and dry ingredients together, adding just enough liquid to make a soft batter. Don't whip, beat, or stir vigorously – it makes the bread heavier.

• Start testing for doneness at the minimum end of the suggested baking time, then check every 5 minutes thereafter until the tester comes out clean. Overbaking will dry out the bread.

Zucchini Bread

1 cup	all-purpose flour	250 ml
1 cup	whole-wheat flour	250 ml
1½ tsp	baking powder	7 ml
½ tsp	baking soda	2 ml
1 tsp	cinnamon	5 ml
½ tsp	allspice	2 ml
½ tsp	salt	2 ml
½ cup	brown sugar	125 ml
¾ cup	butter, *melted and cooled*	175 ml
2	large eggs	
1 tsp	vanilla	5 ml
1 tbsp	lemon zest, *grated*	15 ml
1½ cups	zucchini, *grated*	375 ml
2 tbsp	lemon juice	30 ml

TIP:

• Measure carefully when making a quick bread: Scoop the flours from the bag or canister into the measuring cup with a spoon, then level the cup off with the back of a knife.

Most recipes for zucchini bread produce sweet loaves that go well with coffee or tea. This one is savoury, a delicious accompaniment warm or toasted to salads and soups. Top it with cream cheese and slivered red onion for a wonderful open-face sandwich.

1. Preheat oven to 350°F (180°C). Grease and lightly flour a 9" x 5" (2-L) loaf pan.

2. In a large bowl, combine flours, baking powder, baking soda, spices, and salt.

3. In another large bowl, beat together sugar and butter. Add eggs one at a time, beating well. Add vanilla and lemon zest.

4. Toss zucchini with lemon juice.

5. Stir dry ingredients into egg mixture with quick, light strokes, alternating with the zucchini, just until combined. Do not overmix.

6. Spoon batter into prepared loaf pan in an even layer. Bake in preheated oven 40–50 minutes, or until a wooden skewer or cake tester inserted close to the centre comes out clean.

7. Let loaf stand in pan for 10 minutes, then turn out onto a rack to cool.

Makes 1 loaf.

Index

Recipe variations and Quick Tricks have been indexed; therefore, when looking for a recipe on a page, also check the sections in coloured type.

Recipe variations and Quick Tricks have been indexed; therefore, when looking for a recipe on a page, also check the sections in coloured type.

Recipe variations and Quick Tricks have been indexed; therefore, when looking for a recipe on a page, also check the sections in coloured type.

*Recipe variations and Quick Tricks have been indexed; therefore, when looking for a recipe on a page, also check the sections in coloured type.

*Recipe variations and Quick Tricks have been indexed; therefore, when looking for a recipe on a page, also check the sections in coloured type.

*Recipe variations and Quick Tricks have been indexed; therefore, when looking for a recipe on a page, also check the sections in coloured type.

Recipe variations and Quick Tricks have been indexed; therefore, when looking for a recipe on a page, also check the sections in coloured type.

Recipe variations and Quick Tricks have been indexed; therefore, when looking for a recipe on a page, also check the sections in coloured type.

Recipe variations and Quick Tricks have been indexed; therefore, when looking for a recipe on a page, also check the sections in coloured type.

*Recipe variations and Quick Tricks have been indexed; therefore, when looking for a recipe on a page, also check the sections in coloured type.

*Recipe variations and Quick Tricks have been indexed; therefore, when looking for a recipe on a page, also check the sections in coloured type.

*Recipe variations and Quick Tricks have been indexed; therefore, when looking for a recipe on a page, also check the sections in coloured type.

*Recipe variations and Quick Tricks have been indexed; therefore, when looking for a recipe on a page, also check the sections in coloured type.